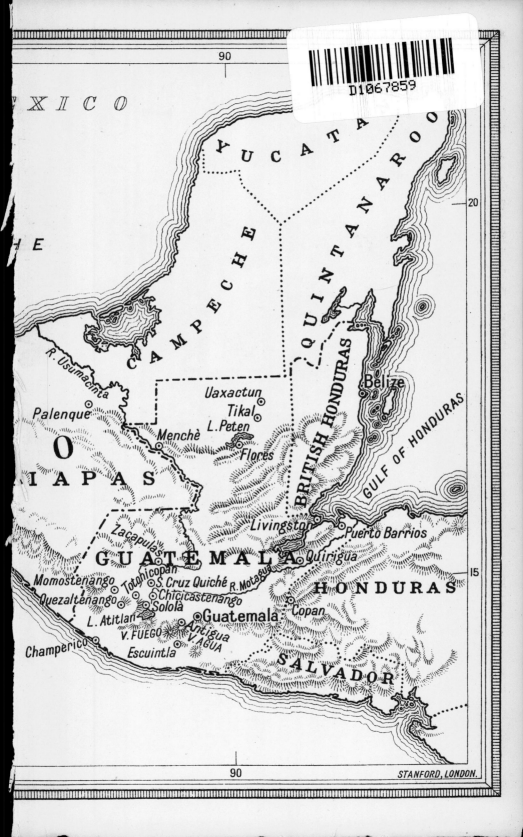

MEXICO

YUCATAN

QUINTANAROO

CAMPECHE

R. Usumacinta

Palenque

Uaxactun

Tikal

L.Peten

Menchè

Flores

O
IAPAS

BRITISH HONDURAS

Belize

GULF OF HONDURAS

Livingston

Puerto Barrios

Zacapula

GUATEMALA

Quirigua

R. Motagua

HONDURAS

Momostenango

Totonicopan

S.Cruz Quiché

Quezaltenango

Chicicastenango

Sololà

Copan

L. Atitlan

Guatemala

v. FUEGO

Antigua

V. AGUA

Champerico

Escuintla

SALVADOR

90

20

15

90

STANFORD, LONDON.

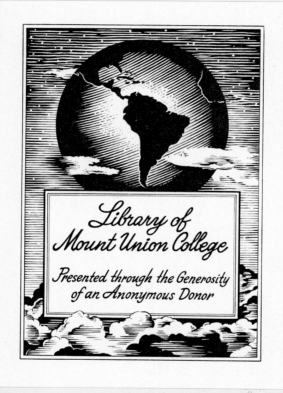

BEYOND

THE MEXIQUE BAY

By Aldous Huxley

NOVELS

Brave New World
Point Counter Point
Those Barren Leaves
Antic Hay
Crome Yellow

SHORT STORIES

Brief Candles
Two or Three Graces
Little Mexican
Mortal Coils
Limbo

ESSAYS AND BELLES LETTRES

Music at Night
Vulgarity in Literature
Do What You Will
Proper Studies
Jesting Pilate
Along the Road
On the Margin
Texts and Pretexts

POETRY

The Cicadas
Leda

DRAMA

The World of Light
The Discovery, adapted from
Frances Sheridan

SELECT WORKS

Rotunda

Chatto & Windus

COPAN   Stela.

BEYOND
THE MEXIQUE BAY

BY

ALDOUS HUXLEY

CHATTO & WINDUS

LONDON

1934

PRINTED IN GREAT BRITAIN
BY T. & A. CONSTABLE LTD.
AT THE UNIVERSITY PRESS
EDINBURGH

917.2
H986b
99063

Contents

v

BEYOND THE MEXIQUE BAY

vi

Illustrations

BEYOND THE MEXIQUE BAY

BEYOND THE MEXIQUE BAY

On the Ship

THE most remarkable thing about a winter cruise is always the preliminary advertising. What a jewelled prose! What images and metaphors! And the staggering gongorisms! Shall the ship be called just 'ship'? Perish the thought of such banality! *Oh eyes, no eyes, but fountains fraught with tears!* And oh liner, no liner, but 'yacht-like giantess,' but 'gay and exquisite hostess of the world's most front-page people.'

And then there are the astonishing places to which these giant hostesses transport you—places where you 'bathe in liquid opal,' where 'quaint native cities hearken far back into old-world history,' where (confronted by the *danse du ventre*) you can hear 'the dead echo of pagan laughter and savage prayer.' And, of course, you never just call at West Indian ports: you 'follow the old *conquistadores* into the glamorous romance of the Spanish Main.' You do not grossly visit the Mediterranean: you 'loll on the pale gold sands of the Riviera' (in the month of February, God help you!) 'watching the sapphire tide'—watching it, alas, in vain, because there is none;

A   I

and when that palls, you go and 'feel your Nordic Personality melt and expand in the riotously colourful *souks* of Tunis and Kairouan.'

As for the people you associate with on board the exquisite giantesses—they are all ' front-page,' ' sophisticated,' ' worth-while ' or, at the very worst, ' a gay charming set who have found a cruise the perfect combination of smartness and thrift.'

It is a thousand pities that steamers have no eyes. Their eyelids, in this delicious literature, would be much more than just a *little* weary. And as for the rocks on which they sit . . . But perhaps in the nautical circumstances it would be more tactful not to mention the rocks.

On the Ship

LIQUID opal, the genuine antique, contemporary golf-courses (twenty of them in Hawaii alone), the last word in cocktail bars and peach-pink sanitary fittings—the blurb-writers promise to take you into the very heart of all these variegated delights. But what they fail to mention—and for me it seems one of the most significant things about the whole business —is the fact that a winter cruise takes you into the future as well. For when you board a giant hostess,

2

you find yourself in the world of your grandchildren.
The five hundred inhabitants of a cruising liner are
in no sense a typical sample of the contemporary
population ; no, they are a typical sample of the
population as it will be, unless in the meantime we
are all blown to pieces, fifty years hence. For the
gay and charming front-pagers who go on winter
cruises are, in the main, elderly people. Retired or
merely tired business men and their wives ; widows
with competences and ageing spinsters, trying to
escape from winter and loneliness in the well-advertised
companionableness of deck life in the tropics ; a
sprinkling of the very old and infirm. The genuinely
young are few ; but, by way of compensation, the
imitation youthfulness of early middle age is plentiful.
Adolescents of five-and-forty abound. Such, then, are
the front-pagers. By no means, I repeat, a characteristic sample of the contemporary population. But,
according to the prophecies of all the experts, a completely typical bunch from the gay nineteen-eighties.

In 1980 the population of the Western world will
probably be somewhat smaller than it is at present.
It will also, which is more significant, be differently
constituted. The birth-rate will have declined and
the average age of death have risen. This means
that there will be a considerable decrease in the
numbers of children and young people, and a considerable increase in the numbers of the middle-aged
and old. Little boys and girls will be relatively rare ;

but men and especially women (since women tend to live longer than men) of sixty-five years old and upwards will be correspondingly more plentiful—as plentiful as they are on a cruising liner in 1933.

So all aboard the giant hostess and Westward Ho for a glamorous adventure into the future ! But, frankly, I prefer the present. Little boys may be an intolerable nuisance ; but when they are not there we regret them, we find ourselves homesick for their very intolerableness. After two or three weeks of a winter cruise (there are some, appalling thought ! which last as much as four months), one would gladly exchange the widows, the bulging ex-stockbrokers, the smart but thrifty young kittens of forty, for a waggon-load of even the most diabolic children, for a wilderness of even the silliest undergraduates.

What a world our grandchildren will have to live in ! Opinions, on the decks of a cruising liner, are unbelievably sound. It would seem impossible to find in any other area of equal size so large a number of right-thinking men and women. If similar causes continue to result in similar effects, our grandchildren's world will be a world of die-hards. As the young grow fewer and the old more numerous, the mistrust of all radical opinions will tend to increase, the desire for change to diminish. It will probably be safer than ours, the world of 1980 ; but it will certainly be less exciting. Go cruising and judge for yourself !

ON THE SHIP   Giant Hostess.

ON THE SHIP

On the Ship

PEERING through the window of the gymnasium, I was rewarded for my inquisitiveness by an astonishing spectacle. Mounted on the electric horse, a stout lady of mature middle-age was riding furiously, all out, as though she were bringing the good news from Ghent to Aix. The mechanical quadruped heaved its wooden loins and rhythmically all the superfluous adiposity of its rider lifted and with a jellied shuddering subsided, lifted once more and subsided, again and again, endlessly.

> At Boom, a great yellow star came out to see,
> At Düffeld, 'twas morning as plain as could be ;
> And from Mecheln church steeple we heard the half
>   chime . . .

But no Joris broke the silence. Determined, her face grimly set—that is, as much set as it could be, seeing that it too was lifting and subsiding along with all the rest—the stout lady galloped on. I walked away, hoping that, when at last she got there, they would have the decency to pour down her throat their last measure of wine. She deserved it.

5

On the Ship

Fun, on our giant hostess, was organized. The amusement front had its duly appointed commissar —a very efficient professional from one of the tourist agencies. He saw to it that the games on deck were played systematically. He, no doubt, it was who decreed that our dinner, every third or fourth day, should be called a Gala Dinner, and that we should be given paper hats, balloons and cardboard trumpets. And his, finally, was the brilliant notion of the children's party. The invitation card has gone into my archives ; it is a document for which future historians will be grateful. The wording of it ran as follows :

The Headmaster and Staff
of
Cruise School
Request the Pleasure of your Company
at a
Children's Party for Grown-Ups
In the School-Room
(Main Lounge, Promenade Deck)
9.15 P.M. Saturday, February 4th.

School or Nursery Dress *must* be worn.
Bring your toys and dollies with you.
Romps, Games, etc., at 9.30. Nannies at Midnight.
Parking for Perambulators provided.

6

ON THE SHIP

Now, the most interesting thing about the Amuse-
ment-Commissar's idea is that it was not original.
The Bright Young People had it first, in 1928, when,
on a certain autumn night, the romping of the adult
children was so uproariously merry that over a large
area of Belgravia sleep became impossible. Some of
the rompers, if I remember rightly, ended in the
police station. And there, too, should have ended
their idea. But no ; there was something in its
quaint peter-pannishness that made an irresistible
appeal to the imagination of English ladies and gentle-
men. The original rompers had mostly been inhabitants of those equivocal marches between Bohemia
and the *Monde*. Five years later their idea was
part of the stock-in-trade of a professional amuser,
catering for as representative a collection of the
elderly *haute bourgeoisie* as you could hope to find.
And with what glee his invitation to the nursery
was accepted ! I never saw such romping among
real children. It was clear that, far from being abnormal, the original inventors of the nursery party
were, in this respect, perfectly representative of their
economic class. It was the Bright Young who first
thought of this particular manifestation of infantilism ;
but the Dim Old took to it as happily as ducks to water.

My objection to anthropologists is the same as my
objection to missionaries. Why do these two classes
of people waste their time converting heathens and
studying the habits of blackamoors, when they can

find, in their own streets, men and women whose beliefs and behaviour are at least as strange as those of the M'pongos and, so far as we are concerned, painfully and dangerously more significant ? Anthropology, like charity, should begin at home.

Barbados

BRIDGETOWN is not a large place ; ten minutes of slow walking brought us to the suburbs. It was evening and the hot air was perfectly still. We walked through a vertical stratification of sewage smells and flowers, through minglings of tuberose and stale fish. Gigantically tall thin palms, bending with their own lankiness, had been drawn, so it seemed, by a very vulgar but extraordinarily accurate and laborious artist—drawn in Indian ink, on the pale orange expanses of the West. There was a yelling of frogs ; and the insects were like an invisible but ubiquitous orchestra, incessantly engaged in tuning up.

It was six years since I had been in a hot country, and I had forgotten how unspeakably melancholy the tropics can be, how hopeless, somehow, and how completely resigned to hopelessness. The feet of the negroes shuffled along the pavements. Small black children played in the gutters, silently. Squatting on the kerb, their fathers were reading the local

8

newspaper by the light of the street lamps. And between the lamps, in the thickening night, every passing form was disquietingly without a face, and handless ; blackness melted into blackness ; men were as suits of clothes walking. Every now and then we passed a chapel—always lighted up and always full of people singing hymns. For half a minute, perhaps, the noise of ' Abide with Me ' would drown the noises of the tropical night ; then, as one moved further away, the frogs and the cicadas would reassert themselves, and one was aware of both noises vibrating with an equal hopelessness under the first stars.

Barbados

INDOORS and out of doors, by night as well as by day, all the women in Barbados were always and invariably in hats. The march of fashion in our colonial empire is slow, and the negresses of Bridgetown were wearing wide-brimmed hats with large, bulging crowns, such as were all the rage in the English provinces four or five years ago. Even when they were carrying burdens, they carried them on their hats. Squelched, those large crowns oozed out round the base of fish baskets and kerosene tins. Hats, I take it, are still in Barbados what they were till quite recently in Europe—emblems of respectability, badges of class. To doff the kerchief or the peasant's cap and put on the hat was to affirm symbolically the principles of the French Revolution. 'Liberty!' you tacitly proclaimed as you took the air in your new head-dress; 'society is no longer divided up into a class of hat-wearing mistresses and kerchief-wearing slaves. Likewise Equality and Fraternity! a hat's a hat for a' that; and my four-and-elevenpenny Marks and Spencer is of the same family as your Reboux.' Among the negroes, I suppose, it is still imperatively necessary to make these affirmations. The theory of their liberty and equality is still all too theoretical.

Barbados

OUR fellow front-pagers had all gone to dine and dance at Hastings, where the fashionable life of the island is concentrated. Greatly to the distress of our taxi-driver, we insisted on feeding indigenously, in the town itself. Protesting, he took us at last to what looked and sounded, from the outside, like a thoroughly forbidding kind of eating-hell. But appearances were deceptive. The dining-room was clean, and the pandemonium of noise was all being produced by a single electric gramophone. Except for one other white diner and a couple of very decorous coffee-coloured billiard players, we had the place to ourselves. The rum cocktail was excellent, so were the stewed flying-fishes and the grilled dolphin steaks ; and so, it turned out, was the company. For our fellow diner, with whom we very soon got into conversation, turned out to be a most remarkable personage.

'Do you often eat at this restaurant ? ' I asked.

He laughed delightedly. 'I own it ! '

And it was not only the hotel that he owned. He had four shops—three in Bridgetown and one at the other end of the island ; he had a filling station, a pawnbroking business, a bus line. All his own creation, worked up out of nothing. It was Napoleonic. And the latest addition to his empire was an undertaking establishment.

'I feed them and clothe them, and then I bury them.' His laughter was infectious. 'Here's a little book on embalming I got the other day,' he added, producing it out of his pocket. But it seemed there was not much demand in Barbados for these refinements.

When we had finished our dinner, he offered to take us for a drive in his car. We accepted with alacrity. The chauffeur was waiting at the door. We drove off —circuitously, so that we might be shown all our new friend's various establishments. His name sprawled boldly across the shop fronts ; under it, in large letters was written, 'THE FRIEND OF THE POOR.'

The road to Speightstown—for that was where we were bound — followed the coast. Between trees, every now and then, we had glimpses of the sea

11

breaking snow-white, under the moon, on beaches almost as white as the foam on the waves. Every mile or so we passed through a village. The houses were tiny shanties of wood or corrugated iron. In chapels the inevitable hymn-singing was going on. Still hatted against the moonlight, women came and went among the houses ; in the dust, outside the doors, squatted groups of men, faceless in the shadow.

Our Napoleonic friend had a shop at Speightstown. On the window was pasted a notice, which I read by the light of the moon as he was unlocking the door. ' Would it not be consoling,' the announcement ran, ' to inherit FOUR THOUSAND DOLLARS from the dear departed ? If you allow me to make the funeral arrangements, you will receive, free of all charge, a ticket for the Turf Club Sweepstake. This ticket may win you a first prize of FOUR THOUSAND DOLLARS. Tickets are given subject to only one condition, which is that the funeral fees be paid before the drawing of the winning numbers.' I made no comment : I could only silently admire.

In a back room behind the shop, lit by a dim oil lamp, a very old negress was sitting, with her hat on, of course, cleaning flying-fish. Snick, snick—off went the long fins, the tail, the head ; another snick, out came the guts and, with a little manipulation, the backbone. The fish was dropped into a basket. An incredibly beautiful, pale brown girl was sitting beside her, sewing. The door behind them was open on to the sea. There was nothing specially curious or remarkable about the scene ; but for some reason it held, and in my memory still holds for me a quality of extraordinary alienness and unfamiliarity, of being immeasurably remote. Nothing I ever saw and— since our fantasies are *ours* and so are always nearer, however extravagant, than the intuitions that reach our minds from without—nothing certainly I ever imagined was so far away as that little room at Speights-town. And the girl, so beautiful, with her face shining in the lamplight, as though it were illumined from within, the old negress, under her battered hat, busy with black hands among the silvery fish—they were the inhabitants, it seemed, of another universe.

Trinidad

A ROPEWAY goes down from the pitch lake to the sea. Its buckets, at the moment, dangle idly ; as of everything else, the world has an excess of asphalt. No work is being done at the lake, and the telpher wires, stretched tightly across the sky, serve only as convenient perches for innumerable black pelicans. They sit there like a passage of semi-quavers on a mile-long expanse of ruled paper. We seemed to be landing at the foot of a gigantic page of Liszt.

13

Trinidad

MY conception of the pitch lake of Trinidad was formed in childhood and had been modified by no subsequent accession of knowledge. I had only to shut my eyes and murmur the words, 'pitch lake of Trinidad,' to see a black tarn, boiling hot, and surrounded by appalling precipices. My private pitch lake looked, in fact, like one of Doré's illustrations to the *Inferno*. Imagine, then, my disappointment with the real, the public pitch lake. For the real pitch lake is simply about two hundred asphalt tennis courts, in very bad condition, set in the midst of some gently undulating green meadows. I felt inclined to ask for my money back.

Trinidad

THE oranges that grow in these tropical islands are particularly juicy and aromatic ; but they never appear on any European or North American market. As with so many of us, their faces are their misfortune ; they have a complexion which nature has made, not orange,

14

but bright green, irregularly marbled with yellow. Nobody, therefore, outside their countries of origin, will buy them. For fruit, strangely enough, is sold on the strength of its appearance, not of its taste. Every grower knows that his product must appeal first to the eye and only secondarily to the palate. Immense pains have been taken to embellish the skin, but how little does any one ever trouble to improve the flavour, of our dessert !

The appeal of bright colours, symmetry and size is irresistible. The sawdust apple of the Middle West is wonderfully red and round ; the Californian orange may have no flavour and a hide like a crocodile's— but it is a golden lamp ; and the roundness, redness and goldenness are what the buyer first perceives on entering the shop. Moreover, both these fruits are large ; and greed is so simple-minded that it always prefers food in large chunks to food in small chunks —prefers it even when the food is being bought by weight, and it makes no difference whether the individual portions are big or little.

But this is not the whole story. Man looks out on reality through an intervening and only partially transparent medium—his language. He sees real things overlaid by their verbal symbols. Thus, when he looks at oranges, it is as though he looked at them through a stained-glass window representing oranges. If the real oranges correspond with the *beau idéal* of oranges painted on the window, he feels that every-

15

thing is all right. But if they don't correspond, then he becomes suspicious ; something must be wrong.

A vocabulary is a system of platonic ideas, to which we feel (illogically, no doubt, but strongly) that reality *ought* to correspond. Thanks to language, all our relations with the outside world are tinged with a certain ethical quality ; before ever we start our observations, we think we know what it is the duty of reality to be like. For example, it is obviously the duty of all oranges to be orange ; and if, in fact, they aren't orange, but, like the fruits of Trinidad, bright green, then we shall refuse even to taste these abnormal and immoral caricatures of oranges. Every language contains, by implications, a set of categorical imperatives.

Trinidad

AT the Imperial College of Tropical Agriculture the geneticists were busy on bananas. The problem was this : to produce a new variety that should combine all the virtues of the Gros Michel, large size, thick skin (for a banana must be its own travelling-trunk) and handsome appearance, with resistance to that insidious Panama Disease, which has ruined so many plantations throughout the Caribbean. The

16

fruit of their labours (which I ate and found, surprisingly enough, much better than the Gros Michel) has now to be tried out by the commercial growers. If the trial turns out to be successful, science will have given the producer yet another source of larger and securer harvests. If only it could give the consumer the means of buying these harvests ! But before it can give him the means of buying, it must first persuade the consumer that being able to buy harvests and live in peace is better than being able to indulge in hatred for the foreigner, pride of race, national and class exclusiveness. Men do not live by bread or bananas alone : they also live by their passions— their good passions and, still more, their evil passions. Which sort of fun does this consumer like best—the fun of being at peace and so able to consume and to create ? or else the fun of boasting, the fun of hating and despising, the fun of mob-intoxication and mob-irresponsibility, the fun of yelling *Deutschland, Deutschland über alles,* and of sobbing, in chorus, over the final scenes of *Cavalcade* ? At present most consumers pay lip-service to peace and prosperity. But they behave as though they preferred the latter alternatives : which means that really, in the depths of their being, they do prefer them. It is the business of men of science to devise a technique for making prosperity and peace as satisfying, psychologically, as nationalistic hatreds and hysterias. It is, in most cases, only from motives of passion that people will

B 17

act reasonably. Very well, then, the science of applied anthropology must discover which are the safest passions to make use of. At present enlightened self-interest is not acceptable to the great majority of civilized men and women. It fails to satisfy them, because it is less exciting than the indulgence of those lusts and urges so richly gratified by nationalism. Moral : enlightened self-interest must somehow be made as thrilling as unenlightened animal impulse. To discover how this may be done is incomparably more important than to discover new varieties of the banana. Yet we have an Imperial College of Tropical Agriculture, but no Imperial College of Applied Anthropology.

Trinidad

OUR friends—and by the end of our single day in Trinidad we had the most charming friends—took us after dinner to a Calypso Tent. Now a Calypso Tent (as I think it almost goes without saying) is not a tent and has nothing to do with Calypso. It is a large shed without walls—a tin roof on posts—in which, during the weeks that precede Shrove Tuesday, the local talent assembles to rehearse certain songs specially composed against the coming of Carnival. The tune to which these songs are sung is always some variant of an old Spanish air called Calypso; the words are home-made and topical. (The singers, who are negroes and have the negro's more than Indian passion for grandiloquence, call themselves ' Calypsonians.' Calypsonians !—it is the sort of opulent word that Greene or Marlowe would have delighted in. Why is it that, to-day, only the vulgarest and most coarse-grained poetasters have the face to ride in triumph through Persepolis ? Good poets would as soon publicly break wind as let fly at their readers with a purple passage. The *Zeitgeist* is a most tyrannous spirit; to evade its imperatives seems, for a sensitive artist, to be all but impossible. The Calypsonians of Trinidad live in another *Zeit*; so the *Geist* they obey is not the same as ours. In that, it may be, they are fortunate.)

The singing was introduced and accompanied by an orchestra consisting of flute, clarinet (the instrument mainly responsible for tracing the melodic line), violoncello and guitar. The performers played by ear and, as the spirit moved them, improvised elaborations on their parts. The resultant sounds were simply astonishing. These four negroes produced music like nothing else I have ever listened to. The orchestral colour was virulently aniline; in the end its very violence and intensity produced a kind of numb fatigue. But for the first minutes the ear was dazzled, as it were, and delightedly amazed.

There were four or five singers, all well known, it

seemed, to the audience, and each possessing a stage name in the grandest negro-Elizabethan style.

' The Duke of Normandy ! ' announced the master of ceremonies. Up climbed a coal-black youth, and with an expression on his face of the most touching seriousness began to sing a song, of which the opening lines ran as follows :

> Oh, wouldn't it be-ee
> A good thing if we-ee
> Supported lo-cull industree !

At the end of every stanza came a refrain in the form of a question :

> Why shouldn' de products of dis island
> Support de popula-ashun ?

This appeal for Trinidadian autarchy was warmly applauded. The idiocies of the greater world have penetrated even into the recesses of the Caribbean.

When he had finished, it was the turn of the ' Lord Executor.' A gnarled, little old man, white-skinned but entirely negro, you felt, in spirit, made his bow, and, pulling his hat down at a very sinister angle over his right eye, began to sing a long ballad about a female burglar, called Ruby, whose trial had recently made a great impression on the public of Port of Spain. Unhappily, I can recall little more than the refrain :

> But when Rub-ee
> Pleaded guilt-ee
> She got two years in custod-ee.

One other passage, from a long catalogue of the things
that Ruby stole, remains in my memory :

> She took boots and she took shoes
> And bloomers such as ladies use.

But the rest, alas, is silence.

Silence, too, is all but the chorus of another song
by the Duke of Normandy about the rail-versus-road
controversy.   The duke was a modernist and all for
the road.

' So what I say,' he sang, while the orchestra improvised an extraordinary accompaniment that ran
up and down the scale like the laughter of a giant
woodpecker :

> So what I say
> Is, wouldn't it pay
> Much better for all of us
> To travel by de r-omnibus ?

After that the Lord Adjudicator sang almost in-
comprehensibly (which was the more regrettable, as
his song was evidently richly obscene) in that queer
French patois which still lingers among the negroes
of Trinidad.   And when the laughter had died down,
the Lord Executor went through a long Newgate
Calendar of all the important crimes of the preceding
year.   Nothing of it remains with me, except the
phrase ' lenient brutality' applied to a particularly
savage murder.

The proceedings ended with a ' flyting.'   Three of
the singers got up on to the stage together and pro-

ceeded to improvise stanzas of derision at one another's expense, attack and counter-attack, to the unspeakable pleasure of all the listeners. The gigantic black matron sitting immediately in front of me heaved with such violent paroxysms of laughter, that I was afraid she would disintegrate. Happily I was wrong ; goodly and great, like a black female Og, she sailed out of the Calypso Tent and in the tropical darkness outside was lost, as though in her native element.

Caracas

THE most immediately conspicuous difference between the British Colonies of the Caribbean and the Spanish American republics is a difference in the women's clothes. Sartorially, the colonies are bits of the English provinces with their provinciality raised to the nth power. The negresses and mulattos have abandoned the eternity of traditional costume for a temporal world of fashions—but of fashions that are never less than four years old and, even in the palmiest days at home, were French only after the school of Stratford-atte-Bowe. The colonial *monde*—to judge at least by such glimpses as one had in the streets—is scarcely more modish than the commonalty. True, the fashions it affects are perhaps only three years old and they have moved, in their march towards Paris, as far, shall we say, as Kensington High Street. But that is all.

How startlingly different is the feminine scene in Venezuela or Panama, in Guatemala or Mexico or Cuba ! At La Guayra I did not see a single heel less than four inches high. Powder was mauve on dark noses and a rich artificial colour mantled the brown cheeks. Against a negro or an Indian skin the buttery glossiness of acetate silk shone, yellow, or peppermint green, or more often tenderly pink—*pâle et rose, comme un coquillage marin.* And what frills, what flounces ! Little sweethearts of the world ; for the cut was a Hollywoodian adaptation from the French. La Guayra is only a provincial town. In Caracas, the capital, we had a sight of Venezuelan rank and fashion ; it looked like the paddock at Longchamps.

Caracas

AT some moment in its history, no doubt, every palace is genuinely palatial. The gilding shines and the mirrors are untarnished, the damask is still fresh and the crimson plush not yet threadbare. None of the palaces I have ever visited has revealed to me its hypothetical state of bright virginity. And I am glad of it ; for, in my eyes, the greatest charm of palaces (and I have a passion for them) consists precisely in the mixture of impossible grandiosity with a kind of dim squalor which no well-brought-up bourgeois would tolerate for a moment. Nor, indeed, would he have to tolerate it. For in a small establishment one can afford periodically to renew and refurbish. But when it is a matter of laying down forty or fifty hectares of crimson carpet, of repainting by the square mile—well, even a king has to think twice about it. And while he is thinking, the squalor continues to creep yet deeper into the heart of the magnificence. Perhaps the place has been redecorated now ; but I remember that when, as a boy, I went round Windsor Castle, the dark blue velvet on the chairs in what I suppose was the Chapter Room of the Knights of the Garter had been so much worn by a long succession of august posteriors that there were mange-spots in the pile and the stringy warp of the material showed through in naked indecency. In another palace, in Europe, I have seen moths rising from the sofa on which the royal personages habitually sat. And how dingy the paint-work invariably is ! What accumulations of dark grey dirt have lodged in the undustable recesses of the gilding ! Each hall and echoing saloon is shabbier than the last. The most improbable treasures meet the eye, whichever way it turns— amber busts of Queen Victoria ; life-sized elephants in rock-crystal ; the Tsar's lapis lazuli dining-table ;

a solid platinum escritoire presented by the first Baron Rothschild. But the carpet is worn, like the linoleum in the corridors of a board school; the forty-foot damask curtains have not been replaced since the Crimean War; and as for the monumental clock on the porphyry mantelpiece—it stopped on the morning of the battle of Sadowa, and has never, from that day to this, marked anything but eleven minutes past nine.

The presidential palace at Caracas is a small but very choice specimen of its kind. The plush seems heavier than elsewhere, and more darkly crimson; the gilding more brassily yellow, the carving more ornate and in more strikingly bad taste. It is like a palace on the late nineteenth-century stage, and the properties are as shabby, when you look at them closely, as those of any theatre.

Behind the throne in the chief reception-room hung a gigantic portrait of the present ruler of Venezuela, prancing, on a white horse as god-like as himself. In another room his photograph, life-size, revealed a shrewd and almost too genial little old gentleman in goggles, bulging pronouncedly about the lower waist. ' Look here, upon this picture, and on this.' But it is not the mythological prancer, it is the bulging and begoggled old gentleman, who is the strong man of Venezuela, and who has been its strong man, almost uninterruptedly, for the last quarter of a century.

Colon

ENGLISH provincial dowdiness at Barbados and Trinidad ; Franco-Californian smartness at Caracas. At Colon, the Country Club had completely prevailed over Paris ; the negresses were all dressed in natty sports clothes and low-heeled shoes.

Prostitution and the sale of curios and antiques seem to be the two staple industries of this very depressing city. And since sailors cannot afford to be too particular, the first industry is, only too often, merely a branch of the second.

We rolled through the *quartier réservé* and the residential suburbs, very slowly, in a one-horse cab. ' I tink, sir,' said the negro driver, with an old-world courtesy that was most engaging, ' I tink, sir, dat we have de honour to be compatriots.'

I said that I was very glad to hear it ; but privately I felt pretty sure that he was wrong. Many thousands of negroes have migrated from Jamaica and the other British islands to the shores of the neighbouring republics. They have had large families in their new homes. But in nine cases out of ten their children are not British subjects, for the simple reason that, in nine cases out of ten, the parents never took the trouble to marry. Britannia has a short way with bastards.

26

JAMAICA

If you are born of British parents outside the Empire, but in wedlock, she will take you to her bosom ; but if you are born outside both the pales, then you stay outside ; and that's that.

The Central American governments have recently had this fact forced upon their attention. In good times they welcomed the influx of negro population from the islands. But now times are bad ; there is unemployment at the ports, in the banana plantations and sugar mills. The various governments would like to repatriate the now superfluous aliens. But to their dismay, they find that most of them are not aliens. If they are bastards—and they almost always are— they are true-born Panamanians, Nicaraguans, Honduraneans, or whatever it may be.

Times are bad in the islands as well as on the mainland ; any sudden accession to the labour reserves would be extremely unwelcome. Our ministers and consuls are proclaiming the sanctity of marriage with a truly missionary zeal.

Jamaica

AT Kingston we said good-bye to our giant hostess. The other front-pagers had twenty-one more days of her. I did not greatly envy them their thrifty smart-

27

ness. The costly squalors of individual travelling have their compensations.

Jamaica

JAMAICA is the Pearl of the Caribbean—or is it the Clapham Junction of the West? I can never remember. But, anyhow, pearl or junction, it made us both feel extremely ill, and we were thankful to be off on a small Norwegian banana boat, bound for British Honduras and Guatemala.

On a clear night in the tropics, a slowly rolling ship has a private astronomy all its own. I used to lie sometimes for hours watching these novel celestial motions. The stars would go slanting up at an angle through the sky, pause at the top of their trajectory and, with a long rush, swoop down again ; then very slowly, as though tentatively, as though reluctantly, would begin to curve sideways and upwards, exploring the darkness, until at last they seemed to have found the path they were looking for, and up they would slant again in strong undeviating flight—and the whole cycle of the movements had begun anew.

British Honduras

On either side of the ship coral islands began to appear, so exactly like the coral islands of childish imaginations that I was reluctant for a time to accept the evidence of my senses. However, there unquestionably they were—little atolls, sunk to the gunwale in blue water, each with its clump of palm trees and perhaps a tiny house or two and a boat drawn up on the white beach. A few hours later we were anchored off Belize.

Walking through the streets, one saw but little traces of the great calamity of 1930, when a hurricane blew the sea in a huge wall of water right across the town. A heap of bricks, it is true, was all that was left of the principal house of God ; but Mammon, Caesar and the Penates had risen fresh and shining from the ruins. Almost all the private residences and all the government offices, all the shops and warehouses, had been rebuilt or repaired. The town as a whole looked remarkably neat and tidy. Even a tidal wave may have something to be said for it. It does at least clear away the slums. Our governments and municipalities are less brutal ; but they are also, alas, a good deal less effective.

The sanitary arrangements at the new hotel were all that could be desired ; but the proprietor, who was a Spanish-American, was evidently unacquainted, not only with English spelling, but also (which was worse) with our English euphemisms. At the top of the stairs I found myself confronted by a door, on which were written, in very large black letters, the words : FOR URIN.

Why not, after all ? Nevertheless, I was a little startled. We are all like Pavlov's dogs—so conditioned that, when the scatological bell rings, we automatically begin to frown or blush. It is absurd, it is even, if you like to think of yourself as a rational being, rather humiliating. But there it is ; that is how the machine happens to work. To know that there *is* a machine and that it *does* work in this particular way is to be, even though still subject to its control, in some sort superior to it. Not a very satisfying triumph, perhaps ; but still, I reflected, as I closed the door behind me, better than no triumph at all.

British Honduras

WHEN I was a boy there was hardly, in all my acquaintance, a single reputable family which did not eat off mahogany, sit on mahogany, sleep in mahogany. Mahogany was a symbol of economic solidity and moral worth. Just as in Barbados the hat proclaims the emancipated and no longer inferior negress, so, in Victorian England, mahogany proclaimed the respectable man of substance. So loudly and unequivocally did it proclaim him, that those whose trade was in luxury could never be lavish enough with their mahogany. In Pullman cars, in liners—wherever, indeed, it was necessary to give clients the illusion that they were living like princes—mahogany fairly flowed like water.

Alas, how quickly such sacred symbols can lose their significance ! For us, to-day, the highest luxury is a perfect asepsis. The new casino at Monte Carlo Beach could be transformed at a moment's notice into a hospital. (Luxurious in the traditional manner, the old is almost infinitely unhygienic.) The Wagon-lit Company's latest coaches are simply very expensive steel nursing-homes on wheels. There is no place here for mahogany. There is hardly more place in the private house. I cannot think of a single modern high-bourgeois home, in which mahogany plays more than a casual and inconspicuous part. My friends eat off glass and metal, sit on metal and leather, sleep on beds that are almost innocent of enclosing bed-steads. If they use wood at all for their furniture, they use one of the light-coloured varieties, or else a cheap soft-wood painted to harmonize with the general colour-scheme of the room. Never mahogany. The dark rich wood, so much beloved by our fathers and grandfathers, has not only lost its symbolic meaning ; it is also (and the Marxians would say that this was directly due to the loss of prestige) regarded with aesthetic distaste. Mahogany, in a word, is now hopelessly out of fashion.

Here, so far as the historian of taste is concerned, the matter ends. For the social historian, however, it is only just beginning. British Honduras used to live on the export of mahogany. But we prefer the lighter woods, we prefer metal and glass and ripolin. Result : a falling off of Honduranean exports and a corresponding rise in the death-rate from tuberculosis. Increase of phthisis in Belize has a contributory cause in the decline of gum-chewing in Chicago and New York. Chicle, like mahogany, but on a smaller scale, is a British Honduras staple. Financial stringency, and perhaps also a change of fashion, cause American typists to chew less than they did. Therefore the chicle-hunters and their dependents—like the mahogany-cutters and theirs—have less money to buy food and so less resistance to disease. Tubercle takes its opportunity.

The inadequacy of man's imagination and his immense capacity for ignorance are notorious. We act habitually without knowing what the more distant results of our actions are likely to be—without even caring to know. And our ability to imagine how other people think and feel, or how we ourselves should think and feel in some hypothetical situation, is strictly limited. These are defects in our make-up as mental

beings. But they are defects which possess great biological advantages. Any considerable increase in our
capacity for knowing and imagining would be likely
to result in the paralysis of all our activities. Take,
by way of example, this little matter of mahogany.
If we knew precisely what were going to be the effects
upon the British Honduraneans of our choice of metal
instead of mahogany; if we could vividly imagine
what it feels like to be chronically underfed, to die
slowly of consumption; if our sympathy with them
were what the word literally means, a genuine ' with-
suffering '—should we then ever have the courage to
buy anything but mahogany? And if we bought
nothing but mahogany, what about the people who
live by the sale of soft-woods, glass and stainless steel?
Knowing the effects on them, imaginatively realizing
their sufferings, how could we resist *their* appeal?
The final result would be a hopeless neurasthenia.

What is true of mahogany is true of anything else.
Excess of knowledge and imagination leads to a kind
of paralysis. (The tragedy of this excess has been
written in *Hamlet*.) The confident capacity to choose
depends on ignorance or, if knowledge is unescapable,
on insentience and lack of imagination. In practice
we are able to do things with a light heart, because
we never know very clearly what we are doing, and
are happily incapable of imagining how our deeds
will affect other people or our future selves. To rail
against destiny because it has decreed that we shall

live in darkness and insensibility is foolish. We should rather be thankful that it has been made psychologically possible for us to choose and to act. If we find that our acts and choices result in damage to others, it is our duty, as human beings, to try to remedy the evil we have caused. It is certainly not our duty to refrain from choice and action because all choices and actions may—indeed must—result in some evil to somebody.

By remote delegation and proxy the English public is trying to make up for the miseries it has unwittingly inflicted on the negroes of Belize. The British Honduras government, for the existence of which we non-chewing despisers of mahogany are at least theoretically responsible, is making great efforts to induce the negro woodmen to go on the land. The task is not easy; for these woodmen have been brought up in a traditional contempt for agriculture. The material difficulties are also great. Still, there is plenty of fertile ground available, and the country, which is about equal in area to Wales, has a population hardly if at all larger than that of Nuneaton. The forests are filled with ruins, and in the palmy days of the Maya Old Empire this territory, which now supports, or rather does not support, forty-five thousand people, may easily have had a million inhabitants. Intensely cultivated, it might again become populous and prosperous. Our refusal to eat our dinners off mahogany is, for the moment, a disaster for the Honduraneans. If it compels them to change their mode of life, it may perhaps some day turn out to have been the kindest thing that has ever been done to them.

British Honduras

IF the world had any ends British Honduras would certainly be one of them. It is not on the way from anywhere to anywhere else. It has no strategic value. It is all but uninhabited, and when Prohibition is abolished, the last of its profitable enterprises—the re-export of alcohol by rum-runners, who use Belize as their base of operations—will have gone the way of its commerce in logwood, mahogany and chicle. Why then do we bother to keep this strange little fragment of the Empire? Certainly not from motives of self-interest. Hardly one Englishman in fifty thousand derives any profit from the Britishness of British Honduras. But *le cœur a ses raisons*. Of these mere force of habit is the strongest. British Honduras goes on being British because it has been British. But this, of course, is not the whole story. We have been educated to personify the country in which we live. A collection of incredibly diverse people living on an island in the North Sea is transformed by a simple mental conjuring trick into a young woman

35

in classical fancy dress—a young woman with opinions that have to be respected and a will that we must help her to assert ; with a virginity which it is our duty to defend and a reputation, which we may never allow to be questioned, for strength, virtue, beauty and a more than papal infallibility. To the overwhelming majority of British voters, taken as individuals, it is probably a matter of indifference whether British Honduras remains within the Empire or without. But the non-existent young lady in fancy dress would be mortally offended by the suggestion that the place should be painted anything but red on the map. Red therefore it remains. The evidence of things not seen is too much for us.

On the Ship

OFF Livingston, which is, somewhat surprisingly, the name of a town in Guatemala, we anchored to take on board a cargo of twenty-four thousand stems of bananas. The loading lasted all night. Under the glare of electric lamps the Carib stevedores came clambering up from their lighters on to the ship. They were black ; they sang as they worked ; sometimes one would break off to execute a few dance steps. Their hats were like those queer shapeless things that beggars in seventeenth-century pictures always wear, and they were dressed in coloured cottons—pinks and blues and yellows, all very pale with age and excess of washing. Against the dark sea the barges were silvery, the banana bunches a luminous green. It was a Teniers—but a Teniers, for a change, of genius—come startlingly to life.

Puerto Barrios

THE Health Officer, the Political Officer, the Customs Officer . . . They sat there in rows. It took us an immensely long time to land. The machinery of bureaucracy worked with a slowness that was partly, no doubt, attributable to the heat, but mainly, I think, to the consciousness, on the part of each individual bureaucrat, of his own dignity as a representative of the Republic of Guatemala. Official dignity tends to increase in inverse ratio to the importance of the country in which the office is held. There are of course exceptions. I have been vilely treated by the minor representatives of the greatest Powers and with courteous alacrity by those of the smallest. But as a general rule the mechanism of over-compensation comes into play, and the official of a small country takes his revenge for political inferiority by personal offensiveness towards foreigners —especially the nationals of powerful states. It is an intolerable bore ; but, then, what else can you expect ?

We got away at last, and walked down the long jetty rejoicing in our freedom. Rejoicing, it turned out, too soon. For at the pier-gates—an enormous bayonet fixed in his rifle—stood an Indian soldier, who demanded peremptorily to see our passports. These, of course, with the accompanying vaccination certificates, tourist's identity cards and all the rest, had been duly examined, stamped and countersigned. But we were foreigners and therefore the legitimate prey of any one in authority. They had given this poor little Indian a real gun and made him a sentry. He was a great man—but a great man who remembered the four hundred years of white oppression. If any one had a right to a bit of compensatory fun at our expense, it was he. We gave him the passports. He studied them very gravely for several minutes, upside down ; then looked from our photographs to our faces and back again with ever-growing suspicion. In another moment he would have arrested us. Only just in time, I took the passports from him, and turning them right side up, showed him the official stamp of the Republic. He might not have learnt to read ; but he ought at least be able to recognize a quetzal-bird when he saw one. The sight of the national emblem produced an immediate effect. Those quetzals proved that Higher Powers had already been at work upon our passports. From a position of exulting superiority, he was suddenly precipitated into abjection. A representative of the Republic of Guatemala, he was to us foreigners as a Brahmin to a pair of Untouchables. But in relation to the Higher Powers he was the most miserable of Outcastes. And now the Higher Powers had hall-marked us with their quetzal-bird as one of themselves. His brief moment of compensatory Brahmin-hood was over ; the full weight of those four hundred years of oppression came heavily down once more upon his shoulders. He saluted and drew back to let us pass. We could afford, now, to feel sorry for him.

Quirigua

AT Quirigua we spent three very pleasant days as the guests of Dr. MacPhail, the head of the United Fruit Company's hospital. The place was astonishingly beautiful, and our host one of the best and most charming of men. The doctor's professional reputation stands very high ; but it is his kindness and his wisdom that have made of him the universal godfather of Guatemala. You cannot travel anywhere in the Republic without meeting people who will

39

talk to you—and talk invariably with affectionate gratitude and respect—of Dr. MacPhail. He is an institution, one of the best in the country.

The brand of malaria that you caught in the Valley of Quirigua was peculiarly virulent. The place was a regular death-trap. To-day, thanks to the work of Dr. MacPhail and his colleagues, Quirigua is almost healthy. The natives have been patiently educated into reporting at the hospital on the appearance of the first symptoms of the disease. Periodical blood-tests are made and the personally healthy, but socially dangerous carriers of infection are subjected to special treatment. Houses are screened and, wherever practicable, the land is drained. Life in the valley is now very nearly safe.

It seems still to be undecided whether malaria was indigenous to America, or whether it was brought from the Old World by the Conquistadores, as a slight return for the Redman's gift (if his gift it really were) of syphilis. Documentary evidence is lacking, and we can only speculate in the abstract.

Here, then, are two theoretical arguments against the indigenousness of the disease. First, endemic malaria tends to keep population low and civilization backward. But the Old Empire Mayas developed a culture that was, in many respects, astonishingly high ; and in the now pestilential regions round Lake Peten their population seems to have reached a density of nearly three hundred to the square mile. (Dr. Ricketson of the Carnegie Institution, arrived at this figure by counting the house mounds on sample clearings made in the jungle round the ruined city of Uaxactun.)

Secondly, there is the case of Cortes, who, in 1525, marched a force from Mexico through Guatemala into Honduras. Mexico, Guatemala, Honduras—names, when one sees them on the map, like any other names. But for those who have walked even a mile or two in the forests of the *tierra caliente*, or ridden up and down the sides of a few *barrancas*, this march must rank as one of the most astonishing of all the feats recorded in the almost unbelievable history of the conquests. Now, if the country had been poisonous with endemic malaria, could an army even of sixteenth-century Spaniards have come through alive ?

Almost all history, up to the present, has been written in terms of politics and economics. The fundamentals of human existence—physiology and psychology—are everywhere ignored. It is a case of *Hamlet* without the Prince of Denmark.

Quirigua

GREEN aisles, and the tattered leaves of the banana trees hung, sunlit or shadowed, like old flags in the chapel of some Order of Knighthood. The aisle darkened to a narrow tunnel ; we were among forest trees. Then, glaringly, the sultry white sky was above us, and there, in the wide clearing, were the great carved monoliths and, at either end of the open space, the pyramid mounds on which the temples had stood. With growing astonishment and admiration, we moved from one magnificent stela to another. This forum had once been thronged. They had burnt copal incense on the altars, perhaps spilt human blood. And every five years, punctually, another of those sculptured stones had been dragged from the distant quarries and hoisted upright into its socket in the ground. And there they still stood, obscurely commemorating man's triumph over time and matter and the triumph of time and matter over man.

Striped like a gaudy convict—and for the same reasons, for he was a dangerous murderer—a large coral snake lay coiled near the foot of the tallest obelisk. At our approach, he woke and oozed slowly away, inch after tricoloured inch, into his hole. And while we were standing in front of the most extraordinary of the monuments—the huge mythological animal that lies at one corner of the southern pyramid—there was a sudden noise in the trees overhead. Looking up, we saw a flock of toucans hopping clumsily among the branches ; grotesque, like a ribald human invention ; and as they moved, their great bills would flash startlingly in the light, like drawn daggers.

QUIRIGUA   Detail of glyph.

Quirigua

FOR an artist the material obstacles in the way of unrestricted self-expression are easier to surmount than the mental. Thus, the Maya sculptors had none but stone implements ; nevertheless, they were as highly accomplished, manually, as the best-equipped statuaries of the age of steel. Skill and an inexhaustible patience had taught them to transcend the limitations of their neolithic technique ; they were free to do whatever they liked with their material. ' Whatever they liked . . .' But what did they like ? The answer to that is that they liked only what they could like, only what they were psychologically capable of liking, only what, in a word, they had been conditioned to like. The *Zeitgeist* is just Professor Pavlov on a cosmic scale.

People who are born into an isolated and homogeneous community are liable to be conditioned much more strictly than the members of a society composed of many diverse elements and in contact with other societies, having traditions different from its own. An Eskimo never sees any one but other Eskimos ; and as Eskimo society is classless and unspecialized, this means that he only sees people who have been brought up in exactly the same way as himself. Comparison

43

is the beginning of criticism, and he has nothing with which to compare the accepted conventions of his small world. With a contemporary European the case is different. He lives in a society divided into a great number of economic, professional and denominational classes ; two hours in an aeroplane will take him to places where people speak a different language, think different thoughts, obey other sexual taboos and have unfamiliar table manners. The circumambient Pavlov rings a great diversity of bells ; there is deconditioning and reconditioning ; there are the conflicts that arise when loyalties are divided and of equal strength. Our minds, in consequence, are much less closely circumscribed than those of the Eskimos. Nevertheless, sooner or later even the most highly civilized and emancipated person comes to a mental frontier which he cannot pass—comes to it, of course, unaware, and does not realize his inability to go further ; for it is of the essence of these inward barriers that they never reveal their presence, unless, as the result of some fortunate or unfortunate conjunction of circumstances, we are shaken out of our second nature and transported violently to the other side of what is thenceforward perceived to have been an arbitrary limitation of our freedom.

The Mayas occupied a position nearer to the Eskimos than to ourselves. The individual was born into a society not much differentiated (it was probably divided into only two classes, the ignorant laity and

the learned priest-rulers) and in contact with other
communities not very different from itself. Conditioning was not quite so strict as it is within the polar
circle ; but it was a good deal stricter than in modern
Europe. Sculptors, as we have seen, could do what
they liked with their materials. But there were certain things which they simply could not like. Perhaps
the most conspicuous absence from Maya sculpture is
that of the female form—*et tout ce qui s'ensuit*. True,
there is, at the Peabody Museum, an incredibly beautiful terra-cotta figure from Campeche of a goddess
with a worshipper resting like a tired child in her
lap. It is a Maya version of the protective Madonna
of Catholic Europe. Piero's at San Sepolcro is perhaps the finest example of the class—a monumental
figure, spreading wide the folds of her cloak to give
shelter to a group of poor mortals, whose helplessness
and unhappiness have symbolically reduced their
stature to that of children. This Maya goddess is a
strong mother, and the artist's treatment of the figure
and the draperies beautifully expresses her character.
There is no hint here of Mylitta or Diana of the
Ephesians. The Maya pantheon included no goddess
of love, and the heavenly person who looked after
the fertility of Central American fields had none of
the female—the all too female—attributes generally
assigned to this deity, but was a man holding an axe
—for he was the god of the thunderbolt as well as
of rain—and grotesquely fitted with the snout of a

tapir. The goddess represented in the Campeche statuette must have been one of the minor divinities, perhaps the object of a heretical cult.

No female principle was active in the Maya universe ; and since Maya sculpture was a religious art, that concerned itself precisely with the divine Nature of Things, no representation of the female form appears among the ruins. I have seen a fair amount of Central American art and can recall only one reference to the act of generation. This was at Monte Alban, near Oaxaca, where there is a bas-relief of an ithyphallic man—the work, so far as I could make out, of the pre-Zapotec occupants of the site. There must, it is obvious, be other objects of the same kind ; but they are certainly rare. Rare enough to justify us in saying that Maya sculptors were so conditioned by their environment that whatever might be their tastes in life, they found sex in art all but unthinkable.

Maya art is florid, but invariably austere ; a more chaste luxuriance was never imagined. It is instructive, in this context, to compare the art of the Central Americans with that, no less richly ornamental, of the Indians. More than any other, Indian art is impregnated with sensuality. From Cape Comorin to the Himalayas, and for the last two thousand years, almost every Hindu artist seems to have been engaged in illustrating the works of Aretino. Even the most sacred persons tend to melt—and at the most solemn moment of their religious life—into suggestive postures.

Buddha among the women of his father's court—here
is a theme that calls for a sensual treatment. But
Buddha taking leave of the world, Buddha resisting
temptation, Buddha preaching—these are another
story. Yet the renderings of these scenes in Indian
art are of the same kind as the renderings of life in
the harem. It is as though a Christian artist were
to paint the Agony in the Garden in terms of Renoir's
Baigneuses, or Bronzino's *Love, Folly and Time*. Indian
art is the same outside the Buddhist tradition as
within it. The boneless limbs—dozens of them, very
often to a single personage—ooze about the picture-
space or the sculpture-volume like a voluptuous ecto-
plasm. The haunches jut to right or left ; the waists
are tapered as though by a delicious process of suction ;
even the men seem as though inflated about the chest ;
and as for the women . . . But language fails. The
very animals are symbols of sensuality. Elephants
have the gracefully bulging appeal of Lakshmi or the
girls in the seraglio of Gotama's father ; and I remember, in the Musée Guimet, a fourth-century marble
of the school of Amaravati surmounted by a frieze
of indeterminate quadrupeds, all kneeling, all with
their bodies bent in the shape of the letter U, and
the succession of their more than human posteriors
raised in curve after luscious curve towards the sky.
A very odd example of the pathetic fallacy.

Of all this treacly and ectoplasmic sensuality there
is, in Maya art, not the smallest trace. The female

47

form, as we have seen, never appears, and the male
body, when it is shown divested of its hieratic ornaments, is always uncompromisingly male and never
takes on those hermaphroditic attributes which distinguish gods and saviours in Indian art. The nearest
approach to the Indian spirit is to be found in the few
statues in the round which have survived among the
ruins of Copan. One of these—a beautiful head and
torso of the maize god—may be studied in the British
Museum. It is a wonderfully graceful and delicate
piece of work : but its delicacy has none of the equivocal, epicene quality of Indian elegance, and its
grace is wholly without lasciviousness.

In Indian art even the ornamental forms have a certain sensual quality. Head-dresses, bracelets, anklets
tend to be conceived as a series of rolls of flesh. A
thigh with two or three tourniquets round it—that is
what the typical Indian tiara looks like. All the lines
in a passage of Indian decoration are curved, all surfaces gently swell and retreat. The straight and the
angular are of rare occurrence in ornament, and even
by the architects they are avoided wherever possible.
In such buildings as the Jambulinga temple at Pat-
tadkal, the Lingaraja temple at Bhuvanesvara, or the
later Kesava temple at Somnathpur (to name but a
few characteristic specimens), the Indians perfected
a kind of organic architecture, whose forms are those,
not of an abstract solid geometry, but of living tissue.
Many of these temples are, in their own way, extra-

48

ordinarily beautiful : but their way is an oppressive
way : they give you a suffocating sense of animal
heat, and their stone flesh seems as though turgid
and pulsating with blood.

Maya decoration is luxuriant like a tropical forest ;
but it is a forest in which one can breathe freely of
an air that is actually exhilarating. The life of the
swarming ornaments—and they are all vehemently
alive—is a life of the mind, of the imagination liberated
from the obsessive warmth and heaviness of material
bodies. Straight lines and angles, surfaces that are
flat and perpendicular to one another—all the abstractions of pure geometry appear among the rich exuber-
ance of the Mayas' symbolic decoration. Their sacred
personages wear no Indian mitres of tight-laced and
bulging meat. No, their head-dresses are sometimes
pure geometrical abstractions, like those metal-smooth
cones and cylinders worn by the people in Piero della
Francesca's frescoes ; sometimes, as on most of the
stelae at Quirigua and Copan, they consist of fantastic
combinations of decorative and symbolic motives ;
sometimes, best of all, they are representations of the
feather tiaras worn by men of rank. These elaborate
haloes of feather fireworks are decorations that are
at once gracefully naturalistic and as austerely abstract
in their formal arrangement as the most mathematical
of cubist designs.

Among the most extravagant of the Mayas' ornamental combinations are the hieroglyphs. The fan-

D   49

tasies of Gothic decoration seem pedestrian by comparison. But however rich and strange, this extravagance is always rigidly disciplined. Each hieroglyph is contained by, and completely fills, its appointed square. The *mise en page* is almost always impeccable. These fantastic and often wildly grotesque symbols are subject to the severest intellectual discipline.

As for Maya architecture—its style is all that is most un-Indian, most abstractly inorganic. An affair of pyramids, of flat walls divided up into rectangular panels, of wide and regular flights of steps, it is an embodiment of man's most distinctively human, his most anti-natural imaginings.

Indian artists, then, liked to use their skill to express sensuality through plastic symbols, to render the emotion accompanying the immediate contact of flesh with living flesh in terms of pictorial, sculptural and even architectural forms. The Mayas, on the contrary, did not like to use their artistic skill in this way. Their decorative forms have no quality of sensuality, and they almost never made direct representations of erotic scenes or of what I may call erotically significant persons. There is no sex in the art of the Mayas ; but, by way of compensation, what a lot of death! From ten onwards, all the glyphs representing numerals in their vigesimal system are variations on the theme of the death's-head. Nine faces, each with its distinguishing character and emblems, but all with the same fleshless lower jaw. The inscriptions on the monuments are mainly concerned with the recording of dates, so that emblems of death are as common among the Central American ruins as numerals upon the stones of a modern cemetery. But death among the ruins is by no means exclusively a by-product of Maya arithmetic. Copan, for example, is full of skulls, or rather of those magnificent skull-symbols, more gruesome than any realistic imitation—those decorative abstractions in stone, by means of which the Maya sculptors expressed the idea of death with a penetrative force only surpassed, in all the history of art, by the Aztecs.

To compare two widely different artistic traditions is to find oneself, inevitably, confronted by a question. Why are the traditions different? Of two artists, both capable, so far as technique is concerned, of doing what they like, why should the one who lives in India like, and the one from Central America dislike, expressing sensuality? Why should one find in death a congenial and stimulating theme, while the other is best inspired by, indeed can hardly escape from, thoughts of sexual pleasure?

In either case, as I have already pointed out, the immediate causal agent is the Local Pavlov—the spirit pervading each particular extent of time and place. But why should the Local Pavlov have chosen to ring just those particular bells which happen to be rung, and no others? The people who believe in a determinism of Race will answer this question by saying that the Local Pavlov had to ring those particular bells, because every Local Pavlov is merely the expression of the fundamental character of the Local Race. Pavlov conditions, but has himself been conditioned by, his victims.

It is possible that there may be some small element of truth in this theory of racial determinism. Congenital differences in metabolism, nervous sensibility and, more doubtfully, intelligence have been observed as characteristics of the members of different races. Certain Melanesian, for example, seem to be, on the average, more sensitive to pain than we are ; Bushmen, Australian Blackfellows and perhaps some races of negroes are perhaps a little less bright in the head than Europeans and Asiatics. But it must be remembered that over large areas of the earth's surface pure races are unknown. In Europe, for example, all talk about the congenital difference of one race from another (let alone its congenital superiority or inferiority) is perfectly irrelevant, for the simple reason that it is only in the remotest recesses and blind alleys of the Continent that anything like a pure race can be discovered : and even here the purity of blood is certainly not untainted. Moreover, even when pure, the race is not, biologically speaking, a true race, but only one of several variations on a single racial theme, the European. Some cultures are, in certain respects, superior to others, but the

explanation of the fact must be sought in the nature
of the cultural tradition, not in the congenital differences between the ' races,' brought up within these
diverse traditions. We are back again with the
Local Pavlov, and the question why one Local
Pavlov should differ from another still remains un-
answered.

It is possible that there are some slight congenital
differences between Indians (whoever the Indians
may be ; for the geographical term connotes every
possible combination of numerous races) and Central
Americans. But I see no particular reason to suppose
that the difference between the two artistic traditions
is attributable to these congenital dissimilarities.
Dr. Gann, it is true, has remarked several times on
the apparent indifference to sexual matters displayed
by the contemporary descendants of the Mayas.
Can it be that the absence of all erotic themes from
Maya art and its prevailing tone of austerity are due
to the fact that the people were, as a whole, congenitally less interested in sex than the Indians or
ourselves ? It may be so, of course ; but I think it
improbable.

In his classical study of ' The Sexual Life of Savages
in North-Western Melanesia,' Dr. Malinowski has
recorded the fact that ' the nervous excitability of
the natives is much less than ours, and their sexual
imagination is relatively very sluggish.' So far as
sex is concerned, the Trobriand Islanders are without

53

faith : only unequivocal contact has power to rouse
them to a state of erotic excitement. Compared
with ourselves they are congenitally undersexed. And
yet, as Dr. Malinowski has shown, the preoccupation
of these people with sexual matters surpasses even
that of the contemporary European.

In the case of the Mayas, it should be remembered
that Dr. Gann's observations were made among the
wretched inhabitants of the Central American low-
lands. Malaria and hookworm, raw alcohol and
malnutrition have reduced these people to a very
low ebb of vitality. It is difficult to make love on
an empty stomach, and still more difficult to make it
on a duodenum that is full of *ankylostoma*. The
Ancient Mayas were masters of the jungle and had
all the land under intensive cultivation. Food, in
their time, must have been abundant, and ' full feasts,'
as the poet has remarked, are ever the ' increasers
of desire.' Properly fed, the Mayas were probably
as amorous as any other people ; and even if their
nervous excitability was not so great as ours, that
would not, as Malinowski has shown, have prevented
them from taking at least as much interest in sex as
we do.

I think, then, that we must attribute the differences
between the Maya and the Indian artistic traditions
entirely, or at least mainly, to culture rather than
racial heredity. If the Local Pavlov behaves in one
way rather than in another, it is not because the

Local Race has such and such congenital idiosyn-
crasies ; it is rather because a number of accidents
have conspired to make him what he is. According
to Marxian theory, the accidents which determine
the nature of the Local Pavlov are all of an economic
kind. But this hypothesis fails completely to account
for the frequently observed fact that two peoples,
whose economic development is fundamentally the
same, have dissimilar cultures. That economics have
some influence on culture is obvious ; but it is surely
no less obvious that their influence is not completely
decisive.

It has been fashionable for some time past to attribute
the formation and development of cultures exclusively
to impersonal forces. Depersonalized, the story of
mankind gains in majestic dignity of appearance, but
loses, unfortunately, in scientific adequacy and veracity.
This august astronomical kind of history just doesn't
happen to be true. Direct observation shows that
accidents of the most trivially personal kind may play
a decisive part in modifying the thought and behaviour of entire communities. For example, the
death of a medicine man during the absence of his
appointed successor has been observed, in one of the
tribes of Pueblo Indians, to lead to a radical change
in the religious ceremonial and beliefs of the entire
community. Knowledge of the rites was a trade
secret reserved to a single man. The man died without having been able to pass on his knowledge to his

official heir ; consequently the religion of a whole tribe was changed.

Socially important secrets are seldom in the hands of a single man ; but there have been, there still are, very many communities in which knowledge and, in general, all the elements of higher culture have been the possession of a few. Consider the contemporary world. The very existence of an industrialized and urbanized society depends on the knowledge and skill of, at the most, one per cent. of its members. A selective massacre of three or four hundred thousand technicians—perhaps of a much smaller number—would bring the whole economic and social life of England to a standstill. True, it would be possible for us to make good this catastrophic loss. But it takes a long time to form a good technician, and while the new men were being trained, most of the population would have died of hunger and disease. Unspecialized agricultural societies are not so abjectly dependent on a class of technicians as are we. Accidents among the guardians of culture do not lead to the physical destruction of the community, but only to a modification of its psychological life.

Maya society consisted, in all probability, of a small ruling class of learned priests and a large, subservient and ignorant laity. In such a community (and even the most democratic and best-educated of modern societies are still fundamentally of this type) the fortuitous appearance among the rulers of an individual possessed of some special congenital ability, or preoccupied for whatever reason with one particular class of ideas, may lead to the formation of a certain tradition of culture that will canalize the thought and behaviour of the whole people for generations. European history provides a striking example of this process. At the beginning of the seventeenth century European thought had broken the banks of its mediaeval conduits and was seething in confused and uncertain flood. The astonishing accident of Galileo reconverted this flood into a river. With ever-increasing impetus thought flowed along the new channels he had prepared for it.

Concerning the history of the Mayas we have no documents beyond the ruins, the dates and the traditions preserved by Landa and in the Popul Vuh and the books of Chilam Balam. One can only speculate about the causes which made their culture what it was. My own conviction is that its distinguishing peculiarities were due to such personal accidents as the birth, in a favoured social position, of exceptional individuals. To what cause, for example, must we attribute that obsessive preoccupation with time, which is such a striking feature of Central American culture? Other agricultural communities have not found it necessary to work out elaborate calendars or to devise an intellectual instrument for thinking back into remotest antiquity. There was nothing, therefore, in their economic development that made

it inevitable for the Mayas to invent the Great Cycle
and establish dates many thousands of years removed
from their own position in time. Personal accident
offers the only plausible explanation of the fact.
We must postulate the appearance among the Maya
priesthood of one man, or a succession of men, haunted
by the consciousness of the perpetual perishing of
things and congenitally equipped to deal with this
obsession in mathematical terms. (The god Itzamma
is possibly the original inventor of the calendar,
deified and worshipped by his compatriots). Once
the practice of calendar-making became established,
it would be as ' natural ' for all succeeding Maya
priests to bother their heads with problems of time
as it was ' natural ' for the Greeks of Herodotus' day
not to bother theirs.

A similar explanation may be suggested to account
for the absence of the female element from Maya
theology and of sensuality from Maya art. The
pantheon of the codices and the monuments is an
elaborate affair, which looks as though it were the
product of a selection and crystallization from some
more primitive folk religion. Significant in this
context is the fact that, in the Archaic Culture which
preceded that of the Mayas, the principle of fertility
is symbolized by a female figure. Why did the Mayas
reject this symbol in favour of the less obviously
appropriate man - with - a - nose - like - a - tapir's ? The
answer, I think, is that somebody, with an anti-

phallic turn of mind, rejected it for them. There was an editing of the old religion—*in usum serenissimi Delphini*. An edited cosmology must necessarily reflect the character of the editors, and this character will become, to a certain extent, the character of all those who accept the edited religion as their guide through life. Philosophy, according to Bradley, is the finding of bad reasons for what we believe by instinct. But most of what we believe by instinct turns out, on analysis, to be merely what we happen to have picked up in childhood. *Instinctively*, the Mayas believed that the god of fertility was a tapir-snouted man. Somebody had once said so and the assertion had been constantly repeated ; therefore they ' felt it in their bones.' In *their* bones, on the contrary, the Indians felt that the principle of fertility was a Yoni-Lingam ; and the Ephesians *knew* (and we may be sure that their intuition had a quality of irrefragable certainty) that the same deity was a woman with four rows of mango-shaped breasts and a swarm of miniature animals crawling up her arms.

The Mayas' preoccupation with the emblems of mortality may also have been due to an intellectual fashion set by a few people. Periods when death was all the rage recurred several times in European history. The fifteenth century, for example, was a time when corpses, skulls and skeletons were extravagantly popular. Painted, sculptured, written about and dramatically represented, the Danse Macabre was everywhere. To the fifteenth-century artist a good death-appeal was as sure a key to popularity as a good sex-appeal is at the present time. The 'forties of the eighteenth century witnessed a revival of this fashionable interest in death. Blair and especially Young were instrumental in making the grave as popular, during a number of years, as the bed. The *Night Thoughts* had an international success comparable to that of the *Green Hat*. The Maya and the later Aztec preoccupation with the more gruesome aspects of death may have been the inevitable result of their economic development or of any other abstraction you like to mention. But it may, even more probably, I think, have been the result of a tradition inaugurated by a few individuals of a peculiar turn of mind. Similarly, the unspeakable horrors of the Aztec sacrifices were a logical outcome of the cosmological speculations of a few philosophers. The sun was alive and required nourishment ; if it were not properly nourished it might die, or at least become angry ; therefore, for the good of humanity at large, human victims had to be bent backwards over a stone and have their hearts ripped out with an obsidian knife. It is the sort of argument that a solitary theologian, brooding over the problems of the world, would first of all devise to account for the existence of sporadic sacrificial rites and then develop, abstractly, to the logical conclusion that, since the sun is large and more than human, solar appetite must be extraordinarily hearty and the supply of victims therefore never sufficiently copious.

We are now in a position to suggest an answer to our original question. Why is one artistic tradition different from another? Geographical, climatic and economic factors play their part. So, perhaps, does racial idiosyncrasy. But the finally decisive element is accident—the accident of an unusual combination of chromosomes and the consequent birth of an unusually gifted person; the accident in an individual's peculiar upbringing or of his finding himself so favourably placed in society that he can exercise an influence on his fellows; the accident of the existence of royal or clerical patronage—and so on, indefinitely. If we care to risk a generalization, we may say that the main features of a culture are predictable by any one acquainted with the impersonal forces at work upon and within the community; but that the details are the result of accident and are therefore unpredictable. For example, we may predict that an agricultural people will have more highly developed arts than a hunting people. But we shall not be able to predict the nature of the traditional forms, nor their artistic quality. No amount of knowledge of the impersonal forces at work will allow us to prophesy that *this* agricultural people will represent the principle of fertility as a phallus or a yoni; *that*, as a man with an axe and the snout of a tapir. All the concrete peculiarities of a cultural tradition are the fruit of accident and cannot be foreseen.

Accident determines not only the traditional themes and forms of a people's art, but also its quality. At first sight it might seem as though artistic ability were a matter of racial inheritance. But when we look more closely we find reason to doubt if this is so. There are no artistic or inartistic races ; there are only, within each social group, certain sets of artistically fortunate or unfortunate accidents. Many facts point to this conclusion. Thus, in the course of its history, the same people may produce works of art of widely varying quality. Egyptian art was sometimes superb ; but at other times (as the contents of Tutankhamen's tomb made only too clear) it could be deplorably cheap, theatrical and vulgar. Italian painting was very nearly non-existent after 1750. English music was once as fine as any in Europe ; with the death of Purcell it evaporated. And yet the English were still the English and, so far from being a decadent race, were displaying immense energy and resourcefulness in almost every other field of human activity.

Again, it is often asserted that the different European races are distinguished by different artistic aptitudes : that the Italians excel in the plastic arts, the English in literature, the Germans in music, and so on. Now, first of all, none of these social entities is a race. The only objective test for difference of race is the Precipitin-Test. Applied to the so-called races of Europe, it shows that ' Nordic,' ' Alpine,' ' Mediterranean ' are the names of inconstant variations, and that all Europeans are fundamentally of the same stock. In the second place, such laudatory or disparaging epithets as ' musical,' ' inartistic,' and so on, do not apply permanently to any social group. The English have had their excellent composers and even one or two first-rate painters. For generations at a time, the Italians have been without decent literature or plastic arts. And so on. We are brought back once again to the accident.

Considered genetically, any given population is a vast roulette table. Every fertile conjunction of a man and a woman is a spin of the wheel. Sometimes there will be, so far as the arts are concerned, an extraordinary run of luck. The literary, or pictorial, or musical lucky number will turn up again and again ; there will be a long succession of artists of genius, of patrons with good taste. Then, suddenly, the luck will turn, and for generations the winning colour or number will obstinately refuse to come out. These runs of luck and of mischance are enough to account for most of the differences in quality between one national art and another. But there is also another factor which must be taken into account. Once established (mainly as the result of personal accidents), an artistic tradition canalizes the activity of artists— and the more isolated and homogeneous the society, the more strict, as we have seen, is their conditioning. Now, it is possible that some traditions are more propitious to artists than others. An extreme case of the unpropitious tradition may be found in Mohammedan India. Here, all representations of human and even of animal forms are against the rules. There is, consequently, no sculpture worthy of the name, and such bootleg miniature painting as exists is on a miserably small scale and qualitatively poor and unsubstantial.

More subtly unpropitious are certain purely formal traditions, such as the Middle Minoan or the recent and very similar Barcelona *art nouveau* traditions. Perhaps a very great artist might be able to surmount the obstacles which these put in his way. I do not know. Anyhow, the difficulty of making something satisfactory out of forms that are a mixture of the naturalistic and the slimily decorative is obviously very great.

In the Train

THE green luxuriance of the coastal belt gave place, as we rolled up the valley of the Motagua, to drought and dust. The river flowed between vast dry hills, golden-tawny except where the shadows of clouds had turned them to indigo. Here and there, the sky-

line was fledged with a brown scrub, bare or with the
withered leaves still hanging on the branches. Under
the blistering sun, the landscape was strangely wintry.

From the bare slopes immediately above the river
huge candelabra cacti rose stiffly into the air. There
was no shade : the dust whirled up as we passed.
Near the villages the shrunken stream of the Motagua
was alive with bathers—men lying in the water
like buffaloes, with only their noses projecting out
of the blessed coolness ; brown children at play ;
women in their shifts squatting in the shallows and,
with a half coconut shell, scooping up the water and
pouring it languidly over their bodies. From our
travelling oven, we watched them enviously.

The train began to climb, up and up interminably
into the parched hills. The villages were few, miserable and far between. On the fringes of a particularly
dismal collection of shanties a large Greek temple
made of cement and corrugated iron dominated the
landscape for miles around. As we steamed out of
the station, I noticed that the place was called Progreso.
The fact annoyed me ; I can detect an irony without
having it underlined for me. Progreso, the shanties
and that tin-roofed temple—it was insultingly too
obvious. Like something in the *Forsyte Saga*. Later,
I was to see a great many more of these Guatemalteco
parthenons. Temples of Minerva, they are called.
Every fair-sized village has one of them. They were
built by dictatorial command, and are the late Presi-

dent Cabrera's contribution to the national culture. He even established a Minerva Day, when such school children as there were marched out to give gymnastic displays and sing patriotic anthems under those tin roofs. But in 1920 Cabrera went the way of all Central American dictators, and since then, I gather, the cult of Minerva has declined.

Guatemala City

THE capital is a pleasant, if rather ugly town, about as populous as Norwich, but more extensive. Earthquakes are frequent, and it is therefore customary to build houses of only a single story. Defect of height has to be made up for by excess of length and breadth ; you can walk a surprisingly long way without coming to the end of this town of only a hundred and twenty thousand inhabitants. In area, at least, it is a metropolis.

The *monde* of Guatemala consists of the local Spanish-American aristocracy, with which, since it tends to keep itself to itself, the casual visitor makes very few contacts, and of the resident foreigners, circling planet-wise, at graded hierarchical distances, around their respective legations. Most of the familiar features of colonial life are reproduced in Guatemala with a punctual fidelity. There are the usual clubs—American, Golf, Country and German—and, between six and eight every evening, in the covered *patios* of the two principal hotels, the usual whiskies-and-sodas. Happily, nobody feels it necessary to keep up prestige by means of ceremonial magic ; there is none of that wearisome ' dressing for dinner,' which is one of the curses of tropical existence under the Union Jack.

The civilized, non-Indian fraction of the Guatemalan community has suffered severely from the depression. Coffee does not sell, or sells at a loss ; and the same is true of bananas, of sugar, of cattle, of mahogany—of everything, indeed, which Guatemala ever exported.

In the streets of the capital you see but few traces of that flashing Parisian modishness which illuminates Caracas. Venezuelan oil, we must presume, is more profitable than Guatemalan coffee. Still, the Guatemalan ladies are not without elegance. They know, at any rate, how to set off becomingly their own peculiar style of beauty. And what lovely creatures some of them are ! A certain amount of Indian blood flows in the veins of practically every European family that has been long established in Central America. Not more than three hundred thousand Spaniards settled in New Spain during the whole colonial epoch —a thousand white immigrants a year, of whom the great majority were men. These men begot children ; but the only women they could beget them on were Indians, or part-Indians. Somewhere in the history of almost all the white creole families there is, inevitably, a copper-coloured ancestress. This slight admixture of Indian blood results in a strange and very striking type of feminine beauty. The eyes are large and expressively Spanish, the cheek-bones Indian and high. Indian or Andalusian, the smooth opaque skin invites an artificial complexion. The shoulders are broad, like the Indians', the bosom deep ; but the arms are slender, the extremities small. A strange beauty, I repeat, and for some reason extraordinarily fragile-looking and precarious, as though it were on the verge of disappearing and to-morrow would no longer be there. And for all I know to the contrary, it probably won't be there. Tough and durable youthfulness is a product of the temperate zone, the modern beauty parlour and the culture of the abdomen. Some of our professional beauties are almost everlasting.

Et, chêne, elle a vécu ce que vivent les chênes. . . .

But here, near the Equator, it is still, as in Malherbe's day it was with us, a matter of roses.

Guatemala City

A NEW session of Congress was to begin that morning, and the President would open his parliament in state.

68

GUATEMALA CITY

On our way to the market we were held up for more than an hour by the mere anticipation of his passage. The route was lined with troops and, even with the great man an hour away in his palace, nobody was allowed to pass. The soldiers were stumpy little men, not much more on an average than five foot three or four in their boots. They were all pure Indians from some village in the highlands ; but at a first glance one might have taken them for Japs, and, after a second, wondered if perhaps they weren't Eskimos. Whites and *ladinos* were conspicuously absent from the ranks. They can afford to buy their freedom from military service. Nor, I imagine, do the authorities greatly encourage them to enter the lower grades of the army. In a country liable to revolutionary disturbances, rulers have always preferred to surround themselves with foreign rather than with native troops. However good their discipline, you can never be quite sure that soldiers will obey when they are ordered to shoot their own people. With foreigners there will be little risk of such compunctious insubordination. A Sikh regiment would hardly have fired on the crowd in the Jalianwalabagh at Amritsar ; but when General Dyer gave his order, the Gurkhas blazed away with perfect equanimity. Every Central American nation is in reality two nations. These Quichés and Cakchiquels from the hills are as foreign in the white and *ladino* capital as Nepalese in the Punjab. They can be relied on to obey any orders. Whether the officers can be relied on to give the right orders is another question which it would be vain in this land of *pronunciamientos* to discuss.

Cavalry at the trot and, in the midst, a top hat, gliding ; some cheers, some military trumpeting, out of tune. The President had passed. We were free at last to cross the road.

The covered market was as large as several cathedrals and crowded. Tiny Indian women, carrying their own weight in farm produce and always with a baby or two slung like haversacks over their shoulders, moved hither and thither silently on bare feet. Whole families of dark-skinned peasants squatted immovably in the fairway. *Ladino* housewives stood bargaining at the stalls. The tone of their voices when they spoke to the Indian vendors was either arrogant or, if meant to be kindly, condescending. Central American half-castes are brought up to be a good deal more Aryan than the Aryans. Their attitude towards those who, after all, are their mothers' people, is almost invariably offensive. They despise the Indians, take no interest in their customs, and feel it as a personal offence that the foreigner should pay so much attention to them. A sense of inferiority calls—with what dismal regularity !—for over-compensation. How much of every human being is an automaton ? Three-quarters ? Four-fifths ? Nine-tenths ? I do not know ; but in any case the proportion is depressingly high. In all our Central American wanderings we did not meet a single *ladino* who was not over-compensating. The mechanism functioned infallibly, like a Rolls Royce.

Meanwhile, we had been slowly jostling our way down narrow aisles whose walls were banked-up flowers and vegetables and tropical fruits. The profusion was fabulous. The market at Guatemala is the only place where I have seen reality outdoing a Dutch still life. The meanest fruit stall was one in the eye for Snyder and the Van Heems. 'Put *that* in your pipe, Weenix,' it seemed to proclaim, 'and smoke it—if you can.'

The display of local handicrafts was meagre and of disappointingly poor quality. A few specimens of native weaving and embroidery were amusing enough in a crude, unsubtle way, and we found some hat bands made of plaited horse-hair which were really astonishingly pretty. But that was all. We consoled ourselves with the thought that there would probably be better stuff in the country plazas.

Outside in an overflow market we saw an old Indian woman selling iguanas. They were cheap ; you could buy a miniature dragon with three feet of whip-lash tail, all alive, for twenty or thirty cents. Flayed and gutted, the dried carcasses of several more lay in a neat row on the pavement, a pale meat crusty with flies. Near them stood an enormous bowl, full of iguana eggs. Curiosity wrestled with prejudice and was at last defeated ; we moved away, leaving the eggs untasted. That evening we happened to

71

pass again along the same street. Business in lizards had evidently been slack ; the old woman's pitch was still crawling with monsters. While we were looking, she began to pack up her wares for the night. One by one, she took up the animals and dumped them into a circular basket. The tails projected, writhing. Angrily she shoved them back into place ; but while one was being folded away, another would spring out, and then another. It was like a battle with the hydra. The abhorred tails were finally confined under a net. Then, hoisting the lizards on to her head, and with the bowl of their eggs under her arm, the old woman marched away, muttering as she went heaven knows what imprecations against all reptiles, and probably, since she shot a furious look in our direction, all foreigners as well.

Guatemala City

THE little Indian soldiers looked very smart in their khaki uniforms ; their equipment was neat and new ; the rifles they carried seemed the last word in scientific murder. The Guatemalan army is reputed to be efficient and, considering the size and resources of the country, it is certainly large. And what is it for ? For police work within the country ? But half a dozen aeroplanes, a few light tanks and armoured cars and a small but highly disciplined force of mounted infantry would be amply sufficient to preserve order even in a land of *pronunciamientos*. No, these big battalions are not for domestic consumption ; they are for export—' for defence against foreign aggression,' as our statesmen more gracefully put it.

In the case of Guatemala the foreign aggression can only come from, and the export of battalions only proceed to, El Salvador, Honduras, Nicaragua and Costa Rica on the one side, and Mexico and British Honduras on the other. The Mexican state of Chiapas long was, and British Honduras still is, regarded by the Guatemalans as an *irredenta*. But Mexico and the British Empire are too formidable for any military export trade to be worth attempting. Before such manifest impossibilities, even passion counts costs, considers self-interest and finally sees reason. No, Guatemala's military exports and imports have been, and for all practical purposes can only be, to and from the other four Central American Republics.

Central America achieved its independence from Spain in 1821, and during the succeeding century the Five Republics into which the old Captaincy General of Guatemala was broken have been at war, in various permutations and combinations of alliance, four or five times, and on two other occasions have escaped war only as the result of foreign arbitration.

To understand European politics, one should read

the history of Central America. This is not paradox, but scientific method. It is by studying the simple that we learn to understand the more complex phenomena of the same kind. The behaviour of children and lunatics throws light on the more elaborate behaviour of adults and the sane. Pavlov's dogs have explained many hitherto inexplicable characteristics of human beings. Most of the little we know about the anthropology of civilized peoples is the fruit of enquiries into the nature of primitive societies. Central America, being just Europe in miniature and with the lid off, is the ideal laboratory in which to study the behaviour of the Great Powers.

The most striking facts about the wars of Central America is that none of them has had an origin which could possibly be interpreted as economic. There has never been any question of capturing markets, destroying dangerous commercial competitors, seizing provinces for the sake of their industrially valuable resources. The wars of the Five Republics have been wars between Conservatives and Liberals, between Clericals and Anti-Clericals, between those who desired a single federal republic and those who claimed sovereign independence for each state. They have not been wars of interest, but of ' political principle '—in other words, wars of pure passion. Wars are now generally attributed to the machinations of rival groups of capitalists. Owning as they do the instruments of propaganda, they first emotionally

involve the dumb deluded public (already prepared
by all its education to be involved) in their private
quarrels ; then, when the emotional temperature is
high enough, proceed, in their capacity as rulers, or
powers behind thrones, to give the order for mobiliza-
tion and slaughter.

This description is probably true enough ; but it
remains a mere description, requiring to be elucidated
and explained. We want first of all to know why
the exploiters quarrel ; and, in the second place, why
the exploited allow themselves to be involved.

The theorists of the left proclaim it almost as an
axiom that, where there is private profit-taking, there
of necessity must also be periodical war. But this
is clearly untrue. If capitalists were interested only
in the efficient exploitation of their victims (as would
to heaven they had had the sense to be !) they would
not waste their resources in fighting one another ;
they would combine to work out the most efficient
scheme for squeezing profits out of the entire planet.
That they do not do so—or do so only spasmodically
and inadequately—is due to the fact that the exploiters
are as much the slaves of the passions aroused by
nationalism as the exploited. They own and use the
instruments of propaganda, but are themselves the
first to believe in, and to act upon, the nonsense they
broadcast. These Machiavels are incapable of seeing
their own best economic advantage. Peace, it is
obvious, and internationalism pay ; war on its present

scale must, in the long run, inevitably harm the capitalists who bring it about. Nevertheless, they *do* bring it about—and believe, under the patriotic cant, that they are bringing it about in their own interests. They make war in order to increase the profits they derive from their particular system of nationalist economy at the expense of the profits derived by fellow capitalists from rival systems. (Nationalism is against the higher economic interests of the exploiters ; but it creates certain particular interests of monopoly which to some extent justify the capitalists in their appeal to arms on business grounds.) They also make and threaten wars on the Machiavellian principle that foreign dangers give the ruler an opportunity for strengthening his position at home. It is for this reason that all the post-war dictators have been scare-mongers and sabre-rattlers. The fear of each people for its neighbours confirms the power of the rulers who happen to be in office. But what is this power compared with the power that would be wielded by an oligarchy of world-rulers ? And compared with the profits to be derived from a world-system of economy, how poor are the profits earned under a mere nationalist system ! Moreover, modern war is demonstrably ruinous to economic activity and disruptive of social order. So far from enriching and strengthening himself by war on the present scale, the capitalist ruler is likely to lose in the convulsion most of such money and power as he possesses. In spite of which, our rulers insist that the political and economic system shall remain (to their own manifest disadvantage) nationalistic. Safe and profitable, internationalism is yet rejected. Why? Because all capitalist rulers are bound by a theology of passion that prevents them from rationally calculating their profits and losses. And so long as such a theology continues to be accepted by rulers, it makes no difference whether these are private profit-makers or bureaucrats representing 'the People.' The development of nationalistic state-socialism is not only possible ; at the present moment, it actually seems a probability.

The truth is that our so-called wars of interest are really wars of passion, like those of Central America. To find a war of pure interest one must go far afield. The Opium War between England and China was one of the very few whose causes were purely and unadulteratedly economic. 'All for Hate,' is the title of every great international tragedy of modern times, ' or the World Well Lost.'

' *Les intérêts*,' writes the French philosopher, Alain, ' *transigent toujours, les passions ne transigent jamais.*' Interests are always ready to compound, passions never. You can always discuss figures, haggle over prices, ask a hundred and accept eighty-five. But you cannot discuss hatred, nor haggle over contradictory vanities and prejudices, nor ask for blood and accept a soft answer. Neither can you argue away the immediately experienced fact that boasting is delightful, that it is bliss to feel yourself superior to the other fellow, that ' righteous indignation ' is wildly intoxicating, and that the thrill of being one of a mob that hates another mob can be as pleasurably exciting as a prolonged orgasm. The exploited who succumb to the nationalist propaganda of the exploiters are having the time of their lives. We have asked what they get out of being involved in their masters' quarrels. In the early stages of being involved they get the equivalent of free seats at a magnificent entertainment, combining a revival meeting with championship boxing and a pornographic cinema show. At the call of King and Country, they spring to arms. Can we be surprised ?

La guerre naît des passions. But before we begin to elaborate this proposition, we must ask ourselves the very pertinent question : whose passions ? The passions of the people as a whole ? Or only of the rulers ? *Of both*, I believe is the correct answer. It is the rulers, of course, who actually declare war ; and they do so, first, because they are moved by passions that the theology of nationalism has taught them to regard as creditable ; and, second, because they wish to defend interests which nationalism has either really created or which they themselves have invented to serve as a rational justification for their passions. But rulers cannot carry on a war unless the ruled are moved by the same passions or the same rationalizations of passions as themselves. Before war can be waged, the mass of the people must be made to imagine that they want the war ; that the war is in their interests or at least unavoidable. This end is accomplished by a violent campaign of propaganda, launched at the time of the declaration of war. But such a campaign would not be effective if the people had not from earliest childhood been indoctrinated with the nationalist theology. Owing to this nationalistic conditioning of all their worst passions, the ruled are sometimes actually more war-like than their rulers, who find themselves reluctantly propelled towards a war which they would like to avoid. At other times, the ruled are less the slaves of nationalist passion and prejudice than the rulers. Thus, I think it would be true to say that, at present, the majority of French and English people are more pacific, less dangerously obsessed by the Moloch-theology of nationalism, readier to think of international politics in terms of reason, than are their governments. Rulers naturally tend to oppose the policy of the ruled. When the French populace was imbued with nationalism, the bourgeoisie was pacific. Now that it thinks of freedom, in terms not of nations, but classes, the rulers are nationalistic.

In the notes which follow, I shall discuss the war-producing passions in themselves, without specific references to those who feel them. In practice, it is obvious, everything depends on the rulers. They

79

can either encourage and systematize the expression of these passions ; or, alternatively, they can prevent the theology of nationalism from being taught in the schools or propagated by other means. Rulers who wished to do so could rid the world of its collective insanity within a generation. Revolution by persuasion can be nearly as swift and ' catastrophic ' as revolution by violence and, if carried out scientifically, promises to be incomparably more effective. The Jesuits and the Assassins have demonstrated what can be done by intelligent conditioning of the young. It is disastrous that the only people who have thoroughly learnt the lessons of Loyola and the Old Man of the Mountain should be the exponents of militant nationalism in Germany and Italy, and the exponents of militant collectivism in Russia. War is the common denominator of all the existing systems of scientific conditioning.

So much for the people who feel the passions. Now for the passions themselves—hatred, vanity and the nameless urge which men satisfy in the act of associating with other men in large unanimous droves.

It is reported of Alain that when, in the trenches, his fellow soldiers complained of the miseries of war, he would answer : ' *Mais vous avez eu assez de plaisir ; vous avez crié Vive l'Armée ou Vive l'Alsace-Lorraine. Il faut que cela se paye. Il faut mourir.*'

Hate is like lust in its irresistible urgency ; it is, however, more dangerous than lust, because it is a passion less closely dependent on the body. The emission of a glandular secretion suffices to put an end to lust, at any rate for a time. But hate is a spiritual passion, which no merely physiological process can assuage. Hate, therefore, has what lust entirely lacks—persistence and continuity : the persistence and continuity of purposive spirit. Moreover, lust is ' perjured, murderous, bloody, full of blame,' only before action ; hate, both before and during action. In the case of lust, the time of action is limited to a few minutes or seconds, and with the ending of the action coincides the temporary or permanent ending of that particular passion of lust. Very different is the case of hatred. Its action may continue for years ; nor does the ending of any particular phase of the action necessarily entail the ending of the emotional state which was its justification.

Hate is not, of course, the only passion behind the theory and practice of nationalism. Vanity—the collective vanity manifested by each individual member of a group which he regards as superior to other groups and whose superiority he feels in himself— vanity is equally important ; and both these passions are combined with, and derive an added strength from, that lust for sociability whose indulgence yields such enormous psychological dividends to the individual of a gregarious species. At ordinary times, indeed, vanity seems to be more important than hate. But it must not be forgotten that hate is the actual or potential complement of vanity. Delusions of greatness are always accompanied by persecution mania. The paeans of self-praise with which the nationalists are perpetually gratifying themselves are always on the point of modulating into denunciations of other people. Hatred, even when not actually expressed, is always there just below the surface. One is therefore justified in speaking of this passion as fundamental in the contemporary theory and practice of nationalism.

So far as the physiology and psychology of individual human beings is concerned, there is nothing to prevent the pleasures of hatred from being as deliciously enduring as the pleasures of love in the Muslim paradise. Fortunately, however, hatred in action tends to be self-destructive. The intoxicating delight of being one of thousands bawling ' *Deutschland, Deutschland über alles*,' or ' *Marchons, marchons, qu'un sang impur abreuve nos sillons*,' is apt to be brought speedily to a close. Bawling in mobs is almost as good as copulation ; but the subsequent action generally leads to discomfort, extreme pain and death all round. *Il faut que cela se paye*, and the payment entails the transformation of hatred from a source of pleasure to a source of misery, and in many cases the transformation of the hater himself into a corpse. This, I repeat, is fortunate ; for if the gratification of hatred were always as delicious as it is sometimes, then there would obviously never be any interval of peace. As it is, the world seems *well* lost only so long as the action dictated by hatred remains successful. When it ceases to be successful, the loss of the world is realized and regretted, and the haters become homesick once more for a quiet life on friendly terms with their neighbours. But once a war has been started, they are not allowed, and do not even allow themselves, to succumb to this natural homesickness. Nationalism is a set of passions rationalized in terms of a theology. When, in the natural course of events, the passions tend to lose their intensity, they can be revived artificially by an appeal to the theology. Moreover, ' tasks in hours of insight—or orgasm—willed can be through hours of gloom fulfilled.' A theology, with its accompanying principles and categorical imperatives, is a mechanism for making it possible to do in cold blood the things which, if nature were left to itself, it would be possible to do only in hot blood.

The commonest, one might call it the natural, rhythm of human life is routine punctuated by orgies. Routine supports men's weakness, makes the fatigue of thought unnecessary, and relieves them of the intolerable burden of responsibility. Orgies, whether sexual, religious, sporting or political, provide that periodical excitement which all of us crave, and which most of us are too insensitive to feel except under the most crudely violent stimulation. Hence (beside all the private and domestic orgies) such public stimulations as gladiatorial games, bull-fights,

boxing matches, gambling ; hence patriotic demon-
strations, hymns of hate, mass meetings and parades ;
hence saturnalia, carnivals, firsts of May, fourths and
fourteenths of July ; hence religious revivals, pilgrimages, miraculous grottoes and all the techniques for
arousing what Professor Otto has called the ' numinous ' emotions. Sensitive and civilized men can dispense with these crude, almost surgical methods for
producing excitement. But sensitive and civilized men
are rare—as rare as the Americans who, after ten years
of prohibition, can enjoy a glass of good wine. The
vast majority can only get their kick out of the equivalent of proof spirit. Consider in this context the
adaptation to popular needs of the religion of Jesus.
For Professor Otto, the essence of religion is the
' numinous ' emotion in all its forms, from panic
terror up to a rapturous awareness of the *mysterium
tremendum fascinans* of the world. And so far as the
religion of the ordinary, insensitive but excitement-
loving person is concerned, this is probably true.
Jesus, however, lays no stress on such emotions, nor
prescribes any technique for arousing them. For him,
it is clear, the surgical stimulation of deliberately
induced ecstasy, of luscious ritual and corybantic
revivalism were all entirely unnecessary. They were
not unnecessary for his followers. These, in the course
of a few hundred years, made Christianity almost as
sensational and orgiastic as Hinduism. If they had
not, there would have been no Christians.

84

The bearing of these facts on Central American wars, and international disputes in general, is obvious. Nationalistic theology is not only a substitute for passion ; it is also an excuse for it. It justifies those periodical orgies of emotion which are, for the great majority of men and women, a psychological necessity. So long as these orgies remain platonic, no harm is done. They are a bit undignified, that is all. But if people need to get drunk, if they cannot preserve their soul's health without occasional orgasms of hatred, self-love and group-frenzy, why, then, drunk they must get and orgasms they must have. The trouble is that the greatest *immediate* happiness of the greatest number too often leads to the greatest *ultimate* unhappiness. The orgies of nationalism are not platonic orgies-for-orgies'-sake. They lead to practical results—to the piling up of armaments, to senseless economic competition, to embargoes on foreign goods, and ultimately to war. *Il faut que cela se paye.* The fundamental problem of international politics is psychological. The economic problems are secondary and, but for the psychological problems, would not exist. The good intentions of such statesmen as desire peace —and many of them do not even desire it—are rendered ineffective by their consistent refusal to deal with the war-disease at its source. To attempt to cure symptoms, such as tariff-wars and armaments, without at the same time attacking the psychological causes of these symptoms, is a proceeding foredoomed to failure. What is the use of a disarmament or a World Economic Conference so long as the people of each nation are deliberately encouraged by their leaders to indulge in orgies of group-solidarity based on, and combined with, self-congratulation and contemptuous hatred for foreigners? Our need is rather for a World Psychological Conference, at which propaganda experts should decide upon the emotional cultures to be permitted and encouraged in each state and the appropriate mythologies and philosophies to accompany these emotional cultures.

Before we enter into the possible activities of such a conference it is necessary to consider the psychoanalytic theory of international relations set forth in Dr. F. Vergin's book, *Sub-Conscious Europe*. Dr. Vergin's contention is that war is an escape from the restraints of civilization. 'It is quite useless to demand higher standards of Christian morality and at the same time to preach peace.' Ethical restraints exact their own revenge. It is no coincidence that, in France, the parties most closely associated with Catholicism should be the most violently chauvinistic. All European parties with a Christian orientation are fundamentally warlike, because the psychological pressure of Christian restraint necessarily urges them on to find emotional relief in hatred. Such, in brief, is Dr. Vergin's theory. It has the merit of being simple and the defect of being perhaps a bit too simple. Ours is not the only civilization that has imposed restraints

86

on the appetites of the individual. Every civilization imposes restraints : otherwise it would not exist. Again, not all restraints are felt to be restraints : people can be so conditioned as to accept certain artificial restraints as though they were part of the order of nature. The restraints which hedge in the individuals of a primitive society are more numerous and less escapable than those by which we are surrounded. In spite of which, many primitive and semi-primitive societies have been on the whole remarkably peaceable. For example, Mexico and Central America before their separation from Spain had enjoyed two centuries and a half of almost uninterrupted peace. And yet the population of these provinces laboured under restraints of all kinds—political restraints imposed from without, and psychological restraints imposed from within, as the result of stringent religious conditioning. According to Dr. Vergin's argument, the psychological pressure generated by such restraints should have driven the people into civil war. It did nothing of the kind, and for several good reasons. In the first place, all members of Spanish Colonial society were brought up in an emotional culture that made them regard submission to King and Church, and reasonably decent behaviour towards their fellow-subjects, as unquestionably right and ' natural.' In the second place, their life was so arranged that they could get all the orgiastic excitements—religious ceremonies, dances,

sports, public executions and private wife-beatings—
for which they periodically craved. This being so,
they had no urgent psychological need for the orgies
of militant nationalism. The dangerous psychological pressure, described by Dr. Vergin, is worked up
only among puritans who disapprove and suppress
all exciting and pleasurable activities whatsoever.
' Righteous indignation ' is the only emotional orgasm
these people allow themselves ; they therefore live
in a chronic state of hatred, disapproval and un-
charitableness. The rulers of Central America were
not puritans and, while imposing socially valuable
restraints upon their subjects, allowed them by way
of compensation a plentiful choice of more or less
harmless amusements. Furthermore, if any of them
wanted to enjoy the pleasures of public hatred there
were always Sir Francis Drake and Morgan and
Dampier ; there were always, besides the buccaneers
and pirates, all the home-country's official enemies ;
there were always heretics, protestants, foreigners and
heathens. Objects of collective detestation in rich
variety—and most of them, very fortunately, a long
way off, so that it was possible, the greater part of the
time, to enjoy the pleasures of nationalism platonic-
ally, without having to suffer the smallest incon-
venience.

At the beginning of the nineteenth century this
vast and, for long generations, peaceable Spanish
colony transformed itself into six independent states,

each in an almost chronic condition of civil war and
each disliking all the rest so intensely that the civil
war from time to time gave place to savage outbursts
of fighting between state and state. The reasons for
this strange and distressing metamorphosis are such
as to deserve the most careful consideration by the
delegates to our hypothetical World Psychological
Conference.

From the very beginning, there had always been
the best possible economic reasons why the Indians,
the *mestizos* and the American-born white creoles
should wish to revolt against the dominion of Spain.
In varying degrees all were exploited by the distant
government and, still more, by its lawless representatives on the spot. During the later seventeen-
hundreds, as a result of Galvez's reforms, the economic
condition of the country and its native-born inhabitants
seems to have improved ; it is probably true to say
that, at the turn of the new century, there were actually fewer economic reasons for revolt than there ever
had been in the history of the colonies. These fewer
reasons were still, of course, many and enormous.
But they would not in themselves have been enough
to initiate a war of independence. The victims of
oppression had been so thoroughly conditioned to
accept the existing situation that they found the idea
of revolt unthinkable. It became thinkable only
when Napoleon deposed the legitimate king of Spain
and usurped the throne for Joseph Bonaparte. Spanish-

American loyalty had been, till then, astonishingly solid—a great arch, as it were, flung, in apparent defiance of all the laws of political physics, across a gulf of bottomless incompetence and iniquity. The millions of its component stones all centred upon, and were held together by, the key-stone of the legitimate king's divine right to rule ; and the art of the psychological engineers who raised it—the priests and the Spanish administrators—had consisted in suggesting the people into the conviction that this divine right was not only their key-stone, but their rock of ages as well, and that without its presence, there, at the crown and centre of everything, they would be lost, non-existent, eternally damned. Napoleon brutally removed the possessor of the divine right to rule the Spanish empire. Deprived of its key-stone, the arch disintegrated. The first symptoms of disintegration was the Indian revolt in Mexico headed by Hidalgo. This was an orthodox economic revolution of oppressed serfs—but an economic revolution made possible only by the removal of divine authority personified by Charles IV. Goya's old figure of fun was God's representative, and his deposition meant that, from being almost or completely unthinkable, revolution suddenly became not only thinkable but actable.

The most curious fact in the history of the Mexican and Central American revolt against Spain is that independence was actually proclaimed by the conservatives and catholics. More royalist than the

king, they were afraid of what would happen to them
if they remained connected with the liberal, constitutional Spain of 1820. To preserve their loyalty to a
non-existent king-by-divine-right, they rebelled against
the actual king, who, at that moment, had been forced
to become a constitutional monarch.

So much for the revolt from Spain. The subsequent
history of the ex-colonials is the history of men with a
traditional culture of the emotions suitable to one kind
of political régime, trying to establish another régime
borrowed from abroad, and failing, because the new
system could not be worked except by people brought
up in an entirely different emotional culture. The
whites, near-whites and *mestizos*, who constituted the
only politically conscious and politically active element
in the population, had been brought up to accept the
divine right of the king to rule them. At the same time
they preserved the anarchic tradition of the Renaissance, regarding themselves as individuals, each having
the right to do as well as he could for himself. Accordingly, we find reverence for the throne accompanied
by evasion of its commands. The people were simultaneously convinced that the king had a divine right
to make the laws, and that they, as individuals, had a
divine right to disobey them whenever they could do
so advantageously and without being found out. After
the Bonapartist usurpation of 1808, the idea began to
dawn upon them that they themselves might make the
laws ; which, in due course, after the declaration of

independence, they proceeded to do. But unfortunately they had carried over from the *ancien régime* the idea that each man had also an inalienable right to break the laws. Such an idea was not too harmful under a monarchy, which provided a certain stability and continuity of rule. But it was fatal under a republic. Democratic institutions can only work where individuals have been conditioned to show public spirit and a sense of responsibility. The correct emotional culture for self-governing people is one that produces a feeling for honour and ' sportsmanship.' Battles may still be won on the playing-fields of Eton ; but, what is perhaps more creditable to those elm-shadowed expanses of soggy turf, colonial empires are humanely lost there. That capacity to see the other fellow's point of view, that reluctance to exploit to the full his chronic weakness or momentary disadvantage, that scrupulosity which Tennyson was already denouncing as ' the craven fear of being great,' and which (in spite of numerous individual and official backslidings) has come more and more to be characteristic of the national policy towards subject races, are all the products of these playing-fields. Cricket and football prepared our administrators for the task of humanely ruling and for the more recent task of not ruling, and scepticism has finished off the job which games began. Of the newly invented Maxim gun, H. M. Stanley, the explorer, remarked : ' It is a fine weapon, and will be invaluable for subduing the heathen.' Nobody could utter such words now, because nobody has the kind of faith professed by Stanley. Given the means of action, all strong faith must inevitably result in persecution and attempts at the domination of others. Scepticism makes for tolerance and peaceable behaviour. All Central Americans were brought up as unsporting believers. Hence, with the disappearance of monarchy, the chronic misgovernment of every Central American state.

The newly fashionable idea of nationalism was imported along with the idea of self-government. Applying the logic of this philosophy of hatred and division to their own immediate problems, the people of Central America tried to make each administrative district into an independent country. There were moments when single departments of provinces (such as the department of Quezaltenango in Guatemala) declared their independence. But such extravagances of folly were not permitted by the other departments, whose representatives insisted on the new countries being at least as large as the old colonial provinces. These, heaven knows, were small enough. The introduction of the nationalistic idea into Central America resulted in the dismemberment of a society which had hitherto been unquestionably one. Fellow-subjects of the same king, speaking the same language, professing the same religion and having every possible economic reason for remaining united, the Mexicans

BEYOND THE MEXIQUE BAY

and Central Americans were constrained by the
emotional logic of an imported theology of hatred to
renounce all their ties of blood and culture. Almost
from one day to another this hitherto united society
divided itself into six arbitrary groups of artificial
enemies.

All enemies, except those fighting for the strictly
limited food supply of a given territory, may be described as artificial enemies. But there are degrees
of artificiality. The artificiality of the enmity between
the Central Americans is of the highest order. Nationalism is the justificatory philosophy of unnecessary and
artificial hatred. Under its influence, and in the
absence of natural enemies, men will go out of their
way to create artificial ones, so as to have objects on
which to vent their hatred. Similarly, in the absence
of women or of a subjective taste for women, men
will imaginatively transform other men into artificial
women, so as to have objects on which to vent their
lusts. Like collective hatred, homosexuality has its
justifying theology, adumbrated by Plato, and in recent
years systematically worked out by M. André Gide.
This author has done for the love of artificial women
what Maurice Barrès did for the hatred of artificial
enemies—moralized its pleasures and endowed them
with a cosmic significance.

All enjoy the warmth that accompanies boasting,
the fierce electric thrill of hatred. Some take pleasure
in the act of fighting. But none enjoy (though it is

94

extraordinary how many are ready stoically to bear) starvation, wounds and violent death. That the Central Americans have derived intense satisfaction from the act of hating their new, artificial enemies is certain. But these moments of fun have been paid for by other moments of misery and pain. Would it not have been possible, the observer will ask, to invent a political system which would have given them all the emotional orgasms they needed at a smaller material and spiritual cost?

With this question upon our lips, we may now return to our hypothetical World Psychological Conference and, guided by the light which Central America has thrown on the problems of international relations, may profitably begin to enquire into the nature of its discussions.

The end proposed by our conference is international peace. The obstacle which it has to circumvent is nationalism. The material with which it has to deal is the psychology of very suggestible, rather insensitive, but emotional and excitement-loving people assembled in vast urban communities. The problem is to devise means for so treating this material that the obstacle may be avoided and the goal definitively reached.

The first thing our delegates would remark is that all governments deplore and carefully regulate the manifestations of lust, but deliberately encourage those of collective vanity and hatred. To boast mendaciously about one's own gang and to slander and defame other gangs are acts everywhere officially regarded as creditable and even pious. It is as though our rulers, instead of merely tolerating prostitution, were to proclaim the brothel to be a place as sacred as the cathedral and as improving as the public library. Doctrines like that of race superiority are the spiritual equivalent of cantharides. Under the Nazis, for example, every German is made to take his daily dose of what I may call Nordic Fly. The Marquis de Sade was condemned to a long term of imprisonment for having distributed aphrodisiac candies to a few prostitutes in Marseilles. But nationalists who devise means for arousing in millions the disgraceful passions of hatred, envy and vanity are hailed as the saviours of their country.

One of the preliminary conditions of international peace is the inculcation of a new (or rather of a very old) scale of moral values. People must be taught to think hatred at least as discreditable as they now think lust ; to find the more raucous manifestations of collective vanity as vulgar, low and ludicrous as those of individual vanity.

Nationalists and militarists have tried to defend their position on ethical as well as on political grounds. War and nationalism are good, they say, because they stimulate individuals to display the more heroic virtues. But the same argument could be brought forward in favour of prostitution. There is a whole literature describing the devotion and tenderness, the benevolence and, positively, the saintliness of whores. But nobody regards this literature as justifying the wholesale encouragement of whoredom. Man's is a double nature and there is hardly any critical situation in which he will not display, simultaneously or alternately, the most repulsive characteristics of an animal and a heroism equal to that of the martyrs. Nationalism and war stimulate men to heroism, but also to bestiality. So far as individuals are concerned, the bad cancels out the good. And so far as society is concerned, the bad—that is to say the harmful—enormously predominates. War and nationalism are without any possible justification.

But ethical justifications are not what our hypothetical delegates have come together to discuss. They have come together to discuss the psychological conditions for international peace. Ethical justifications are mainly useful after the fact—to confirm individuals in certain types of socially useful behaviour.

I will assume—what, alas, is sadly improbable— that our delegates have agreed in principle on the need for all governments to discourage the manifestations by their subjects of collective hatred and hatred-producing vanity. Having done this, they find themselves immediately faced by the problem of Prohibition. The prohibition of any activity that gives people great psychological satisfactions is very difficult to carry out and, if carried out, may lead to

G   97

all kinds of unexpected and distressing consequences. Zeal to convert and civilize the Melanesians is leading to their extinction ; deprived of all that, for them, made life worth living, they simply cease to live. The effort to make Americans more sober resulted in an increase of alcoholism and criminality. Puritanism carried to its logical conclusions notoriously leads to sadism. And so on ; the dangers of untempered prohibition are everywhere apparent. Many activities are psychologically satisfying, but socially harmful. Suppression of these should always be accompanied by the offer of an alternative activity, as rewarding to the individuals engaged in it, but socially harmless or, if possible, beneficial. This is the principle behind all enlightened colonial administration at the present time. Thus, the head hunters in New Guinea have been persuaded to use for all ritual purposes the heads, not of human beings, but of wild boars ; this modification accepted, they are at liberty to perform all the elaborate and psychologically rewarding ceremonies prescribed by their religion. Psychologically, the abolition of militant nationalism in Europe is the equivalent of the abolition of head hunting in Papua. Our imaginary delegates are depriving the people of a great many opportunities for emotional excitement. What alternatives do they propose to supply? This is a difficult problem, completely soluble, I imagine, only by an experimental process of trial, error and retrial. 'Hate,' as Dr. Vergin has justly remarked, 'pays a higher psychological dividend than can be obtained from international amity, sympathy and co-operation.' Benevolence is tepid ; hatred and its complement, vanity, are stinging hot and high-flavoured. That is why National Socialism is so much easier to popularize than the League of Nations. It will be the task of the psychological engineers to see how far co-operation can be combined with socially harmless, but psychologically rewarding, competitions and rivalry. Rivalry, for example, in industry. (The Russians have exploited this kind of friendly competition in the attempt to get more work out of their factory hands.) Rivalry in sports. Rivalry—but this, alas, would probably arouse not the smallest popular enthusiasm—in scientific and artistic achievement. The substitutes for militant nationalism may be almost as exciting as the things they replace. Thus, at Constantinople, feeling at the chariot races ran so high that Greens and Blues were ready to kill one another by the thousand. It is clear that the homœopathic remedy for militant nationalism can be made as fatal as the disease.

In the course of their labours, our delegates will be called upon to answer a number of very difficult questions. Here are a few of them.

In what circumstances and by means of what technique can you persuade people into the placid acceptance of prohibitions ? When and how can you condition them into regarding artificial restraints as inevitable and 'natural' limitations of all human life ?

Again, what sort of emotional compensations must be given in exchange for specific kinds of prohibition ? And how much emotional excitement, how many orgies, do people need to keep them contented and in health ?

Finally, can the benevolently intelligent ruler dispense altogether with collective hatred ? Or is it a necessary and irreplaceable instrument for the welding of small societies into greater wholes ?

To the first question our delegates would probably be unable to return a definite answer. They would observe that, as a matter of historical fact, the members of isolated and homogeneous communities have often been persuaded to accept the oddest and most arbitrary restraints as natural limitations. Members of heterogeneous communities in frequent contact with foreigners tend to lose unquestioning faith in the local mythology, and are therefore less amenable to the powerful instruments of persuasion provided by religion. There is a sense in which modern society can say with M. Valéry, '*la bêtise n'est pas mon fort.*' True, the intrinsic and congenital stupidity of the majority is as great as it ever was. But it is a stupidity which has been educated in the ideas invented by the relatively free intelligence of exceptional individuals. The result of this education is that stupid people are now no longer able to swallow the sort of theology

which their predecessors unquestioningly accepted.
Universal education has created an immense class of
what I may call the New Stupid, hungering for certainty, yet unable to find it in the traditional myths
and their rationalizations. So urgent has been this
need for certainty that in place of the dogmas of
religion they have accepted (with what passionate
gratitude !) the pseudo-religious dogmas of nationalism.
These are more obviously false and mischievous than
the dogmas of religion ; but they possess, for the
New Stupid, the enormous merit of being concerned,
not with invisible, but with visible entities. Nationalism is not the theory of a God whom nobody has
seen. It is a theory of some actual country and its
flesh-and-blood inhabitants. The theory is demonstrably untrue ; but that does not matter. What
matters to the New Stupid is that the subject of
the theory is real. The New Stupidity is positivistic. One of the tasks of our delegates will be the
devising of a mythology and a world-view which shall
be as acceptable to the New Stupid as nationalism
and as beneficial as the best of the transcendental
religions.

To the two questions in the second group no definite
answer can be given, except on the basis of a specific
research. The balance sheet of psychological equivalents has yet to be drawn up ; nevertheless, a rather
vague, but useful, generalization is possible. Rulers
can impose many prohibitions, provided that the

people on whom they are imposed have been given sufficiently lively and interesting orgies. The problem, obviously, is to define ' sufficiently.' But there is no one definition ; for what is sufficient for people in one set of circumstances is insufficient for people in another. Thus, the orgy-system of the Central Americans, simple and unpretentious as it was, seems to have been quite sufficient for their needs. The fact that they bore, almost without complaint, the enormous oppression of their rulers, is evidence that, psychologically, they were satisfied. To-day we have a choice of diversions incomparably wider than theirs. Nevertheless, our elaborate orgy-system is probably insufficient for our needs. Living as we do in an age of technological progress, and therefore of incessant change, we find that we cannot be amused except by novelties. The traditional orgies which, without undergoing the smallest modification, refreshed our ancestors during long centuries of history, now seem to us intolerably insipid. Nothing can be new enough for us. Even the most exciting and elaborate of our amusements cannot satisfy for long. Nor is this the only reason for the insufficiency of our orgy-system. The processions, dances and even the sports of the Central Americans were related to their mythology. It was to do honour to St. Joseph that one marched round the town with candles and a drum ; one fought cocks or baited bulls to celebrate the Assumption of the Mother of God ; one danced for St. Francis or, on the sly, for the

Feathered Serpent of the old dispensation : one did magic in the name of St. Peter and got drunk because it was All Souls' Day. What was, and still is, true of Central America used to be true, until quite recent times, of Europe. To-day all diversions have been laicized. This has happened partly as a result of the positivistic tendencies of the New Stupidity ; partly owing to the fact that all entertainments are in the hands of joint-stock companies, whose interest it is that people shall amuse themselves, not only on mythologically significant occasions, but every day and all the time. The result is that ' our laughter and our tears mean but themselves,' and, meaning but themselves, mean curiously little. Hence the prodigious success of the entertainments organized by up-to-date mob leaders in the name of nationalism. Mussolini and Hitler have restored to the New Stupid some of the substantial pleasures enjoyed by the Old Stupidity. Can these pleasures be restored in some other and less pernicious name than that of collective hatred and vanity ?

We have seen that people will put up with all kinds of prohibitions, provided that they are given psycho-logically ' sufficient ' compensations. Granted quali-tative sufficiency, what is the amount of emotional stimulation necessary for health ? How many orgies —or rather, since it is the minimum that interests us, how few—do human beings require ? Only pro-longed field-work would permit one to return a scientifically accurate answer. At present, all one can say is that the appetite for emotional stimulation varies greatly from individual to individual, and that populations at large seem to be able now to support very large doses of emotional excitement, now to content themselves with very small doses.

Some people have a very powerful appetite for emotional excitement—or else, which is perhaps the same thing, are cursed with an insensitiveness that only surgical methods can awake to feeling. These, in a peaceable state, are apt to be a nuisance. In the past, most of them could be counted on to destroy themselves by crusading, duelling, piracy and, more recently, by exploring and colonial adventuring. Unhappily, the last of these overseas outlets for violence are being closed—in some cases have been closed already. Germany, for example, has no colonies as a safetyvalve for her more ferocious young men. Perhaps that is why Hitler found such a rich supply of them in the streets of Munich and Berlin. The Jews and the Communists are paying for the annexation of Tanganyika and German South-West Africa. For the Nazi gunmen they provide, so to speak, a Colony in Every Home. Among the Indians of Central America, a good deal of what would otherwise have been dangerous political violence was probably absorbed in the domestic circle ; wives, children and village delinquents were the ' Jews,' the ' Reds,' the ' Coloured Races,' on whom they vented their native brutality and wreaked vengeance for the wrongs done them by their conquerors. With us, wives and children are pretty effectively protected by the law ; that immemorial safety-valve is tightly screwed down. Moreover, darkest Africa is rapidly ceasing to be dark, and its inhabitants are beginning to be treated almost as though they were human beings—or, better, almost as though they were Our Dumb Friends. Soon the violent individuals of even the imperialistic nations will have to look elsewhere for their dangerous adventures and, lacking real Hottentots to bully, will be forced to transform the more helpless of their unpopular neighbours into artificial Hottentots. (In this context, it is not the colour of a posterior that counts ; it is its kickableness.) One of the minor tasks of our conference will be to provide born adventurers and natural slave-drivers with harmless and unharmable blackamoor *Ersatzes*, with safe, humane but satisfying Putumayo-surrogates.

That communities have flourished for centuries without the stimuli of militant nationalism is certain. But the trouble is, that such peaceable societies (of whom the Old Empire Mayas seem to have been one) lived in circumstances very different from those of to-day and were composed of individuals, in whom consciousness had developed along other lines than those by which the modern European mind has advanced. So far as we are concerned, they are Utopias, admirable but fundamentally irrelevant. My own conviction is that, in this matter of emotional stimulation, quantity is strictly a function of quality. If routine is easy, comfortable and secure, and if all the organized emotional stimulations are qualitatively satisfying, then the number and variety of orgies can safely be reduced. Nationalism flourishes among the New Stupid of our contemporary world for two reasons : first, because the common orgies of daily life are of such poor quality ; and, second, because the routine, which is the complement and necessary background of such orgies, has been disturbed. This disturbance is due in large measure to the practical application of nationalism to politics, and results in a state of mind that welcomes nationalism for the sake of the exciting distractions it creates and theoretically justifies. The movement is, as usual, circular and vicious. Routine and orgies. Or, as the Romans preferred to put it, bread and circuses. Still, as always, the universal demand. Men cannot live by bread alone. But neither can they live only by circuses. To some extent, however, a shortage of bread can be made up for by a surfeit of circuses. All the mob-leaders of the post-war years have pursued the same policy : they have organized political circuses in order to distract people's attention from their hunger and the prevailing social uncertainty. Unable to fill empty bellies with bread, they aim instead at filling empty heads with flags and verbiage and brass bands and collective hysteria. The Nazis are preparing, as

I write, to hold a hundred and fifty thousand political meetings in two months. We may parody the words of the old song and ask :

> Will the hate that you're so rich in
> Light a fire in the kitchen,
> And the little god of hate turn the spit, spit, spit ?

Alas, he won't ; and one day the public for whom these political circuses are so lavishly organized will grasp the distressing truth and say, with Queen Victoria, ' We are not amused.'

This brings us to a very interesting point. The amount of emotional stimulation which a given society can tolerate varies within very wide limits. There are times when the whole, or at any rate a large part of, the community will tolerate violent emotional stimulations and even deliberately seek them out. Under the influence of this excitement, difficult tasks will be accomplished and heroic acts performed. But after a certain time fatigue seems to set in ; people cease to be moved by the old stimuli, cease even to wish to live heroically ; their highest ambition is a quiet life, well supplied with the creature comforts. This fatigue, it should be noticed, need not be experienced by the same people as originally cultivated the fatiguing emotions. One generation lives an intensely emotional life and the next generation is tired. The community behaves as though it were a living organism, in which individuals play the part of cells. It is the organism as a whole that feels fatigue ; and this fatigue communicates itself to the new cells which, in the natural course of growth, replace those originally stimulated. 'The fathers have eaten a sour grape and the children's teeth are set on edge.' What is the mechanism of this curious process ? There is no reason to suppose that it is physiological. The children are not born tired ; they become tired by psychological reaction to their parents' enthusiasm. But why do they react ? Why are they not conditioned to share the enthusiasm ? And why is it that when enthusiasms are not too violent there is no reaction, but acceptance on the part of the children ?

To answer these questions with any precision one would have to undertake a campaign of intensive field-work and specially directed historical research. Lacking precise data, one can risk a vague generalization and say that it is impossible so to condition people that they will permanently accept a state of things that imposes an unbearable strain on their psychology ; and that where such an attempt is made, the reaction to conditioning will ultimately be negative, not positive. The image of the social organism once more imposes itself : the community is a creature that can survive only when its constituent parts are in a state of equilibrium. Excessive stimulation has to be compensated by repose. The stimulated cells are one set of individuals ; the reposing cells another. Why and how do the individuals of the second generation realize that a negative reaction to parental conditioning is, socially speaking, necessary? It is impossible to guess. But the fact remains that they apparently do realize it.

Periods of intense general excitement never last very long. The social organism does not seem to be able to tolerate more than about twenty years of abnormal agitation. Thus, the thrilling, heroic period of the religious revival, set going by St. Francis of Assisi, was over in less than a quarter of a century. The great animal that was Europe could not stand the strain of sitting up on its hind legs and performing primitive-Christian tricks. Within a generation it had settled down once more to a comfortable doze. Every violently exciting religious or political movement of history has run much the same course. It will be interesting to see whether the revivalist enthusiasm worked up by Communists, Nazis and Fascists will last longer than the similar mass emotion aroused by the first Franciscans. True, the technique of propaganda is much more efficient now than it was in the Middle Ages. St. Francis had no printing press, no radio, no cinema, no loud-speakers. Hitler, Stalin and Mussolini have them by the thousand. Nevertheless, it may be doubted whether they will really do better than St. Francis. An orchestra can make louder music than a single fiddle. But if you are tired, and bored with dancing, the orchestra will not set you capering more effectively than the fiddle. On the contrary, the very insistence of its appeal will anger you into an obstinate refusal to make the smallest answering gesture.

It should be the policy of every ruler never to allow the emotions of his subjects to be for any length of time systematically over-stimulated. Nor, if he is wise, will he ever make use of emotional over-stimulation to carry out any ambitious, long-range plan of his own. The finally negative reaction of the social organism to such over-stimulation is likely to stultify the plan and may lead at the same time to a temporary lowering of the vitality of the whole community, most undesirable and, in certain circumstances, even dangerous. The aim of the ruler should be to discover exactly the right dose of bread and circuses, and to administer just that, no more and no less. Where the dosage is correct, as it evidently was in Egypt, in Babylonia, in India, in China, a society can remain for centuries astonishingly stable, even under the stress of attack and actual conquest by alien peoples.

Ours is a world of rapidly changing techniques ; education has tinged our congenital stupidity with positivism, and we are therefore impatient of faith in any kind of invisible transcendental entity. In such a world and for such a people what is the perfect dose of bread and circuses ? It is hard indeed to say. But though perfection may be unattainable, it should be fairly easy to improve on the wildly incorrect and dangerous practice of the present time. The formula for permanent health is doubtless beyond us ; but at least the temporary avoidance of sudden death is within our power.

We come now to the last of our questions. Can hate be used for producing unification? Or, rather, can unification be produced without using hatred? Carrera, the Indian chieftain, who ruled Guatemala from 1840 to 1860, made his first entry into the capital under a banner inscribed with these words : *Viva la religión y muerte a los extranjeros*. Uneducated, he knew by mother-wit that the two most effective instruments for uniting men are a shared mythology and a shared hatred.

Carrera did not aim very high ; he wanted, first of all, to unify the army of savage Indians under his command, and later, when he had achieved dictatorial power, to consolidate Guatemala into a sovereign state. His enemies, the Liberals of Salvador, were more ambitious. They aspired to unite all of Central America into a single federated republic. A more considerable task than Carrera's, for which they were equipped with less adequate instruments. For, being educated anti-clericals, they could not exploit the unificatory mythology of a religion they regarded as pernicious ; and being believers in progress, they could not preach hatred of the foreigners whose capital and technical knowledge they hoped to use for the development of their country. Still, some sort of unifying hatred was urgently desirable ; so an attempt was made to work up patriotic feeling against England, on the score that its government had ordered the occupa-

tion of the island of Roatun in the Gulf of Honduras
and was secretly planning to annex the whole of Central
America. Unfortunately perhaps for Central American
unity England was not planning to occupy the country.
Had such an attempt actually been made, it is quite
possible that the Five Republics might have been fused
together by hatred of the common enemy.

Europe possesses no shared mythology, and it will
obviously take some time to fabricate such an instrument of unification. A shared hatred is also lacking,
but could be worked up in next to no time. There is
a possibility, for example, that dislike and fear of
Hitlerian Germany may result in a movement towards
the unification, or at least the rational co-operation,
of the other national states. If this were to happen
we should have to bless the Nazis for being the un-
intentional benefactors of suffering humanity.

But hatred for a near neighbour easily becomes
unplatonic. Almost as effective as a unifier, shared
loathing for people at a distance has this further
merit : it need not involve the hater in any unpleasant
practical consequences. It may be that our delegates
will think it worth while to unify Europe by means
of hatred for Asia. Such hatred would have excellent
economic justifications. Combining efficiency with a
lower-than-European standard of living, the Japanese
can undersell us in every department ; directly or
indirectly, they threaten to take the bread out of
innumerable European mouths. Nothing would be

easier than to work up hatred for these formidable rivals ; and as they live a very long way away, there is a chance that the hatred might remain, so far as most of us are concerned, relatively platonic—an excuse for collective orgies with no ' morning after ' of high explosives and mustard gas.

Orgies with no morning after—paradisial vision ! But meanwhile the tariff walls are raised a little higher and yet another embargo is placed on foreign goods ; more bombers take the air, the new tanks do their forty miles an hour across the countryside, the heavy guns throw their shells still further, the submarines travel ever faster, the dye-works are yet better equipped to manufacture poison gas. And the insanity is infectious. It rages in Central America as it rages in Europe. Never have the Guatemalteco soldiers been so well equipped as they are to-day. And what discipline ! It seems a shame that they should have nothing to do but line the streets on ceremonial occasions. But, patience ! a time will doubtless come, quite soon. . . .

Guatemala City

My knowledge of Central American history had been mainly derived from books of travel and was therefore

H   113

patchy in the extreme. I had read Stephens and so could form a vivid picture of the country during those distracted years at the beginning of the eighteen-forties ; Gage had shown me what the Guatemala of the Captains-General was like in the seventeenth century, and through the eyes of Mr. and Mrs. Maudslay I had had a glimpse of the same region as it was only forty years ago. But between these spots of light were large areas of all but utter darkness. I thought myself fortunate, therefore, in discovering at a friend's house the latest edition of the *Encyclopædia Britannica*. Under the heading ' Central America ' I expected to be able to find just that succinct and accurate summary of the local history that I needed. But, alas, I was disappointed. This is the sort of historical narrative I found, ' The bitter struggle which began in the 'twenties continued finally under the leadership of the great Guatemalan Conservative, Rafael Cabrera, and the equally able and more spectacular liberal leader of Honduras, Francisco Morazan. Morazan was finally defeated and executed in 1842, and the federal union, which he had made his battle cry, was dissolved. A union dominated from Guatemala was formed in the same year, but without Costa Rica. This dissolved in 1825, and in 1850 Honduras, Salvador and Nicaragua formed another union which was broken up by the Guatemalans under Cabrera.' I say nothing of the language in which this is written ; one has learnt not to expect euphonious prose from a scientific specialist—to be grateful when one gets plain grammar. But what one has been led to expect is accuracy. In the *Encyclopædia Britannica* one doesn't get it. Here, for example, is a union formed in 1842 which is dissolved in 1825. A misprint, no doubt ; but why not read the proofs ? And for the gross blunder of calling the Indian leader, Carrera, by the name of the twentieth-century dictator, Cabrera, there would seem not even to be the excuse of bad proof reading ; for the name is repeated several times *en toutes lettres*. Cabrera is just a howler.

I wish now that I had made a note of all the misprints and mistakes I have found in the latest edition of the *Encyclopaedia*. I do not consult the book very frequently ; but it seems to me that I hardly ever open it without finding some stupid slip or other. To these sins of commission one must add numerous and enormous sins of omission. My experience is that if I want information on any subject unaffected by the scientific discoveries of the last twenty years, I am much more likely to find it in the old than the new edition. The old edition was in twenty-eight volumes ; the new is in twenty-four. By some curious dispensation, these four additional volumes seem to have contained almost everything I ever want to find out. Skilful writers could probably have crammed the same amount of information into the reduced space. But in many cases, as I have personally tested, no attempt has been made to do this. The old articles have not been rewritten in a more compressed style ; they have simply been cut down. I have had the curiosity to compare articles in the eleventh edition with the corresponding articles in the fourteenth. Again and again I have found that the article of 1929 is just the 1911 article rather incompetently blue-pencilled. New priest is but old presbyter minus three of its letters. Instead of being compressed into a narrower space, whole chunks of information have simply been cut out. This disgraceful kind of editing is doubly pernicious : valuable facts contained in the old edition disappear and the old articles, many of which were well-designed and well-written wholes, read in their new form like the 'essays' of sixteen-year-old schoolboys.

No, decidedly, the new edition of the *Encyclopædia* reflects little credit on its editors and publishers. The latter seem to have been more interested in selling a lot of copies on the instalment plan than in producing a first-rate class book of reference, and the former have been remiss in not insisting more firmly on a proper standard of accuracy and adequacy. The chief editor, Mr. Garvin, is doubtless a very eminent journalist. But, then, does eminence in journalism qualify a man for preparing a survey of universal knowledge ? In newspaper work, accuracy is the last consideration. Carrera . . . Cabrera ? What

earthly difference does it make which name you
print in a publication that leaves the presses in the
small hours of the morning and by sunset of the same
day is already in the fire, the dustbin or the cess-
pool? Obviously, it doesn't matter two pins what
you say in a newspaper. But in a work which is to
serve for at least ten years as the standard reference
book of English-speaking people all over the world,
this sort of carelessness does matter—matters, indeed,
quite a lot.

Note.—The editorial methods of those responsible
for the Fourteenth Edition of the *Encyclopædia* are
well illustrated in the article on Alexander von Humboldt. The original notice was written by Agnes
Mary Clerke, a competent scientific journalist and
popularizer, who died in 1907. Miss Clerke did her
job efficiently; all the main facts of Humboldt's
career are duly recorded in the Eleventh Edition.
Turn now to the Fourteenth. The article on Humboldt is still signed with Miss Clerke's initials. But
a nameless collaborator, X, is also represented. X
does well to conceal his identity; for his sole contribution to universal knowledge consists in turning
Miss Clerke's sense into nonsense. For example, this
is what Miss Clerke wrote about the later stages of
Humboldt's travels in the New World.

'At Callao Humboldt observed the transit of
Mercury on the 9th of November, and studied the

fertilizing properties of Guano, the introduction of which into Europe was mainly due to his writings. A tempestuous sea voyage brought them to the shores of Mexico, and after a year's residence in that province, followed by a short visit to the United States, they set sail for Europe, etc. . . .'

X abbreviates and amends the passage thus : ' At Callao Humboldt observed (*c.* Nov. 9) '—that *circa* is a beautiful touch—' the transit of Mercury, and studied the fertilizing properties of guano, the introduction of which into Europe was mainly due to his writings. After a year in that province, and a short visit to the United States, they returned (1804) to Europe.'

By a single stroke of his blue pencil X keeps Humboldt a year in the province of Callao (fourteen square miles in area) and takes him thence directly to the United States, presumably round Cape Horn. Mexico is entirely blotted from the record of the explorer's life and the reader is left to imagine that the *Essai politique sur la Nouvelle Espagne* and the *Atlas géographique et physique du royaume de la Nouvelle Espagne* were composed by one who had never been nearer to Mexico than Callao or New York. Editorial ineptitude could go no further.

CIUDAD VIEJA

Guatemala City

In the Guatemala of 1840 Stephens could hear performances of music by Mozart. The visitor of 1933 may think himself lucky if he hears a *marimba* orchestra discoursing tangos in the *patio* of his hotel —may think himself still luckier, I may add, if he doesn't hear it. For the *marimba* is a gigantic xylophone, played with large drum-sticks by three, four, even five performers ; and an orchestra of several of these rattling contrivances, accompanied by saxophones and trumpets, make a greater volume of more piercing noise than can be produced by any other combination of instruments. *Marimba* days at the hotel were always a nightmare. But, except for the canned syrup of the talkies, they provided the only music that one could hear in Guatemala. 'Bad money drives out good.' Is there also, as Sir Norman Angell has suggested, a Gresham's Law for taste ?

Ciudad Vieja

The inhabitants of the valley of Antigua have had, in George Herbert's words, ' afflictions sorted, anguish of all sizes.' Violent death came to them (and still comes) in a rich variety of forms. There is lava to burn and volcanic ash to smother them. Sometimes the earth trembles and they are swallowed up or buried under the ruins of their dwellings. And, occasionally, to vary the monotony, there is a bit of drowning. Antigua was abandoned in 1773 after a particularly destructive earthquake, and the seat of government removed to its present site. But Antigua itself had originally been a place of refuge from other perils. Ciudad Vieja, the earliest capital, stands at the foot of the extinct volcano of Agua, three miles from Antigua on the road that leads down to the Pacific. In 1541, after days of torrential rain, an immense mass of water came rushing down the side of the mountain and overwhelmed the town. Houses were thrown down, and many of the inhabitants were drowned. Chief among these was Alvarado's widow, Doña Beatriz de la Cueva, who had just been elected governor in the room of the recently deceased conquistador. The survivors of the catastrophe packed up and moved to what is now Antigua.

Ciudad Vieja is to-day a mere village, with no trace of its former splendours (if, indeed, it ever had any splendours) except a handsome church founded in 1534—and therefore one of the oldest in this part of America.

The only person in the plaza when we arrived was an old *mestizo* in white cotton trousers, a military tunic and a large straw hat. This last he courteously took off to us. We returned the salute, entered into conversation and discovered that we had the honour of talking to the colonel of the local garrison. The job, it seemed, was not a very strenuous one ; and, pleased to have at last something to do, the colonel offered to show us the sights. We accepted, gratefully.

Like so many of the churches in New Spain, San Francisco at Ciudad Vieja must have been designed and periodically restored only by amateurs. No professional architect could ever have had anything to do with that homely version of a baroque façade, with that ill-proportioned interior, those rustic decorations in stucco. A mason who knew how to turn a vault, a friar who remembered, rather dimly, the churches he had seen at home—these were the makers of San Francisco. The temple is built in a kind of classical patois—an absurd, rather slovenly, but none the less engaging dialect of a noble language.

We found the *convento* attached to the old church abandoned, its *patio* overgrown, its fountain dry. Like so many villages in Guatemala, Ciudad Vieja is evidently without a resident priest. But the rites of religion—not necessarily of the Roman Catholic religion—are still performed by the inhabitants. A minor one was being celebrated while we were visiting the sights. Squatting at the church door was an Indian. With one hand he was beating a little drum, like an elongated jam pot, and with the other he played a *chirimiya*. This is a squeaking penny whistle, with a range of four or five notes, indistinguishable in sound and appearance from those pipes which are still played (also with one hand, while the other taps the drum) on festal occasions in out-of-the-way villages in Provence. In all probability the *chirimiya*, like most of the other traditionary elements of present-day Indian folk-art, was originally imported from Europe. The tune he was playing was also unquestionably an importation. (I never heard any in Central America that was not.) It was a melancholy little affair, about six bars long, with a close resemblance to that old London street cry—'Who'll buy, who'll buy my sweet-scented lavender?' When he got to the end of it, the Indian began again, *da capo ad infinitum*. He was playing it as we entered the church, he was playing it when we came out again ; he was playing it as we went to look at the ruins of the oratory where Doña Beatriz was drowned, and he was playing it ten minutes later when we walked back.

'Do the Indians often play this music?' we asked the colonel.

'Every Friday.'

'And for how long?'

'Oh, about twelve hours,' he answered, as though it were the most natural thing in the world.

'And why do they play it?' we asked. 'What does it signify?'

He shrugged his shoulders. '*Quien sabe?*' And that was the end of our ethnological researches—that would be the end, if one had to depend on the *ladinos*, of all ethnological researches in Guatemala.

On our way to the car we had to pass quite close to the musician. Lifting his chin a little, he blew, for perhaps the eight-hundredth time that morning, the first notes of 'Who'll buy, who'll buy.' Above the barrel of his whistle his eyes stared fixedly into space, black like boot-buttons and no less perfectly inexpressive. I found myself suddenly rather disquietingly reminded of a photograph I had once seen of a giant tortoise eating a snake. The serpent hung, like so much living spaghetti, from those toothless and scissor-like jaws, and the tortoise's eyes were gazing with a bright unwinking fixity into the *Ewigkeit*. Two round black nothings focussed upon nothing. Automatically the mouth continued its labours. Bite, bite, bite; the wildly struggling body was slowly masticated. The eyes continued to stare into vacancy. Everything was totally irrelevant to everything else. It was the same here at the church door in Ciudad Vieja. Nothing gazed at nothing. The drum beat; the thin squeaking of the melody drooped to its conclusion; then, for the eight hundred and first time, began again. And still, above the penny whistle, those black buttons beamed with the same impenetrably meaningless brightness. I was glad to see the last of them.

Frankly, try how I may, I cannot very much like primitive people. They make me feel uncomfortable. '*La bêtise n'est pas mon fort.*'

Antigua

THE Gothic revival in England was a product of the Oxford Movement. Pointed arches seemed better than round ones, because they were the emblems of a certain kind of newly fashionable religion, a certain way of life. Ruskin persuasively rationalized this ethico-religious preference in terms of aesthetics; and on these aesthetic grounds ogival architecture was preferred to the Renaissance and baroque by whole classes of people, who would thoroughly have disapproved of the original reasons for the Gothic revival. My parents, for example, had no great love for the Oxford Movement; but I was brought up in the strait and narrow way of Ruskinism; and so strict was my conditioning that it was not till I was at least twenty and had come under the influence of the aestheticians of a newer school that I could perceive the smallest beauty in Saint Paul's cathedral. Till then, its dome and its round arches had acted on me like a Pavlovian bell: at the sight of them I had shuddered and the thought,

ANTIGUA   La Merced.

ANTIGUA

'How ugly!' had immediately presented itself to my consciousness.

Mr. and Mrs. Maudslay, who wrote their *Glimpse at Guatemala* in the late eighteen-nineties, had never had a chance to be deconditioned from Ruskinism. Their reaction to Antigua was one of unequivocal disapproval. 'If only,' was their reflection, 'if only the Conquistadores had come, say, eighty years earlier! Then Antigua might have been filled with lovely Gothic ruins.' The Antigua of actuality is all baroque and colonial rococo; the Maudslays were so much distressed by it, that they found it necessary to draw a veil: its horrors are passed over in silence.

To those who, like myself, have been deconditioned, or who have never undergone the Ruskinian training, Antigua must seem one of the most romantic towns in the world. I will not pretend that it contains any great masterpiece of architecture: that would be absurd. There is nothing grand at Antigua; but there is much that is charming; much that is surprising and queer; much—indeed everything—that is picturesque and romantic in the most extravagantly eighteenth-century style. Piranesis confront you at every corner; there is hardly a back garden without its Hubert Robert or its Panini. Wherever one looks fantastic ruins fill the foreground and behind them rise, not modest Alban hills, not poor little Soracte, but gigantic volcanoes, as high as Monte Rosa and

almost as shapely as Fuji-yama. It is a thousand
pities that his pilgrimage never took Childe Harold
as far as Guatemala, and that Chateaubriand's knowledge of the New World should have been confined
to the sea-board of the northern continent and the
descriptive writings of Father Charlevoix. What
splendid musings either of them would have sent home
from Antigua ! Musings on the transitoriness of
human glory, on the grandeurs and eternities of
nature ; musings on tyrants ; musings on liberty ;
musings on volcanoes and the cochineal insect ;
musings on the beauties of Christianity or the baseness
of popish superstition, whichever the case might be.
There would have been a cataract of pensive eloquence.
To-day it is too late. On all these incredibly romantic
ruins the Time-Spirit has posted his warning notice :
NO MUSING, BY ORDER. To the outward eye
the letters are invisible ; but, for the inward, they
glare as enormously as Citroën's signature on the
Eiffel Tower.

> Look on its broken arch, its ruin'd wall,
> Its chambers desolate and portals foul :
> Yes, this was once Ambition's airy hall,
> The dome of Thought, the palace of the Soul :
> Behold . . .

But suddenly, just as we are warming to the task
of describing ' the gay recess of Wisdom and of Wit,'
suddenly the writing on the wall starts out at us : NO
MUSING, BY ORDER. Guiltily, we put away our

ANTIGUA   Ruin of Jesuit church.

fountain pens and our notebooks, and address ourselves to the more contemporary business of taking snapshots.

Antigua

THE Valley of Antigua is darkly green with coffee bushes and umbrageous with the tall shade trees under which they are planted. Ninety years ago, in Stephens's day, there was not a coffee berry in all Guatemala. The two great export crops were cochineal, much cultivated round Antigua, and indigo (the best, according to Humboldt, in the world), which grew lower down on the rich, hot lands of the Pacific slope. Cochineal and indigo were killed by William Perkin and the German chemists. Ruined by aniline, the planters were forced, after the 'fifties of the last century, to look for something else to plant. The new staple was coffee. Guatemalan coffees rank among the finest in the world ; and certainly I never drank a cup of anything that could compare with the ambrosial stuff that was served us after dinner by the friends with whom we stayed near Escuintla. It was made from berries grown high up on the flank of the volcano of Fuego. Coffee will flourish in these latitudes up to about five thousand feet, and the higher the finer—also, unfortunately, the fewer. Quality is at the cost of quantity.

For some years after the war, coffee boomed; the planters did very well. What always happens in such cases duly occurred. News of the profits that were being made produced a coffee-rush. Thousands of people migrated to the tropics and sank their capital in laying down several million acres of new plantations. Even if all other prices had remained what they were in 1928, coffee would inevitably have slumped. If you suddenly double the output of a commodity without doubling its consumption, you cannot expect to get as much for what you sell as you did before. Too many geese, in a word, spoil the golden egg. This truth is obvious enough; but the knowledge of it has not sufficed to stop our Yukonesque stampedes into any business that seems, at any given moment, to be doing well. Cotton-rushes, wheat-rushes, radio-rushes, automobile-rushes—we have had all these in recent years, and a dozen more besides. The moment the producers see what they suppose to be ' a good thing,' they fling themselves into it and thereby automatically convert it into a bad thing. All know, in theory, that this is bound to happen; but each believes that, in economic as in all other matters, he is the happy exception to the rule. In our sort of world, this is, no doubt, a necessary delusion; if most people did not have it, things would never get done, or at any rate would only get done very slowly.

ANTIGUA   Doorway.

ANTIGUA

Certainly nothing much gets done in societies in which
taboos are unquestioningly accepted and nobody even
dreams that he can escape from the operations of any
rule whatsoever. It may be that, if there is to be
progress, or at any rate rapid change, the delusion
of individual exceptionalness is indispensable. In a
society rationally planned on equitable principles
this delusion would be discouraged, and such active
manifestations of it as a coffee-rush, severely checked.
This would certainly make for social stability. But
whether social stability may not in its turn make for
the return to the mental stagnation of the primitive
stable society remains to be seen. At present we are
very far from being in a position to judge.

Will coffee ever again be, for Guatemala, the source
of prosperity it was before the slump? It seems a
little doubtful. Trees have multiplied faster than
consumers. The Brazilian planters are said to spend
about a million pounds a year on propaganda ; and
perhaps, if they had a free field, they might increase
the number of coffee addicts sufficiently to make it
unnecessary for them to burn the greater part of their
crop. But propaganda produces counter-propaganda.
The tea-growers are organizing their forces, the battle
of the stimulants promises to be lively. Personally,
I back tea, which seems to me both a wholesomer and
more efficient drug than coffee. And of course it is
quite on the cards that at any moment the chemist
will step in again and kill them both, by synthesizing

a pick-me-up that is cheaper and more palatable than any of the natural caffeins. In any case, I cannot believe that the outlook for the Guatemalan plantations is particularly good. Another ninety years, and it is likely that coffee will have gone the way of cochineal and indigo. What will have taken its place? Perhaps castor oil ; for, as the supply of petroleum declines, it will be necessary to replace mineral by vegetable lubricants. Perhaps by some luxuriant tropical weed, from which alcohol may be distilled for fuel. The palmy days of tropical agriculture are probably yet to come. It will be called upon to supply the greases and the combustibles which at present we take out of the ground, the paper and the artificial fibres which we so wastefully derive from the cellulose of northern forest trees. Golden prospects ! But meanwhile hard-pressed coffee-planters cannot live on their grandchildren's hypothetical prosperity.

Antigua

I FOUND it extraordinarily hard to guess the date of any building in Antigua. The regular succession of architectural fashions is not observable here as it is in Europe ; and I was never sure if the ruin before me was of the sixteenth, the seventeenth, or even the eighteenth century. All were just indistinctly colonial baroque. One explanation for the apparent contemporaneity of churches built at widely separated periods may be found, perhaps, in the fact that Antigua is a place of earthquakes. Every few years, no doubt, façades got cracked and called for extensive repairs ; there must have been frequent excuses for bringing old-fashioned details up to date.

Earthquakes influenced the Antiguan style of architecture in another way. In their attempts to build something that would withstand the constant tremors, the local architects evolved an almost Saxon style. Thus, the convent of the Capuchinas dates from the eighteenth century ; but its cloisters, with their immensely thick round pillars might have been built in the twelfth. The sixteenth-century palace of the Captains-General has the same strangely anachronistic appearance ; and there are many other specimens of this queer anti-seismic architecture, so barbarously massive that it seems incredible that they could have been built by the contemporaries of Borromini or Christopher Wren. Considered technically, the history of ecclesiastical architecture is the history of the increasingly successful efforts of engineers to build a stone-roofed greenhouse. The problem was solved in late Gothic times. In King's College chapel all the space between the buttressed piers is glass, and the roof is a stone vault. A minimum of masonry has been made to carry a maximum of weight. Le Corbusier himself could hardly have done the trick better : King's is the perfect machine-for-praying-in. At Antigua, a secular process was reversed, and the architects retreated from the greenhouse towards the massive artificial caverns of their barbarian predecessors.

Antigua

Two arms crossed ; one, naked, of the crucified Christ, the other in its wide monastic sleeve, St. Francis's. The palm of either hand is marked with the print of nails. It is an emblem one sees on many churches in Antigua, and indeed all over Guatemala. Here, in Central America, it seems to be the regular coat-of-arms of the Franciscan order. In Europe, the Minorites were much more chary in their use of this striking emblem. Indeed, I remember to have seen it only once outside Central America—in the archaeological museum of Aix-en-Provence. Perhaps it was only in the New World, where their power and wealth were so prodigious, that the Franciscans ventured to state the claims of their founder so openly and in such unequivocal terms.

ANTIGUA   Franciscan emblem.

MIAHUATLAN
Flying angel in the church.

ANTIGUA

Antigua

I TRIED to do some painting in the woods behind the hotel, but soon gave up in despair. The hot sun and the insects were too much for me. Or was I perhaps merely using these ordinary plagues of the landscape-painter as excuses for not prolonging the parade of my own incompetence? For there was no doubt about it : here, at Antigua, I felt more than ordinarily incompetent. The problem was fundamentally the same as that which had confronted, and defeated, me so often in Provence : how to render a brilliantly coloured landscape in equivalently brilliant tones without making the thing look like a railway company's advertisement of the Riviera. A number of contemporary painters simply evade the difficulty. They ignore the brilliance in front of them and transpose the whole scene into a much lower and quieter key. Landscapes, which nature has daubed with the most gaudy strontian yellows, cadmium reds and cobalt violets, are rendered by them in terms of black, white and the earth colours. The result, I admit, is often very agreeable. But I resent the agreeableness ; for it seems to me that a difficulty has been shirked. It is relatively easy, as I know by amateurish experience, to achieve a pleasant harmony when you are using a few quiet colours. But oh, how difficult it is to harmonize the many and brilliant tones which actually exist—maddening as it is to admit it—in external nature ! I myself have never succeeded ; which is why I stick to the easily manageable earths. But it irks me to have to make a virtue of incompetence, and from time to time I have yet another shot at rendering cadmium with cadmium and genuine sky-blue with the appropriate cerulean. Always, alas, in vain. Putting away my painting things I cursed the insects and the sun ; but when I looked again at what I had painted I secretly felt rather grateful to them.

Antigua

THE modern Gothic church at San Felipe, a mile out of town, would have rejoiced the Maudslays' hearts. The sight of it, as I stepped out of the bus, carried me back in an instant to Parks Road at Oxford. Instead of chocolate-coloured Indians, I seemed to see the sons of the clergy coming and going through the Gothic portals of their appointed college ; and across the way stood Ruskin's Museum, spikier than any church, but stuffed with science— a wolf in sheep's clothing. Home thoughts with a vengeance !

134

ANTIGUA   Church of S. Francisco.

ANTIGUA

We entered Keble Chapel and found, not *The Light of the World*, but the gruesomely realistic image of a cadaver, in a glass coffin. It was miraculous and this was its feast day. Indians had come from all the country round to pray and burn candles. Behind the high altar, on which the coffin was laid, some hundreds of people were queued up to take their turn to kiss the hand that projected from the crystal box. Most of the worshippers were Indians ; but there were also a certain number of *mestizos* and near-whites in European dress. One of these, a widow in the most elegant of Parisian weeds, took her place just in front of us. Approaching the image, she was torn, I could see, by a painful conflict between the dictates of religion on one side and hygiene on the other. She longed to kiss the hand and so participate in the *mana* with which the miraculous image was charged : but the thought of the thousands of other people who had kissed it, each with his or her peculiar dirt and special brand of microbes, produced a repulsion that was even stronger than her longing. She stooped, as though she were going to deposit her kiss ; but the recollection of all those greasy Indian lips, the inward vision of the innumerable spirochaetes and cocci and filter-passing bacteria that must be swarming all over the sacred hand, checked her in mid career, and she straightened herself up again. Then, improvising a graceful compromise between godliness and cleanliness, she passionately kissed the tips of her black-gloved fingers and wafted the devotion across the intervening space. Touch wood !—but by wireless.

On the Road

FROM Antigua, the road to Lake Atitlan mounts gradually to a rolling plateau. The car bumped slowly across it. Rising high above the intervening mountains, the volcanoes of Agua and Fuego haunted our creeping progress, like the unescapable phantoms of a guilty conscience. Every few miles we would find the table-land slashed across by an immense *barranca*, or ravine. The *barranca* is a Central American speciality. Deep river valleys exist in other parts of the world ; but nowhere, at any rate in my experience, are there so many of them and of such inordinate depth as in Guatemala and Mexico. Even on the motorist these horrible gashes in the earth make a disquieting impression. And when you are on mule-back, you come to hate them with a quite extra-ordinary intensity of passion. You are ambling quietly along, with the church towers of your destination shining on the sky only a mile or two in front of you, when suddenly, without warning, you find yourself at the edge of a *barranca*. A great gulf two or three thousand feet deep divides you from your

136

goal. You pull up your mule and look first wistfully across at the village, so near and yet so horribly distant, on the opposite lip of the ravine ; then down into the depths, where the solitary house by the stream is like a toy and the patches of cultivation are laid out as though on the six-inch ordnance map ; and finally you examine the track—all those weary loops and hairpins of slithering stones going down to the ford and those still wearier loops and hairpins climbing up on the other side. And at long last, resigning yourself to the inevitable, you spur your mule—that is, if your legs are short enough ; my rowelled heels always clanked together under the creature's belly— and, standing up in your stirrups to give a momentary respite to your galled buttocks, you let yourself be carried, lurch after lurch, down the break-neck descent into the valley.

Nature worship is a product of good communications. In the seventeenth century all sensible men disliked wild nature. One has only to read Pepys's account of a country tour to understand the reason why. But a change was at hand. During the earlier years of the eighteenth century the French road system was completely overhauled ; and from 1725 onwards General Wade was engaged in giving to Scotland and the Border their first decent highways. It began to be possible to look at wild nature in comfort and without serious risk. Poets responded to the invitation of the engineers. Rousseau was contemporary with Trésaguet, the reformer of the French *chaussées* ; Wordsworth, with Telford and Macadam. Richard Jefferies was born during the railway boom of the 'forties, and Meredith wrote his poems when the system then inaugurated was at its highest development. Edward Thomas was working in the early Ford epoch, and Giono lyrically ruminates among the Bugattis and the aeroplanes.

Had you seen the country before the roads were made,
You'd hold up your hands and bless General Wade.

It is only *after* the making of the roads that people begin to hold up their hands and bless the country. Untamed, nature seems not so much divine as sinister, alarming and, above all, exasperatingly obstructive. To go hiking across the mountains when you know that at any moment you can slip down into the valley and find a good road, with motor buses, and a service of *wagon-lits*—this is a most delightful pastime. But if you have to traipse across these same mountains, not on pleasure, but on business, and for the sufficient reason that there is no other means of getting where you want to go—why, then, the case is altered. The sublimities of Nature—and these damned *barrancas* are unquestionably sublime—come to be regarded, not with adoration, but with rage, not as evidences of God's handiwork, but as booby-traps put in your way by some insufferably waggish devil. In Central America one learns to understand the classical attitude to nature.

Atitlan

LAKE COMO, it seems to me, touches the limit of the permissibly picturesque ; but Atitlan is Como with the additional embellishment of several immense volcanoes. It is really too much of a good thing. After a few days in this impossible landscape, one finds oneself thinking nostalgically of the English home counties.

Panajachel, the village nearest to our inn, proved to be a squalid uninteresting place, with a large low-class *mestizo* population and an abundance of dram shops. *Aguardiente* and a lick of the white-wash brush go together in these parts. The Indians till the soil and act as beasts of burden, and the half-castes sell them raw alcohol. Commerce is higher in the social scale than manual labour.

San Antonio Palopò, which we visited by water (it being almost inaccessible on the landward side, except to goats and the indefatigable natives), is a purely Indian village. There seemed to be only a single family of *mestizos* in the place. Painfully squalid in their ragged European clothes, a couple of sluttish women came and went about their house ; and it was sadly characteristic that the only child who tried to beg from us should have been a little boy belonging to one of them. The lower-class *ladinos* feel themselves

139

vastly superior to the Indians, and have therefore scornfully rejected the traditional decencies of their behaviour, without, alas, acquiring any of ours.

San Antonio has its own private national costume. The men are dressed in a shirt and drawers of striped cotton, with a long female-looking kilt made of a checked blanket wound round the waist, and a jacket of blue cloth. The women wear a red bodice with full sleeves, striped in red and white, a dark-blue cotton skirt, and quantities of beads and buttons made of gold and silver glass. These last are from Woolworth's or its equivalent, and have presumably taken the place of the old necklaces of coins. Aesthetically, the change is for the better. These gaudy, Christmas-tree ornaments make a splendid showing.

There is no weaving at San Antonio. All the cloth required by the inhabitants is made in two villages at the other end of the lake. San Pedro and Atitlan are the Manchester and Bradford of this small, isolated world. San Antonio is the local Argentine or Saskatchewan ; its inhabitants exchange the surplus from their almost perpendicular maize fields for the manufactured products of the other villages.

Cloth is not San Antonio's only import. In the middle of the little plaza between the church and the *cabildo*, or municipality—the only level place in the whole of the village—an itinerant vendor of pottery was showing his wares to a group of women. From the covered terrace of the *cabildo* the chief men of the village looked on at them and at us with that magnificently dignified aloofness which is characteristic of the Indians. Compared with these utterly impassive aristocrats, the English milord of old French novels is a chattering and gesticulating dago. *Nil mirari* is a motto they constantly live up to ; and they have carried the art of looking through people, of treating them as though they weren't there at all, to a higher pitch than it has ever reached elsewhere.

The pottery seller was from Totonicopan, sixty miles away across two passes of over ten thousand feet and heaven knows how many *barrancas*. But sixty miles among the mountains is, for these wandering merchants, a slight and easy journey. They will walk two hundred miles with a load on their back of as many pounds—a whole kitchen dresser of assorted earthenware, from enormous spherical water jars to children's whistles. The total value of such a load is probably not more than about two pounds. Any vendor who comes back from his round with a clear ten shillings of profit in his pocket will have done very well indeed. The truth is, I suppose, that profit, for these Indians, is only a secondary consideration. What they chiefly desire is not money so much as a bit of fun. Carrying a couple of hundredweights twenty miles a day is hardly our idea of fun. But the Indians enjoy the wandering, the contacts with strange people, the novel sights, more than they dislike the burdens, to which in any case they are accustomed. A vendor will sell his pots in a village a hundrd miles from Totonicopan for the same price as he sells them at home. Trade here is disinterested and platonic ; commerce is practised for its own sake.

Atitlan

THE story of the Spanish conquest is true but incredible. That Tenochtitlan was taken, that Cortes marched from Mexico to Honduras, that Alvarado broke the power of the Quichés and Cakchiquels—these are facts, but facts so immoderately unlikely that I have never been able to believe them except on authority ; reason and imagination withheld their assent. At Panajachel, I made an acquaintance who convinced me, for the first time, that everything in Prescott and Bernal Diaz had really happened. He was an old Spaniard who lived with an Indian wife and their family in a large rambling house by the lake, making his living as a taxidermist and dresser of skins. He was wonderfully expert at his job and had a first-hand knowledge of the birds, mammals and reptiles of the country. But it was not what he did or said that interested me most ; it was what he was. As I watched him moving about the terrace of his house, a gaunt, bony figure, but active and powerful, his

142

black beard aggressive in the wind, his nose like an eagle's, his eyes glittering, restless and fierce, I suddenly understood the how and the why of the Spanish conquest. The strength of the Indians is a strength of resistance, of passivity. Matched against these eager, violently active creatures from across the sea, they had no chance—no more chance than a rock against a sledge - hammer. True, the Indian rock was a very large one, but the hammer, though small, was wielded with terrific force. Under its quick reiterated blows, the strangely sculptured monolith of American civilization broke into fragments. The bits are still there, indestructible, and perhaps some day they may be fused together again into a shapely whole ; meanwhile they merely testify, in their scattered nullity, to the amazing force behind the Spanish hammer.

The old taxidermist went into the house and returned a moment later with a large bucket full of a glutinous and stinking liquid.

' Look here,' he said ; and he drew out of this disgusting soup yards and yards of an enormous snake-skin. ' *Qué bonito !* ' he kept repeating, as he smoothed it out. ' Like silk. Nobody here knows how to tan a snake-skin as well as I.'

I nodded and made the appropriate noises. But it was not at the skin that I was looking ; it was at the old man's hands. They were big hands, with fingers long, but square-tipped ; hands that moved with a deft power, that reached out and closed with a quick, unhesitating rapacity ; the hands of a *conquistador*.

He asked too much for the skin he finally sold us ; but I did not grudge the money ; for, along with two yards of beautiful serpent's leather, I had bought the key to Spanish-American history, and to me that was worth several times the extra dollar I had paid for my python.

On the Road

OUR good friend, Don Alfredo Clark, came early to fetch us, and by nine we were off, climbing up out of the valley towards the highlands. At Sololà, which stands on a shelf of land a couple of thousand feet above the lake, it was market day, and the steep road was almost crowded with the Indians who were tramping up to the town to buy and sell. Men, women and even the little boys and girls had burdens on their backs. For the poorer Indians in this part of Central America it is as though the Spaniards had never introduced the horse, the mule, the ass and the ox. They are as completely without large domesticated animals as were their pre-Columbian ancestors. In other parts of New Spain practically every family has its donkey ; here, not. For some reason fodder is particularly difficult to come by in the highlands of

Guatemala—though why there should be less of it here than at corresponding altitudes in southern Mexico, where asses and mules abound, I cannot imagine. Anyhow, there the fact remains : among the Quichés the ordinary pack animal is still man. The Maya cities, the tombs and temples of the Zapotecs, the gigantic Toltec pyramids, the palaces and *teocallis* of Tenochtitlan—all were raised without the help of a wheel or beast of burden. Pre-Columbian civilization is remarkable as a monument of speculative intelligence and artistic sensibility ; it is perhaps even more remarkable as a monument of muscular energy. In no part of the world has the unassisted red flesh of man performed such enormous labours as in Central America. One admires and one is also rather appalled.

On the Road

NOT far from Sololá we passed a group of Indians working on the road. Two or three soldiers, rifle in hand and with fixed bayonets, were superintending the operations. Convicts ? Not a bit of it : tax-payers and volunteers. Most of the Indians still pay taxes in labour, and when any considerable job needs doing, the authorities send word to the neighbouring villages that they have need of so many volunteers.

K   145

The soldiers are there to see that the volunteering spirit does not cool down.

Voluntary labour at the point of the bayonet—the notion, to us, is extremely distasteful. But, obviously, when you are confronted with the urgent problem of domesticating a wilderness, you cannot afford to be very squeamish in your methods of getting the work done. The development of an undeveloped land will ultimately (we hope) be of good to all the inhabitants. But this potential good cannot be made actual without a large amount of systematically applied human effort. Every colonial power has found itself obliged to systematize the efforts of its subjects by compulsion. Naked or in disguise, as slavery or in some less brutal form, forced labour has everywhere been employed in the development of wild countries. And it is exceedingly difficult to see how they could have been developed without it.

Sololà

THE market at Sololà was a walking museum of fancy dress. Unlike the Indians of Mexico, who have mostly gone into white cotton pyjamas, with a blanket slung over the shoulder in lieu of greatcoat, the Guatemaltecos of the highlands have kept their old costumes.

SOLOLA   Indian Types.

SOLOLÀ

This conservatism has been to some extent affected
by the slump and the persuasive salesmanship of
shopkeepers and commercial travellers. Nobody
starves in this self-supporting agricultural community ;
but money is a great deal scarcer than it was a few
years ago, when the coffee *fincas* were in full production
and called, during the picking season, for whole
armies of workers from the hills. Those were the
glorious times when a man could earn as much as
twenty-five or thirty cents a day. The Quiché villages
were rich : their *fiestas* were grand events, and the
more elaborate of their old dances were staged on a
lavish scale ; *aguardiente* flowed like water, and when
a man needed a new suit of the traditional clothes
he could afford to buy the hand-woven cloth, the
richly patterned sashes and kerchiefs, the hat bands
and tassels. To-day he has to think twice and three
times before he renews his wardrobe. A new outfit
will cost him the equivalent of four or five pounds,
and at the present moment this is, for a Quiché
Indian, an enormous sum. At the local store the
price of a suit of blue dungarees is only a few shillings,
and when it is worn out, which it will be very soon,
he will be able to afford to buy another. It looks, I
am afraid, as though the traditional dress of the
Indians were doomed. All the forces of industrialism
are arrayed against it. Conservative prejudice cannot
long resist the assaults of economics.

Meanwhile a majority of highlanders still wear the

147

old costumes—a different one in every village. The most curious feature, for example, of the Sololà costume is the black varnished hat, which is a strangely flattened version of John Bull's topper. From another village (I never discovered which ; but it cannot have been far from Sololà, for I saw several of its representatives at the market) came men in large mushroom-shaped hats, exactly like those worn by very distinguished old English ladies when they go gardening. I had a slight shock each time I saw one of them. It was as though Miss Jekyll had suddenly gone mad and taken to staining her face with walnut juice and wearing, with her old hat, a grey monkey-jacket and white cotton pants.

The most remarkable thing about these Indian costumes is that they are not Indian at all, but old European. Little scraps of seventeenth- and eighteenth-century Spain have been caught here and miraculously preserved, like flies in the hard amber of primitive conservatism. The Chichicastenango Indians, for example, wear a short-waisted embroidered jacket and knee-breeches of brown cloth, a gay woven sash and an embroidered kerchief tied round the head. It is, almost without modification, the costume of Sancho Panza. Elsewhere one finds a number of small variations on the Spanish theme. Thus, long kilts will sometimes be worn below a neatly tailored bull-fighter's jacket—a reminiscence, perhaps, of the loin-cloths of an earlier dispensation.

The women's dress has been much less profoundly

CHICHICASTENANGO   Procession.

affected by Spanish fashion than the men's. There is no sign here of the long trailing skirts and Lancashire-lassie shawls of the Mexicans. The Filippino lady's low-cut corsage and puffed sleeves, her white petticoat and coquettishly looped-up skirt are unheard of. True, the Quiché women's embroidered bodices may have borrowed something from European peasant costume ; but their short skirts, reaching in many cases only to the knee—these are unquestionably Indian. Perhaps their colour has changed since the conquest ; for they are now dyed with indigo, which was introduced by the Spaniards. But the cut is surely the same as it was when Alvarado passed this way.

Chichicastenango

OF the larger and more accessible Quiché villages Chichicastenango is the most conservative. In spite of hard times, practically all the male inhabitants wear the traditional Sancho Panza dress ; and in spite of relatively close contact with the outer, sceptical world, all of them firmly believe and diligently practise. Believe and practise what ? Nobody quite knows. But anyhow there are no better Catholics and scarcely any better heathens in the whole of Guatemala.

The village is built round a large square plaza of

about two hundred yards a side, planted with eucalyptus and jacaranda trees, the latter in brilliant blue blossom during all our stay, and with two churches facing one another across the intermediate space. The larger, which is the parish church, stands on the east side, and immediately opposite is the Calvario. Both are built at a certain height above the level of the plaza and approached by considerable flights of steps. These steps might have been expressly designed as a stage setting for the religious ceremonies which are for ever ebbing and flowing across the square and up into the churches. They heighten the spectacular quality of the processions and dramatically emphasize every act of individual worship. For the onlooker, those steps are an essential element in the religious life of Chichicastenango. And not of Chichicastenango alone. Steps have played an important part in most of the highly organized religions. The Teocallis of Mexico and the Babylonian Ziggurats were just staircases and nothing more. So was the Pergamene altar of Zeus. So were the pyramid temples of Tikal and Chichen-itza and Teotihuacan. Steps play a considerable part in Christian architecture. And wherever a despot desires to make himself seem god-like, there almost inevitably appears the staircase, and along with it the ritual of worship to which the staircase lends itself. The throne is the traditional ally of the altar, and both, for the same ceremonial reasons, have steps.

CHICHICASTENANGO   Procession.

CHICHICASTENANGO

Chichicastenango

To associate with other like-minded people in small, purposeful groups is for the great majority of men and women a source of profound psychological satisfactions. Exclusiveness will add to the pleasure of being several, but at one ; and secrecy will intensify it almost to ecstasy. At Chichicastenango this social appetite is satisfied by the religious confraternities. These are small groups, each of which is devoted to the cult of some particular saint and is responsible for the embellishment of the saint's image and the upkeep of his altar in the church. Every confraternity has its chapter-house and meetings take place regularly. What happens at these meetings ? *Quien sabe ?* It is not the Indians who will tell you.

On the day of our arrival one of the *confradias* was taking its patron for a processional walk round the town. Draped in pink and blue bunting, the image advanced unsteadily on the shoulders of its bearers. The drum and penny whistle marched in the van and forty or fifty people followed. The final destination of the procession was the confraternity house, where the image would be deposited, left for a day or two so that it might impregnate the air with its *mana*, and then brought back to its place in the church.

Later in the day Don Alfredo took us to pay a call on an Indian, whose house was the headquarters of another confraternity. The man was out ; his wife and children spoke almost no Spanish and were too shy to come near us ; we were able to inspect the chapter-house at our leisure. It was a large room, spotlessly clean, with benches round the walls and an altar, with a cheap modern image, at one end. The ceiling was festooned with strips of coloured paper, folded and fancifully cut, so as to make friezes of little men and birds and stars. Pinned to the wall were a number of coloured advertisements. I admired particularly the calendar given away at the New Year by the makers of Cafiaspirina Bayer. Above was a chromo-lithograph of the Trinity, flanked by groups of saints, with the inscription, GLORIA PATRI, FILIO ET SPIRITUI SANCTO ; in the centre a calendar for 1933 ; and below, in Spanish, a lyrical paragraph about the virtues of aspirin in combination with caffein. The whole thing was beautifully calculated to make an Indian believe that his pills were somehow guaranteed by God Himself, and that along with his Cafiaspirina he was swallowing a bit of the divine substance. These German salesmen know their business, know it better, I thought, as I looked at the advertisement next to the Cafiaspirina Trinity, than the Americans. This large and luscious picture of a young lady showing one armpit and a considerable part of two breasts would be regarded by civilized men as a perfectly

sufficient reason for buying Lucky Strikes, or a week-
end ticket to Florida, or Bodies by Fisher. But the
poor Indians have not yet been trained up to understand the subtleties o the white man's emotional logic.
They are more su ject to God-appeal than to sex-
appeal. Bathing beauties may be all right in the
literate, film-going city ; but not in the highlands.
The country Indians still believe that the world is full
of *miasma*—of vague but powerful forces of evil which
must constantly be guarded against. It is not a pair
of large blue eyes, not a bosom, however deliciously
pneumatic, that will keep the devil at bay. That can
only be done by a properly accredited saint. If
Luckies are to sell here, they will have to be put under
the patronage of Saint Joseph, or Our Lady of Guadalupe, or (better) the national miracle-worker, Nuestro
Señor de Esquipulas.

Chichicastenango

SUNDAY is the more important of the two weekly market
days, and the plaza, when we walked out this Sunday
morning, was densely crowded. There must have been
the best part of five thousand Indians buying and selling
in the open space beneath the trees. Most of them
were in the brown knee-breeches and embroidered

brown jacket of the local uniform ; but a few wore the costumes of Sololà and other neighbouring villages, and from Santa Cruz Quiché came a fair sprinkling of people who had succumbed to the economic pressure of the times and taken to white or blue imported cotton.

The Indians' more than Anglo-Saxon impassivity is specially remarkable when they are bargaining. I never heard a voice raised, or saw a gesture made. No seller ever exhibited the smallest anxiety to sell. Potential buyers would come and examine the wares, rapping the water jars to make them ring, poking the hairy flanks of the little pigs, unfolding the elaborately woven head-clothes and *huipiles*, fingering the fruits ; the seller would look away and seem to be thinking of something else. A price would be proposed and a counter-proposition put forward—almost in whispers. Then a long silence. Then, after a silence, another casual suggestion, and another. It was as though Sir Rodolphe Brown in *Indiana* were doing business with Phileas Fogg. I have never seen such a perfect exhibition of *le phlegme anglais*.

A little altar stood at the foot of the church steps, and before it a family of Indians was worshipping. The smoke of the copal incense rose in thick blue-black clouds. The father prayed and made ritual gestures ; his wife and the children squatted beside him, unparticipating spectators. It is the rarest thing in this country to see a woman taking part in any religious ceremony. He for God only, she for God in

CHICHICASTENANGO   Indian women in the Market.

him : Milton would have liked the spirit of Chichicastenango.

The dim, barn-like church was alive with sound
and movement. From door to high altar stretched a
double row of glimmering candles, and beside every
batch of lights knelt an Indian, who prayed and signed
himself and, in accordance with some private ritual
of his own, illumined and extinguished, added more
candles from the store in his bag or took away, scattered the petals of flowers, and even surreptitiously
poured libations of *aguardiente*. Squatting (for they
were psychologically so far away from the supernatural beings on the altars before them that they did
not even take the trouble to kneel) squatting beside
their men, the wives looked on, blankly, as though
all this were none of their business. Meanwhile, the
prayers went up with a loud and earnest fervour. In
their dealings with the supernatural, the Indians forget
their Anglo-Saxon impassivity. Shrill sometimes with
complaint and sometimes harsh with indignation and
protest, their voices rose and fell. They put their
case, they implored, they even menaced ; if the gods
could not be persuaded to give what was asked of
them—a male child, a good harvest, a restoration to
health—then they should be compelled. ' The kingdom of heaven suffereth violence and the violent take
it by force.' In their high niches above the altars the
gaudy Indian-baroque idols waved their arms, flapped
their painted draperies. Lifted towards them, the

dark faces of the worshippers seemed to glow with the violence of inner feeling—violence of longing and of faith, violence of adoration or of angry resentment. ' O San Josè ! ' the voices would cry aloud, and then —' abra cadabra cadabra '—a stream of incomprehensible Indian eloquence. ' San Francisco cadabra cadabra Santisima Trinidad.' And all the time, through the interminable orations, the hands performed their ceremonial gestures, putting down and taking up, retracting and advancing, as though busy with some mysterious game of chess. And at last the game was finished ; the player was satisfied that he had checkmated his invisible opponent. Leaving his candles to burn there on the floor, he would rise and walk out, his wife and children trailing unregarded behind him, out into the other, unmysterious, sunlit world beyond the church doors.

From time to time the *padre* came in from the convent and, over the candles of all who desired it, pronounced his blessing—a separate Latin benediction for each candle. A little Indian boy in a surplice bent down to collect the offerings of the faithful—a peso (worth now about three-halfpence) for every candle blessed. Some Indians would spend as much as ten pesos—a good day's wage—for this strong Christian magic. Magic that could convert every pawn in their endless game against the devil into a queen : it was worth the money. Worth still more money, in the eyes of the Indians, is the more elaborate magic of

CHICHICASTENANGO   Water Jars.

baptism. We were still in the church when, at noon, the *padre* came in to christen the usual Sunday batch of babies. More than a dozen Indian mothers stood in a line along the northern wall near the font. The *padre* moved from one to the other, making the same gestures over each small squeaking creature, repeating the same reverberant Latin formula. *Accipite salem sapientiae*, he intoned ; and willy-nilly the brown Quiché babies accepted it. The salt, the water, the Latin words—these constitute, for the Indians, the essential opening gambit in their lifelong game against the powers of evil. They can do without the magic rites of burial and marriage. (At Chichicastenango, for example, hardly a dozen native couples have been married in church during the last twenty years ; and even at funerals the priest is rarely invited to officiate.) But christening remains indispensable. Without that liminal magic the Indians would think themselves foredoomed to lose the game.

There are other magics of almost equal importance. Don Alfredo took us that afternoon to the top of a little hill about a mile outside the village. There, in a clearing among the pines, stood an untidy altar of heaped-up stones and potsherds. At one end of the cairn was an image between two and three feet high, very primitive in type ; and, at the other, two crosses. Crosses and idol were impartially blackened with the soot of incense and sacrificial fires. Nobody was about when we arrived ; but the ashes before the

altar were still warm, and in a little niche at the back
of the idol we found a quantity of pine needles, carefully tied up into little bouquets—the prayer bundles
of a recent worshipper.

The country is full of such altars, and always has
been. During the 1630's Thomas Gage was the parish
priest of Mixco, between Antigua and the present
city of Guatemala. In his *New Survey of the West Indies*
he has left an excellent description of his inquisitorial
search for, and discovery of, one of these idols. Gage
'provided a good gammon of bacon, and some fowls
roasted, cold, and others boiled, well peppered and
salted'; and thus supplied, set out with five Spaniards,
a blackamoor and an Indian guide. The idolaters'
temple was a cave in the mountains. The first clues
they found were 'some pieces of earthen dishes and
pots, and one piece of a chafing dish such as the Indians
use to burn frankincense in, in the churches before the
saints.' After much hunting, Gage and his companions
at last came upon the cave : a light was struck, and
they entered. 'Within two rods we found the idol
standing upon a low stool covered with a linen cloth.
The substance of it was wood, black shining like jet,
as if it had been painted or smoked, the form was of a
man's head unto the shoulders, without either beard
or mustachios ; his look was grim with a wrinkled
forehead and broad starting eyes. We feared not his
frowning look, but presently seized upon him.' Later,
Gage came near being murdered by the indignant

idolaters ; but he was saved in the nick of time, and subsequently the Inquisition got to work on his enemies and he was left in peace. After that, no doubt, the Indians chose a yet remoter cave.

In Guatemala the Catholic Church is now disestab-lished. It exists on sufferance and without any political power. Priests are few. The *padre* of Chichicaste-nango, for example, has thirty thousand parishioners and serves a dozen widely scattered villages. One curious result of this state of things is that the Indians practise their ancient rites much more openly than in the past. Pagan altars have been built within sound of the church bells ; the priests know that they are there, but are powerless to suppress them. Cere-monies (such as the *tun* dance), which the Church had prohibited and placed outside the law, have now come out from their hiding places, and are performed for all to see in the village plaza. And that, so far as the Indians are concerned, is the chief result of the pro-gressive legislation of anti-clerical reformers. Two hundred years ago ecclesiastical slackness had pro-duced exactly the same effects as disestablishment is producing to-day. The old religion came so boldly out into the open that in 1745 the Inquisition thought it necessary to launch a special campaign of anathemas against all heretics and backsliders.

What exactly are the Indians' religious beliefs ? I put the question to priests, to native and foreign resi-dents, to visiting anthropologists, but never got a very satisfactory answer. And perhaps there is no one answer—only a number of partial answers. For there is no single religion in Guatemala ; there are many. Every district, almost every village, seems to have evolved its own particular practices and (presumably) beliefs. Elements of Christian and pre-Christian worship have been selected and combined in an endless variety of ways. The Catholic pantheon has received the most surprising additions, the gospel story been treated to all kinds of the oddest emendations. There are villages, for example, where Judas, instead of being burnt on Easter Saturday, as is the case in the more orthodox cities, is worshipped as a god. At Atitlan, according to S. K. Lothrop, it is currently believed that St. John and the Virgin had a love affair on the night of the crucifixion. To prevent a repetition of this event, their images are locked up, on Good Friday, in separate cells of the town prison. The next morning, their respective Confraternities come and, for a couple of hundred pesos apiece, bail them out of captivity. Honour is safe for another year ; the saints are taken back to their altars. Nor is it only Catholicism that is subject to local variations. At Mixco in Gage's time, and at Chichicastenango to-day, images are worshipped at the rustic altars. Further to the north, at Momostenango, the people practise what the German anthropologists describe as a *philosophischer Cultus* ; their god is called Mundo, the World, and is not represented in any visible form.

CHICHICASTENANGO   The drummer.

There are, then, many different types of practice and belief—a diversity of roads leading, however, to the same place. For the point, the fundamental purpose of all these variations on a religious theme is the same. The worshippers want, first, good luck and protection against the powers of evil ; and, second, an excuse for a bit of fun in company. Catholicism and the old religion offer them a pantheon of specialized gods—a sort of celestial Harley Street equipped to deal with all the ills that flesh is heir to. With these specialist gods go special forms of worship—a host of magical formulas, of ceremonial gestures, of fetishistic, ' touch-wood ' rites.

Psychologically it makes not the least difference which gods the Indians choose to invoke or which rites they choose to perform. The only essential is that they shall believe the divine specialists to be properly qualified and the rites magically effective. It is the same with the excuses for having a bit of fun in company. The important, indispensable thing is the fun. If that is satisfying, then it makes not the smallest difference in whose name, or in commemoration of what event, the *fiesta* is celebrated. The chief purpose of a mythology is to provide occasions for *fiestas*, themes for dramatic performances and excuses for dressing up and doing things in a crowd. People are glad of any justification for a bit of sociable amusement, and, in response to this demand, the mythology of every living religion is constantly being added to.

Sometimes the additions are for the entire Church. (The definition of the doctrine of Transubstantiation in 1215 led, after the vision of the Prioress of Mont-Cornillon and the miracle of Bolsena, to the establishment of Corpus Christi, which became the world-wide excuse for pageantry and amateur theatricals.) Sometimes the additions are purely local. (The imaginary landing of the Saintes Maries in Provence is made a local reason for having a gypsies' party.) In Guatemala certain of the Indians' additions to religious mythology are remarkable inasmuch as they are made, so to speak, at the centre, not at the periphery. Well-drilled Christians would have too much respect for the accepted mythology to add to it a love-affair between the Virgin and the Beloved Disciple. But the Indians of Atitlan are not well-drilled Christians, and as they needed a justification for doing something dramatic and interesting on the night of Good Friday and the morning of Easter Saturday they emended the gospel story in what would be, for Europeans, a most blasphemous and disgusting way. It did not seem blasphemous and disgusting to them, first, because they had not been conditioned to regard the gospel story as inviolably sacred, and, second, because they did not, and do not, think of it as having any particular moral or spiritual significance. For such simple-minded people Christian mythology is simply an excuse for *fiestas* and the theoretical justification of their faith in the magical efficacy of particular pictures and

CHICHICASTENANGO   The Drum.

statues. As almost every story with a supernatural element can be made to supply such excuses and justifications, it follows that their choice of rites and mythology is a matter of almost complete indifference.

It ceases to be a matter of indifference only when worshippers are sufficiently self-conscious and individualized to be interested in the problems of personal salvation and social improvement. The Indians, as a class, do not seem to have reached this level of psychological development. The few priests with whom I had an opportunity of talking all told the same story. They had found that their parishioners were simply not interested in what we should regard as the essence of Christianity. In many cases, indeed, they actively disliked it, and, when told about the moral and spiritual significance of their religious rites, were so much disgusted that they refused to go any more to church.

Christianity for these people of the Guatemalan highlands is no more than an equivalent alternative to the aboriginal religions. Their catholicism is just an affair of magic, fetishism and sociable activity. The Indians are primitives—but primitives who have been, for four hundred years, in contact with Europeans. Accordingly, their primitiveness expresses itself, to a great extent, in terms of our culture. This is what makes them so uniquely interesting.

Chichicastenango

WE spent the morning in the *convento*, looking at Father Rosbach's remarkable collection of objects found among the ruins of the pre-conquest Quiché cities. There were painted jars, like those dug up at the Old Maya site of Uaxactun ; there were strange anthropomorphic vases, some grotesque, some executed with a dashing realism ; there were beads and ear-plugs and carved plaques and pendants of jadeite ; there were little animal figures in some dark hard stone. Perhaps the most interesting piece in the whole collection was a round, slightly convex plaque of hammered gold, almost unquestionably of Peruvian origin.

Thirty degrees of latitude separate the Quiché country from the valley of Cuzco. A long and arduous journey. But none the less it was probably made relatively often in pre-Columbian times. The Chimu, who built up an advanced civilization in northern Peru, and who were finally exterminated by the Incas about a century and a half before the arrival of Pizarro, may have been an offshoot of the Maya stock. All their South American neighbours were longheaded ; the Chimu were brachycephalic. But the Mayas were also brachycephalic. So perhaps the Chimus were Mayas. If so, they either walked from

164

TERRACOTTA URN   Collection of Father Rosbach.

Guatemala to Trujillo or paddled there by easy stages in canoes.

Movements of whole peoples are a rare occurrence. But there is good evidence to show that long journeys were undertaken by isolated individuals. Pilgrims to the shrine of the Black Christ of Esquipulas undoubtedly came, in Spanish times, from enormous distances—from Mexico to the north and, it is said, from as far as Ecuador and Peru to the south. The road was no easier after 1520 than before ; and if Christians could walk a thousand or fifteen hundred or two thousand miles through Central America, there was no reason why pagans should not do the same. Moreover, the custom of going on pilgrimage was certainly not introduced by the Spaniards. Guadalupe, near Mexico, was a pilgrimage place long before the Indian, Juan Diego, had his vision of the Virgin in 1531. Indeed, *post hoc* in this case was *propter hoc*. It was *because* of the existence of an Aztec Loreto that Juan Diego had his vision, and that the ecclesiastical authorities were so prompt in accepting its supernatural validity. The pilgrimage habit existed ; all that the Spaniards did was to direct it into Christian channels.

Chichicastenango

In one of the richly carved and gilded altar pieces on the southern side of the church are framed two very interesting Indian primitives—the only pictures of their kind I saw anywhere in Guatemala or Mexico. Primitive sculptures abound in Central America ; but practically all the religious paintings seem to have been done by Spaniards, or at any rate by artists long and carefully trained in the European tradition. Dismal imitations of Murillo, with perhaps a touch of Ribera thrown in by way of spicy condiment, moulder darkly and almost invisibly in every church. Even in out-of-the-way villages the pictures are always, by the standards of Sir Joshua, real pictures. Bad, no doubt ; but genuine attempts at the *beau idéal*, with perspective and chiaroscuro, all correct. Whereas every carving in the place may be manifestly the work of some pious little *indito* from next door. The fact is queer, and seems explicable only on the assumption of a deliberate ecclesiastical policy ; though why the Church should have tried to prevent the natives from painting God and the saints in their own image, when it had no objection to their Indianizing the sacred personages in three dimensions, it is difficult indeed to imagine.

166

CHICHICASTENANGO

Indian Primitives.

Chichicastenango

THE *rancho* stood in the fields outside the village and consisted of two shanties at right angles to one another. The larger was divided by a partition, on one side of which lived the father and his family, on the other the grown-up son and his. Two couples and about ten children in all. The second shanty was used as a workshop—a studio one would have called it, if the owners had been a little richer and had had a differently coloured skin. Yes, a studio ; for Diego, the grown-up son, was an artist. A very spirited lion of his painting adorned the outside wall of the studio, and, within, was an imaginary landscape. But Diego's speciality was the painting of masks for the ceremonial dances. He showed us some bull masks for the dance of the *Toritos*, and a whole collection of human faces, pink and gilded, for the *baile de los conquistadores*—that dramatic ballet in which the Indians celebrate the defeat and enslavement of their own people at the hands of Alvarado. The Serbians, in their folk songs about Kosovo, also commemorated a national disaster —but commemorated it as good Serbians, proud of their race, exulting in the valour of the national heroes, hopeful of deliverance from the oppressors. Very different is the spirit of the *baile de los conquista-*

167

dores. According to all the accounts I have read or heard, its tendency is entirely pro-Spanish. The Indians have chosen to exalt the heroism, not of their own people, but of the men who reduced them to peonage, not of those who resisted the tyrants, but of the tyrants themselves. This is a very extraordinary fact, and the more one thinks of it, the queerer it seems. What is the explanation? Without a knowledge of the social history of the Indians it would be absurd even to try to guess. One would have to know, for example, how soon after the conquest and in what circumstances the dance of the conquerors assumed its present form. And, of course and alas, this is the sort of information for which one searches the existing histories in vain. Nine out of ten of the facts, with which Bancroft's great work is so tightly stuffed, are just those facts that nobody really wants to know. 'In August 1609 Antonio Peraza Ayala Castilla y Rojas, conde de la Gomera, was appointed by royal cédula to succeed President Castilla.' This is doubtless true ; but it is a truth that, so far at any rate as we are concerned, is not susceptible of being made good or beautiful ; whereas a bit of truth about the origins and history of the *baile de los conquistadores* would have been potentially both. Good because instructive, because useful to any one who undertakes the proper study of mankind ; and beautiful inasmuch as it could be made to round off a harmonious system of thought, because it is the sort of truth that demands

CHICHICASTENANGO Diego.

to be reduced to order and which also lends itself to this aesthetic treatment. Valéry has called philosophy ' an attempt to transmute all we know into what we should like to know.' But a great deal of what we know is simply untransmutable. The fact that the conde de Gomera was called Antonio Peraza Ayala Castilla y Rojas is beyond the power of our mental alchemy ; no philosopher's stone known to us can turn it into philosophy. Whereas a set of facts about the Indians' dances fairly asks to be transmuted.

It would be foolish to blame Bancroft for having filled so much of his *History of Central America* with truth that we cannot render good or beautiful. In the first place, he had no other alternative. He could only collect the facts of which some documentary record existed. It is likely that, with the best will in the world, he could not have written the history of the *baile de los conquistadores*—for the good reason that the materials for such a history do not exist. Spanish colonists were not the men to waste good ink and paper on descriptions of Indian customs. Their records are mainly concerned with the, for them, all-important subjects of precedence, official rank, titles of nobility, salaries and perquisites.

Labours like those of Bancroft may seem to us largely unnecessary and fruitless. But our judgment, it goes without saying, is not final. We lack the alchemical equipment required to transmute his truths into the goods and beauties of a coherent system of thought. But that is not to say that they are absolutely untransmutable. It may be that thinkers possessed of a better technique than ours will find a means of turning even Antonio Peraza Ayala Castilla y Rojas into a philosophically significant fact. Bancroft is now almost unreadable ; but for the sake of what he may be made to mean by future alchemists of the mind, he deserves all respect.

Chichicastenango

Two American ethnologists were at work in the *patio* of the convent. Utterly miserable, but resigned, like sheep being led to the slaughter, half a dozen Indians permitted themselves to be taken, one by one, measured, weighed, tested for their reactions, inked for their finger-prints. The spectacle was ludicrous and pathetic. It was absurd that people should make such an agonized face about so little. Absurd, and yet the agony was obviously genuine. These poor creatures really suffered from being just looked at.

The men of earlier cultures were tactually aware of external reality. Their relations with it were, so to say, marital ; the world was their wife, and a wife in the full enjoyment of her conjugal rights. Whereas the moderns are *voyeurs*. A squint through the binoculars and then good-bye. Peeping Tom of Coventry was the first representative of scientific culture. Alas, he was born before his time. For boring a hole in his shutter and looking at Lady Godiva, as she rode naked along the street, he was struck blind. To-day he would have been given the Nobel Prize for his studies in dermatology.

England has its leopards, France its lilies, America its eagle, and Civilization its—what? Its lens. The heraldic emblem of the modern world can only be something made of optical glass.

Chichicastenango

THE Bull Dance is celebrated round about Christmas time; but already, though we were only in Lent, the Indians had started their preparations for it. News came that a rehearsal was to be held at a *rancho* somewhere in the hilly country to the west of the town. The chance was too good to miss and, with Don Alfredo and one of the ethnologists, we set out to see the fun. Against all the laws of Central American meteorology, it was raining; but Diego, who was our guide, assured us that the *rancho* was only half a league away. ' *Media legua*,' he kept repeating, ' *media legua*.' Another Indian, who had attached himself to our party, wouldn't hear of this *media legua* ; it was a league, he insisted. They fell into a long argument which Diego brought to a conclusion by saying : ' Well, it may be a league to you ; but for me it's only half a league.' It was peace with honour ; both sides had won. The rain came down harder and harder ; but like the Light Brigade, we kept indomitably going. Half a league, half a league . . . And at last, after an hour and three-quarters of hard walking, we reached the appointed place. We had covered at least a league and a half.

The *rancho* was built round three sides of a square, and about fifty Indians were assembled in the *patio*. Under the porch a large *marimba* was being played by three performers, and indoors was a second smaller instrument discoursing an entirely different music. The noise was astonishing. Ignored by all the Indians, we sat down on a bench near the larger *marimba* and almost immediately another movement of the dance began. The performers were divided into two groups. Shaking rattles and occasionally letting out a yell, they came dancing up towards one another, then retreated, then advanced again. One was reminded of all the children's parties one had ever attended, ' Here we come gathering nuts in May, nuts in May, nuts in May.' But the toddlers of those far-off Christmases had turned into full-grown copper-coloured savages, shaking rattles and uttering loud concerted whoops. It was curious and faintly disquieting.

Two or three minutes passed, and then 'Nuts in May' turned into the Grand Chain of the Lancers. The two opposed groups merged into a single serpentine procession. Slowly it circled the *patio*, slowly, while the couples who composed this creeping chain hopped round one another in narrow epicycles of swift and violent movement.

The dancing came to an end, and it was the turn of the stage manager to teach the performers their parts. Yes, their parts; for the Bull Dance is a drama in goodness knows how many dozens of rhymed Spanish couplets. The plot I never fathomed; all that I could make out was that it had something to do with a bailiff who entrusts the master's bulls to some herdsmen. The dancers came up one by one; the stage manager read out the words and they repeated them after him, making at the same time— some easily and with conviction, some in an agony of clumsy shyness—the traditional gestures with which the recitation was supposed to be accompanied.

The lesson was over at last. The rattling wooden music of the *marimba* broke out anew. The dancers fell into opposing lines and it was 'Here we come gathering nuts in May' all over again.

There seemed no reason why such a performance should ever come to a stop. But we were not to be given the opportunity of matching our endurance against that of the Indians. After the third or fourth bout of dancing, the proprietor of the *rancho* came up to us and firmly but still, though he was manifestly rather drunk, politely asked us to go away. 'You wouldn't like *us* to come and look on while you were busy with your *costumbres*,' he said.

The argument was unanswerable. I can imagine few things that would embarrass me more than to have a party of Quichés looking on in observant silence while I went through the curious old custom, say, of taking tea in Bloomsbury. Moreover, the man had had more *aguardiente* than was good for him, and a drunken Indian is apt to become unpleasantly violent. With as much dignity as we could muster, we retreated. Diego came running after us. The owner of the house, he explained apologetically, had been selling liquor without a licence. Our race allied us to the authorities ; in this country a white skin is almost an official uniform. Nobody likes to break the laws in the presence of policemen, and so long as we were there, the owner of the *rancho* had been unable to dispose of his liquor. No wonder if he resented our inquisitive prying into his people's *costumbres* !

Chichicastenango

INDIAN men are often handsome ; but I hardly ever saw a woman or young girl who was not extremely ugly. Endemic goitre does not improve their native homeliness ; and without exaggeration, I should

CHICHICASTENANGO   Indian types.

guess that at least a third of the women of Chichicastenango have bulging necks. One would expect to find cretins in a population so much afflicted with goitre. But I never saw a single one. Doubtless they are born, but fail, in the unmerciful environment of an Indian *rancho*, to survive.

Chichicastenango

At Chichicastenango Stephens and Catherwood stayed only long enough to eat their lunch ; but it was a crowded hour. ' In front of the *cabildo* was a new whipping-post. There was not a word spoken ; but a man was brought up before it, his feet and wrists tied together, and he was drawn up by a rope which passed through a groove at the top of the post. His back was naked, and an *alguazil* stood on his left with a heavy cowhide whip. Every stroke made a blue streak rising into a ridge, from which the blood started and trickled down his back. The poor fellow screamed in agony. After him a boy was stretched up in the same way. At the first lash, with a dreadful scream he jerked his feet out of the ropes and seemed to fly up to the top of the post. He was brought back and secured, and whipped till the *alcalde* was satisfied. This was one of the reforms instituted by the Central Government of Guatemala. The Liberal party had abolished this remnant of barbarity ; but within the

175

last month, at the wish of the Indians themselves, and
in pursuance of the general plan to restore old usages
and customs, new whipping-posts had been erected in
all the villages. Not one of the brutal beings around
seemed to have the least feeling for the victims.'

Guatemala in 1840 seems to have been startlingly
like Germany in 1933. The ' remnants of barbarity '
abolished by the German Liberal party have been
reintroduced by their opponents. There has been
a 'general plan to restore old usages and customs,'
and it is noteworthy that all the Nazi leaders
have been particularly eloquent about the necessity
of being ' hard,' of ' learning once more to punish.'
Their followers have gleefully obeyed them, and
large sections at least of the general population
have undoubtedly approved their brutality. The
whipping-post at Chichicastenango was set up ' at
the wish of the Indians themselves ' ; and the beating,
kicking, shooting, starving of Jews and Communists
in Germany goes on because a majority (so it seems)
of German people desires it to go on.

In his *Confessions* St. Augustine tells a still distress-
ingly topical story of a young man called Alypius
who had (thanks to Augustine's own teaching) conceived a horror for the then universally popular
gladiatorial games. It was a theoretical horror,
conceived on principle ; for Alypius had always
refused to witness a fight. One day, however, in the
streets of Rome he met a party of sporting friends on

their way to the fourth-century equivalent of a cup-tie. 'They with a familiar violence haled him, vehemently refusing and resisting, into the Amphitheatre.' The performance began ; but Alypius kept his eyes resolutely shut and declined to be a witness of the iniquities going on before him. Then, suddenly, as one of the combatants was wounded and fell, a great howl of ferocious glee went up from the crowded benches. Alypius' curiosity was roused ; he could resist no longer. Uncovering his eyes, he looked. ' But so soon as he saw that blood,' writes St. Augustine, ' he therewith drank down savageness ; nor turned away, but fixed his eyes, drinking in frenzy unawares, and was delighted with that guilty fight, and intoxicated with the bloody pastime.'

Civilized people are now trained, as Alypius was trained by St. Augustine, to regard cruelty and the infliction of avoidable suffering as morally wrong and aesthetically disgusting. Moreover, society is so organized that they seldom have an opportunity for gratifying their more ferocious passions. Such savage displays as the gladiatorial games are prohibited by law ; and cruelty even towards animals is punished. (If certain sadistic and sentimental old maids had their way, it would be punished by further cruelty, in the shape of flogging. There is no inward, psychological contradiction between a maudlin regard for poms and pekes and a bloodthirsty hatred of human beings.) Thanks, then, to the system within which

M   177

we live, we have but the rarest opportunities for being actors or spectators in a scene of savage cruelty. But if this opportunity were suddenly given us, how would we behave? My belief (and it seems to be confirmed by recent events in Germany) is that a good many of us would behave as Alypius did. We should come, see, and be conquered. 'The strongest oaths are straw to the fire i' the blood.' And lust is by no means the only fire, nor by any means the worst. The impulse to cruelty is, in many people, almost as violent as the impulse to sexual love—almost as violent and much more mischievous. Early training can fix principles and inspire a theoretical disgust. But, given free play, a sudden impulse can undo in a minute the work of years. Moreover, by what seems at first sight a paradox, civilized men succumb more easily to forbidden impulses than do primitives. The reason for this is obvious. In a civilized society, early conditioning can never be nearly so strict as it is in a small, isolated, homogeneous and ignorant group. No member of a large and variegated community can be persuaded to accept any given ethic or world-view with the unquestioning faith of a primitive, for whom the folk-ways of his tribe are the only ways of living and thinking ever invented. Nor can any one who has even heard of science believe in the absolute validity of taboos, or in the sanctions which are supposed to follow the breaking of them. When a primitive society forbids, its members obey; the

178

Circumambient Pavlov has conditioned them so that they cannot do otherwise. But when a civilized community commands, no such automatic obedience can be expected.

> Lord, with what care hast thou begirt us round !
> Parents first season us ; then schoolmasters
> Deliver us to laws ; they send us bound
> To rules of reason, holy messengers . . .
>   Yet all these fences and their whole array
>   One cunning bosom-sin blows quite away.

Which is why the rulers of civilized communities take such good care not only to condition their subjects during childhood, but also (since such conditioning cannot in civilized circumstances be adequate) to deliver them, so far as that is possible, from dangerous temptations when they are grown up. In most countries Alypius would simply not be given the chance to become intoxicated with bloody pastimes. Hitler, however, knows better than the consensus of civilized opinion and, in Germany, Alypius is encouraged not only to look on at, but also to act in, the gladiatorial show. The Nazi movement is a rebellion against Western civilization.* In order to

* To rule efficiently one must have 'faith,' *i.e.* an irrational conviction of one's own rightness and of other people's wrongness ; one must be intolerant; and one must be able to persecute with equanimity. Open-minded and humane rulers can carry on in fair weather. But a crisis comes and they are helpless ; the less civilized members of society seize the power they are too humane to wield. Can decency be combined with strength? Past history gives a discouraging answer to the question. To reconcile these incompatibles is the major task of statesmanship.

consolidate this rebellion, its leaders are doing their best to transform modern German society into the likeness of a primitive tribe. Homogeneity is being forced on a people that was enjoying the blessings of variety. Proximity in space cannot unfortunately be abolished ; but psychological gulfs can be and are being deliberately opened on every side. Mentally and emotionally, Germany is to be made as remote from Europe as New Guinea. The last and perhaps the most formidable obstacle to the strict conditioning process of primitive societies is, as we have seen, the scientific attitude. Nazi philosophy has a short way with the scientific attitude. The duty of all Germans is, in Hitler's own words, ' not to seek out objective truth in so far as it may be favourable to others, but uninterruptedly to serve one's own truth.' An ethic of head-hunters is to be justified by a philosophy of paranoiacs. The result promises to be extremely *gemütlich*.

The French are the people most immediately menaced by Nazi fanaticism ; and there is in this an element of poetic justice. For the two cardinal points in the philosophy, by which the Nazis justify their violences, were both invented by Frenchmen. Gobineau was responsible for that doctrine of race superiority used by the Nazis as an aphrodisiac to arouse hatred for Gobineau's own countrymen. And it was Bergson who led the intellectuals' disastrous attack on the intellect, and so prepared the way for the systematized

CHICHICASTENANGO   General view.

paranoia of Hitler. The sins and errors of the Brahmins are visited in a most disquieting way upon the low-caste masses of their fellow-men.

Chichicastenango

HERE, by way of appendix to the preceding note, are two quotations. The first is from one of the innumerable pieces of humane legislation promulgated by successive Kings in Spain and systematically ignored by their subjects in America. ' *Mandamos que en ningun caso se ejecute en los negros cimarrones* (runaway slaves) *la pena de cortarles las partes, que honestamente no se pueden nominar.*' The second is from Bancroft's account of the atrocities committed by the Welsh buccaneer, Henry Morgan, after the capture and sack of Panama. ' A cord was then twisted round his forehead until,' to use the words of Exquemelin, ' his eyes protruding from their sockets appeared as big as eggs. . . . He was then hung up by the private parts and flogged in that position.'

' *Ach, lieber Sulzer,*' Frederick the Great once remarked of a Prussian official who had waxed eloquent about the fundamental goodness of human beings, ' *lieber Sulzer, er kennt nicht diese verdammte Rasse.*'

Zacapulas

WE made an early start, and forty minutes later drew up in the plaza of Santa Cruz Quiché, the capital of the department. While Don Alfredo went to pay his respects to the Jefe Politico and to ask his permission to use the new road to Zacapulas, which was not yet officially open, we strolled into the church. A good deal of praying and candle-burning was going on ; but the worshippers were all in imported cotton, and the scene lacked the queer anachronistic beauty of similar pieties in Chichicastenango. In a few minutes Don Alfredo rejoined us. The governor had given him all the necessary permissions, and along with them the information that we would not be able to drive into Zacapulas. The last bridge was still unbuilt ; we should have to leave our car and walk. A few steps that was all. The bridge was only *dos cuadros* from the plaza of the town. *Dos cuadros*—two blocks ; from Central Park South to Fifty-Seventh Street. One visualized an agreeable urban stroll.

The road took us first across open agricultural country, then through oak woods, brown in the blistering drought of early spring, as though after a frost. A few miles more, and the woods thinned out into a kind of barren park land, and finally the occasional

182

trees gave place to occasional cactuses ; the park had turned into a desert of stones and dust and desperate vegetable ferocity. The ground fell away beneath us, and there, far down, appeared a river, and beyond it rose range upon range of mountains. The road wound down into the valley, and at last flattened out on a stretch of level ground just above the river. It was the dry season, and the Rio Negro flowed shrunken through a wide expanse of stones ; but even at this low ebb it was an imposing stream. A hundred miles or so below Zacapulas it joins with the Rio de la Pasion to form the great Usumacinta which empties itself into the Gulf of Campeche. Here in the valley, the prevailing golden grey of the dusty landscape was patched with brilliant green. There were cultivated fields, and here and there an Indian shanty. And then suddenly we found ourselves at the unfinished bridge. We got out, climbed the high bank above the road and looked around. *Dos cuadros :* Central Park South to Fifty-Seventh Street. But the dry desolation rolled away, it seemed, interminably ; there was no sign of Zacapulas.

The governor's two blocks of Americanized wish-fulfilment were not, I am thankful to say, quite so long as Diego's subjective half-league. Forty minutes of brisk walking through the dust and under the perpendicular mid-day sun brought us at last to the town. We were directed to the inn, and there, in a shady garden, were given the inevitable eggs, black beans and tortillas, and all the bottled beer we desired and, after those blocks, deserved.

The river at Zacapulas is spanned by a fine bridge, solid enough, to all appearances, to last for centuries. Unfortunately, at the time it was built, some thirty years ago, it seemed so utterly inconceivable that any wheeled vehicle should ever come to Zacapulas that the roadway was made wide enough only for pack animals. If cars are ever to cross the Rio Negro, the bridge will have to be rebuilt.

Accompanied by a little *ladino* boy, we crossed it after lunch on a wild-goose chase in search of pre-Columbian antiquities. It was incredibly hot, and the path along which our guide conducted us was shaded only by enormous phallic cactuses. We panted for perhaps a mile through the thick dust, and were rewarded at last by the sight of several large pyramidal mounds, standing on the flat ground between our road and the river. There had been a settlement here, with temples and perhaps a chieftain's house and burial place. At the foot of the mounds stood a wooden hut. We approached it, and were received on the doorstep, very suspiciously, by the owner, a young Indian of about thirty. We put our question: when he dug his fields, did he ever find things buried in the ground? Reluctantly—for he seemed to hate to give the information, to hate even to possess it— the Indian nodded. Yes, he often found old pots. We looked at one another, smiling with gleeful anticipation. Might we see some of the pots he had dug up ? But this time he shook his head. They were *old* pots, he insisted, and he had new ones of his own—better ones. Old pots were of no use to him : he always broke them and threw the pieces into the river.

There was nothing to do but to trudge back through the dust to Zacapulas. The church, when at last we reached it, was a blessed oasis of cool twilight. And what surprising treasures it contained ! The high altar was fronted with eighteenth-century hammered silver, and the lateral altars were alive with a whole people of gesticulating Indian-baroque saints, all of them charming, and some genuinely beautiful. A very primitive Christ, with shapeless limbs all dribbled with blood, stood against the wall between two remarkably elegant seventeenth-century crucifixes. Opposite was a pair of wooden soldiers dressed in the doublet and armour of, I guessed, about 1580. In the loft above the entrance door were the ruins of a fine organ. In its palmy days the church of Zacapulas must have been really splendid. The Indians, of course, paid for the splendours—paid with goodness knows how much painful labour. But at least—and this is more than can be said for their labours in other fields—they did get some return for their spent energy. The physical work that went into the, economically speaking, useless and wasteful monuments of ancient grandeur was rewarded by the psychological satisfaction which the labourers derived from these monuments. All the excitements of religion, all the imaginative pleasures of being grand by proxy, of being vicariously exalted in the person of one's gods, one's priests, one's kings—these were the rewards. The Indians must have worked very hard to make and keep the church of Zacapulas so splendid ; but at least it was *their* church, and the gilded idols on the altars, *their* saints. They themselves lived in huts ; but the rich and glittering temple in the plaza was their spiritual home. A spiritual home, moreover, having the additional merit of being physically there ; a castle in Spain that was visibly present in Zacapulas. Nobody can deny that the church squeezed an unconscionable tribute out of the long-suffering Indians ; but it gave something in return. Whereas the lay taskmasters, from Alvarado's day to the present, have taken quite as much and given nothing.

Momostenango

MOMOSTENANGO means ' the place of the altars.' And, sure enough, there they are, scores of them, hundreds even, all round the village. Altars of stone, altars of heaped-up earth and broken crockery ; solitary altars standing secretly half-way down the precipitous side of a *barranca* ; altars in groups, almost in crowds, along the open hillside.

No idols stand on these altars. The god to whom they are dedicated is too great to be represented. He is the world at large, Mundo—a lineal descendant, no doubt, of the old Maya-Quiché deity, Huracan, whose name signifies ' Heart of the World.' Once every two hundred and sixty days (the Mayas' sacred year) the Momostecos celebrate, in honour of Mundo, a great feast called the Uajxaqip Vats. (The pronunciation —Washakip, for all practical purposes—is not so forbidding as the orthography). As many as thirty thousand Indians assemble from all the country round, burn incense at the altars, pray, perhaps offer sacrifice. Having done due honour to Mundo, they repair to the parish church, and there confess their sins to the representative of the white man's God. In the intervals of their religious exercises they get drunk and otherwise amuse themselves. And after two or three days of piety and jollity they go home.

Christianity, Judaism and Islam all claim to possess a monopoly of truth. And as these are the three religions with which we happen to be best acquainted, we regard such claims as normal and natural. Statistically, however, they are abnormal. A majority of the world's religions have never made such claims. People have generally believed that the other man's gods, though possibly dangerous, were unquestionably efficient and therefore worthy of respect. The

Indians' impartial and simultaneous practice of two religions seems to us queer and rather immoral. But it is in the grandest of classical traditions. The Greeks and Romans would have behaved exactly as the Momostecos do.

Momostenango

Our host at Momostenango, and our omniscient and indefatigable guide, was Don Ernesto Lange. Don Ernesto is a German who came to Guatemala some fifteen years ago, set up at Momostenango as merchant and storekeeper, married (in very romantic circumstances) a young and remarkably beautiful Indian wife, and now, at the head of a family of six superb children, is the principal citizen of the town and as learned an amateur ethnologist as you can find in Guatemala.

A small man, incredibly active in mind and body, and talking nineteen to the dozen in German and colloquial Central American Spanish, he showed us the queer sights of his adopted city and expounded their still queerer significance. My mind responds adequately enough to about a hundred and fifty German or Spanish words a minute. But Don Ernesto's ordinary rate was at least three hundred.

188

MOMOSTENANGO

Always four or five sentences in the rear, I floundered after him. It was a most exhausting steeplechase ; but I was glad I had the energy to stay the course. The prize was worth the labour : Don Ernesto was a mine—but no, that is entirely the wrong metaphor ; a mine is static, a mere hole in the ground—Don Ernesto was a spate, a cataract of valuable information.

There was, for example, his account of the Momosteco sorcerers. We had climbed up to one of the altars, which stand in a group on the hill just outside the town. Great mounds they were, some of them nearly twenty feet high ; and on each mound were four or five niche-like hearths of broken potsherds, blackened with smoke—the *quemaderos,* or burning places of the Indians.

' Look at this,' said Don Ernesto, and out of a recess among the potsherds he pulled a little bag and from it shook on to his palm a few beans and some quartz crystals. These, he explained, were the stock-in-trade of a sorcerer—the divining apparatus, by means of which he could foretell the future. When a sorcerer dies, his beans and his crystals are laid on one of the altars. Nobody touches them, for they are protected by a taboo ; they lie there in mystical safe deposit. The dead man's appointed successor must wait until the bag which contains them has completely rotted away. Only then may he take possession of the sacred objects and practise the traditional rites.

Moving among the altars, we saw several bags in

various stages of decay. During the last influenza epidemic, Don Ernesto told me, there were literally scores of them. A bad mark, it would seem to people of our way of thinking, against sorcery. But then, in this matter, at least, primitives are not of our way of thinking. The death of sorcerers in an epidemic is, to them, proof positive of the effectiveness of sorcery and of the reality of the evil powers, which sorcerers exploit and resist. Why do sorcerers die? Because the evil powers have been too strong for them, because some other, hostile sorcerer has been practising against them. The moral of all this is clear : the number of friendly sorcerers must be increased and their sorcery made more efficient. Transferred from the realm of international politics to that of magic, it is just the familiar argument of those who clamour for bigger and better armaments.

There are, it seems, more than three hundred medicine-men practising in Momostenango. They form a regular professional body, half priesthood, half Medical Association, doubtless under the protection of some Christian saint. At Jocopila, near Santa Cruz Quiché, the *ladino* secretary of the municipality told us that the medicine-men were all devoted to St. Peter. The Momosteco sorcerers are probably under the same patronage.

Every respectable Indian household has its family sorcerer, who acts as director of conscience, fortune-teller and physician. The two latter functions are inseparably fused together. Before prescribing in his capacity of a doctor, the sorcerer must, as a fortune-teller, discover whether his prescriptions are likely to do any good. With his beans and quartz crystals he plays three games of mystical solitaire. If all three games ' come out,' then it means that the patient is certain to get well ; if two, that he may recover, and that it is still worth while trying what medicine and nursing can do to help him. But if only one game comes out—or, worse, none at all—then the case is hopeless : the higher powers have decreed death and human art can effect nothing. The patient is abandoned to his fate. Convinced in advance of the uselessness of everything they can possibly do, even his own people desert him. He is left alone without food or drink. Not unnaturally, the sorcerer's prophecy is soon fulfilled : the patient dies of thirst and hunger. Yet another proof of the efficiency of magic.

As a young girl, Don Ernesto's wife fell ill and was condemned by the family sorcerer. Her mother could not resign herself to let the child die inch-meal and appealed to Don Ernesto, who boldly asserted that proper treatment would result in a cure. It did and the young *miraculée*, or rather *démiraculée*, is now Señora Lange and the mother of six charming and intelligent children.

After a delicious and gargantuan dinner, Don Ernesto took Don Alfredo and ourselves to see a *compadre* of his, a colonel in the national army.

Momostenango is the recruiting ground for the most efficient of the Indian regiments, and a considerable percentage of its male inhabitants spend several years as soldiers in one of the distant garrisons. It is a testimony to the unshakeable conservatism of the Indians that, even in the metropolitan atmosphere of Guatemala City, they remain as staunchly heathen and devoutly Catholic as in their native village. Stationed in the capital, they will send money to their friends at home that prayers may be said for them at one of Mundo's altars or in the parish church ; and when their service is over, they fall back without any apparent intellectual or emotional difficulty into the traditional grooves of Momostecan life. The fact is interesting and significant.

Don Ernesto's *compadre*, the colonel, turned out to be very nearly, if not quite, a pure Momosteco Indian. He was a heavy-faced man, very quiet, and strangely detached, as though he were separated from you by a thick sheet of plate-glass. Indians' eyes have a blank reptilian glitter, signifying, at any rate to the white observer, nothing at all. But the *coronel's* regard was, even by European standards, fully human : it expressed a profound and hopeless melancholy. He had had, I suppose, enough of our education to make him aware of his own Indianness and of the fact that it is no joke to be self-conscious, but copper-coloured in a world dominated by white men.

A table and six kitchen chairs were all the furniture

of the room in which he received us. A naked electric-light bulb bleakly illumined the white-washed walls, the grey cement floor. From behind the closed doors one heard the noises of people going to bed—a secret ant-hill of unavowable family life. Surprisingly, the colonel produced a bottle of whisky and poured us all a drink. The incongruity between our Indian host and his Anglo-Indian gesture was somehow rather painful. Why should the world be so full of unnecessary miseries, of avoidable agonies and humiliations ?

Later in the evening the colonel tuned his guitar and treated us to a couple of songs. The music had been composed by a local amateur, the words, both in Spanish and Quiché, were his own. The theme of the first was the death of the Quiché king at the hands of Alvarado ; of the second, the Guatemalteco Indian. Unlike the folk-drama of the *baile de los conquistadores*, the colonel's songs were pro-Indian. By a strange irony, it would seem that Indians can become patriotically conscious of their race only when they have had a white man's education.

The local composer's melodies were extremely commonplace little Spanish tunes, and the colonel's verses were more uncompromisingly prosaic than any I have ever heard. I remember only two lines. Alvarado had beaten the Quichés, and then—

> Cambió la situación
> De nosotros aquí.

It did indeed ! And the most piercingly beautiful lyric could not have brought the fact home more effectively than did the *coronel's* prose, when declaimed in that bleak poverty-stricken room, with the Anglo-Indian bottle on the table and the soft Amerindian noises behind the fast-shut doors ; declaimed, to the twang and rattle of an ill-played guitar, in a hoarse cracked voice, and to a frivolous incongruous tune, by this member of the conquered race to whom the conquerors, along with the privileges of rank and schooling had given the agonizing knowledge of his own people's impotence and degradation.

On the Road

SAN FRANCISCO EL ALTO stands in the biting mountain cold, high, high above the great valley in which lie Totonicopan, San Cristobal and Quezaltenango. It seems the end of the world. But its plaza was so tightly crammed with bartering Indians that we had the greatest difficulty in pushing our way through the crowds ; and the church, when at last we had fought our way to it, displayed an almost metropolitan magnificence. Still grander was, or rather had been—for it was in a sadly ruinous state—the great church of the Franciscans at San Cristobal in the valley

194

below. This must be one of the largest churches in the country ; one of the richest too. Its huge gilded altars are incomparably splendid.

Most of the figures carved by Indian sculptors tend to be distorted in the same characteristic fashion. They are stumpy, short-limbed, steep-featured ; it is as though an effort had been made to compress them so as to fit into an imaginary box, rather too short and rather too narrow to accommodate them comfortably. The figures of primitive sculpture are often stumpy ; for the head, being the focus of interest, tends to be enlarged at the expense of the body. But the stumpiness of this American-Indian sculpture is peculiar inasmuch as the compression, applied as well to the features of the large face as to the limbs and trunk, is a compression exercised by invisible flat surfaces at right angles one to another. An Indian saint is a person who has been put into one of those machines for packing cotton into cubic bales. I like to fancy that this characteristic Guatemalan distortion is dictated by an ancient artistic tradition. Nobody who has looked at the Maya stelae can have failed to be struck by the way in which human forms are distorted so as to fit into the square framework of the hieroglyphs. To fit into and also to fill the frames. For there is a fundamental aesthetic difference between Mayan and Egyptian hieroglyphs. The Egyptian glyph is just a little picture, having no structural relations with a frame and therefore under no necessity to undergo any particular kind of distortion. Among the Mayas, the word-picture (generally a human head) is, mathematically speaking, a function of its frame. The thing represented is made coterminous on three sides with the enclosing square, and on the fourth side, though rarely reaching to the boundary of the frame, is brought against a line parallel to it.

In order that it may fill a rectangular frame, a head must be flattened above and below, and steepened fore and aft ; in a word, it must go through the cotton-bale-making machine. Even when they were working in three dimensions the Mayas often treated their subject as though it were placed inside a cube or a parallelepiped which it had to fill. The frame of the hieroglyph added depth to its length and breadth and became an imaginary, but definitely visualized volume, conditioning the forms of the sculpture within it and imposing certain necessary distortions.

The Indian sculptors who carved such saints as those in the Franciscan church at San Cristobal seem to have worked within the same sort of imaginary cubes and parallelepipeds. Perhaps, unconsciously, and by mere force of tradition, they were still thinking of those square frames into which their ancestors, a thousand years before, had compressed the pictures that served them as numerals and writing. It is only a fancy ; but I should like it to be true.

We lunched at Quezaltenango in a most forbidding German hotel. Pretentiousness, dirt, expense—one

was painfully reminded of inedible lunches in South
Shields, of a week-end in Middlesborough, with a
dark tide-mark of grit and the pubic hairs of commercial travellers running round the bath. Escaping
to the market, we were distracted from these unappe-
tizing home thoughts by the discovery, at the stall
of a drink seller, of some really beautiful gourd cups.
The painting of gourds is a considerable peasant
industry both in Guatemala and Mexico. The nature
of the objects made is dictated by the shapes of the
vegetables. The commonest are cups, bowls, rattles
and ornamental fish. In general the colours are
extremely gaudy. Pale blue and white flowers painted
on a scarlet ground ; or else there will be patterns in
red, blue and yellow on shining black ; sometimes of
scarlet on white. The general effect is Tyrolean or
Bavarian-Alpine. It is a typical semi-sophisticated
peasant art, fundamentally European in style. But
these gourd drinking vessels at Quezaltenango were
entirely different. Unvarnished, and painted in only
two colours, black and ochre, they bore no resemblance
to the art-and-craft gourds of ordinary Central American commerce. The designs painted on them—con-
ventionalized birds and women—were like the drawings
made by neolithic men, when they first began to think
in verbal concepts. Palaeolithic man put a line round
his untransformed memories ; neolithic man, on the
contrary, put the line round his concepts and arranged
these Platonic Ideas of reality in patterns that would

satisfy his soul's desire for order. Later, men were able to return from conceptual abstraction to naturalism and to embody a large amount of naturalistic art in their patterns. The Tyrolean gourds of Mexico are painted in a late tradition of peasant art ; the decoration is tinged with naturalism. Our Quezaltenango artist was still in the first flush of neolithic conceptualism. The traditions of modern naturalistic art had not affected him at all : which was the more remarkable as he was evidently a man of some education. At any rate, he could write. On one of the cups was scratched, in a careful but rather uncertain lettering : *un triste recuerdo del jobencito D.* A sad reminder of the young man D. Poor young Mr. D ! I hope he got some satisfaction out of his exquisite neolithic talent. I certainly did. For ninepence I bought two small masterpieces of his creation, and my pleasure in them more than made up to me for the horrors of the all-too-English hotel.

Copan

To the ordinary Englishman, how little the aeroplane still means ! He lives as though the Wright brothers had never existed, moves and almost uninterruptedly has his being in a pre-Blériot world. When he travels it is always by train or car, over a network of rails and metalled roads. The plane is for him superfluous, an unjustifiable and slightly inconvenient luxury.

Profoundly different is the state of things in Central America. The plane has come and, quite suddenly, transformed an immemorial mode of life. There are hardly any railways in the Five Republics, and the roads are mostly mere bridle-paths. Over the greater part of the country one travelled, until very recently, as the Britons travelled before the coming of Julius Caesar. Maudslay possessed but one advantage over the Old Empire Mayas, whose ruined cities he explored—he had a horse to ride and pack mules to carry his luggage. In Maya times his beasts of burden and his mounts would all have been bipeds. (Even under the Spanish dispensation some people preferred the human beast of burden. Stephens thus describes the mode of travel favoured by distinguished ecclesiastics in 1840. ' He set off on the back of an Indian in a *silla*, or chair with a high back and top to protect him from the sun. Three other Indians followed as relay carriers, and a noble mule for his relief if he should become tired of the chair. The Indian was bent almost double, but the *canónigo* was in high spirits, smoking his cigar, and waving his hand till he was out of sight.')

Mules, porters, mud-tracks through the jungle. . . . Then, from one day to another, people were hurtling through space in tri-motored air liners. A long,

199

laborious epoch of history was suppressed, and without transition men passed from a neolithic technique of transportation to the most advanced twentieth-century practice.

Measured on the map, distances in Guatemala are absurdly small. Measured by human effort and fatigue, they are enormous. Ten years ago, for example, it took you anything from twelve days to three weeks to travel from Guatemala City to Flores in the north-eastern corner of the country. You had to go down to Puerto Barrios on the Atlantic, take ship to Belize in British Honduras, paddle up the Belize river in a canoe for four, six, seven, even ten days—it depended on the amount of water that was coming down—and finish up with four or five days on a mule, riding through the jungles of Peten. Now you step into your plane at half-past ten and step out again at Flores in comfortable time for lunch.

By rail and what, by courtesy, we will call road, Copan is about four days from Guatemala City ; by aeroplane, about an hour and a quarter. Unfortunately there is, for political reasons, no regular service between the two points. Copan is a village just across the frontier in Honduras. In the Five Republics the local air services are all strictly national ; and Pan-American Airways, which are responsible for the long-distance international services, call only at the more important towns. The gulf dividing Copan from Guatemala City seemed therefore impassable.

But an enterprising acquaintance, Dr. Harris, the American biologist, had discovered that the journey could be made. True, no pilot from Guatemala had ever landed at Copan ; but it was reported to possess a flying field. A plane could be chartered from the local company, and, armed with the necessary visas, vaccination certificates, flying permits, and what not, we could drop down into the neighbouring republic, look at the ruins and be back, if necessary, in time for lunch.

The theory of nationalism is one of the grandest labour-creating devices ever invented. To fly from point A to another point B a hundred miles away is, physically, a simple matter. But if the two points lie on opposite sides of a national boundary, how difficult the business at once becomes ! The theory of nationalism makes it necessary for each State to create huge, expensive organizations, whose function is, first to prevent and then, at a price and under absurd conditions, to allow, the performance of such physically simple acts as flying from A to B. And how much time and trouble must be wasted by innocent individuals in circumventing the obstacles which are so carefully put in their way ! A mitigation of nationalism would save the world millions of hours of wasted time and an incalculable expense of spirit, physical energy, and money.

To the rare travellers who visit these far-away countries of Central America, the resident diplomats show a boundless kindness. Mr. Lee, the British consul and acting minister, wrote me a letter of recommendation so glowing that, when at last I found the Honduranean minister, he gave me all the necessary visas at once and—what I thought uncommonly handsome—free of all charge. I was grateful ; and would have been a good deal more grateful if I had not had to make about four blisteringly hot journeys to his legation before finding him at home. Meanwhile, the officials of the aeroplane company had not been idle. Through the Guatemalan Foreign Office they had approached the Honduranean Foreign Office at Tegucigalpa ; the Honduranean Foreign Office had communicated with the Honduranean Ministry of War ; and after due consideration it had been decided that the safety of the State would not be seriously imperilled by our visit to Copan. Telegraphically, we were authorized to go. The arranging of our little trip had consumed about six man-hours of valuable official time and about as many of (I flatter myself) still more valuable unofficial time.

The sun had just risen when we took off from the air-port of Guatemala. We climbed into a flawless sky, but down in the valleys the mist lay impenetrably white. There was sunlight only above four thousand feet. The mountains were islands, and here and there the cone of a volcano rose like Stromboli from the level expanse of that shining sea. We flew on. The valley of the Motagua wound away beneath us, a fjord between mountains. In the interminable and meaningless wilderness of peaks and *barrancas* and volcanoes, it was the only clear and significant geographical feature.

Time passed ; we were approaching our destination. Somewhere below us lay the ruins. But where? Which of these narrow rivers of white mist was the valley of Copan? There was nothing for it but to go down and look. Three times our pilot swooped down out of the blue—two thousand feet of steep and sickening descent—down into the fog between the closely crowding mountains. But there was nothing to be seen and after the third attempt he turned back. Twenty minutes away, in Guatemalan territory, was the landing field of Esquipulas—a plateau lying high enough to be free of mist. We landed. In an hour the sun would have scoured the lowest valleys and we could start again.

Esquipulas is the home of a Black Christ of such extraordinary sanctity that every January pilgrims came, and still come, from enormous distances to worship at his shrine. It seems that in the eyes of all the aboriginal American races, black is traditionally a sacred colour ; so that what draws the worshippers from as far as Mexico in the north, and as Ecuador in the south, and even as Peru, is probably less the saintliness of the historic Jesus than the magical sootiness of his image. With us, black is symbolical only of grief. The black uniform of our clergy is a kind of chronic mourning that is meant, I suppose, to testify to the essential *sérieux* of their official character. It has no magical significance ; for on all ceremonial occasions it is discarded for a praying costume of white linen, or of cloth of gold, or of gaudily embroidered silk. But though black is not with us a sacred colour, black images of exceeding holiness are none the less fairly common in Europe. The reason, I suspect, is that such statues have a somewhat sinister appearance. (The Holy Face of Lucca is very nearly black and, with its glittering jewelled eyes, is one of the strangest and most terrifying sculptures ever made.) In Otto's terminology, black idols are intrinsically more ' numin- ous ' than white. Numinosity is in inverse ratio to luminosity.

Most regrettably we were unable to see the image. The village of Esquipulas stands some two or three miles from the landing field, and to have walked there and back would have taken too long. Our pilot was anxious to reach Copan as soon as possible, so that we could get away again before the afternoon wind sprang up and made starting difficult. We had to content ourselves with a distant bird's-eye view of the huge white church, towering high above the almost invisible huts of its attendant village, a landmark in the wilderness.

An hour passed ; the sun was already high in the sky and very hot. We climbed into the plane again and started off. The mist had all melted away and,

COPAN   Stela and altar.

in a little while, there below us, clear as a map, was the valley of Copan, narrow between hills, with its village, its fields of dust-coloured stubble, its winding river, its tree-grown Maya acropolis rising sheer in a great wall from the water's edge. We came spiralling down. A small bald patch not far from the ruins was evidently the landing field. A herd of cows scattered in hysterical agitation as we descended. Avoiding these animals as best he could, and steering clear of the larger of the numerous rocks with which the airport was strewn, our pilot, who was fortunately a most skilful flyer, brought us safely to land. We stepped out and, accompanied by some small boys who offered to be our guides, walked off to see the ruins. Our pilot took the road to the village ; the local authorities would be anxious, he knew, to prove their importance by lengthily examining his papers. If he did not indulge them, they might turn savage.

Time and its allies in destruction, vegetation and weather, play curious tricks on the works of man. A city left to their tender mercies is generally destroyed as an architectural and engineering whole, but spared in its decorative details. The great masses of masonry are buried and disrupted ; tend, if the vegetation is strong, to vanish altogether, dissolved into their component parts ; the statues, the reliefs, the fragile pots and jewels survive, very often, almost intact. At Copan, for example, a few mounds covered with trees, a wall here and there, some rubbish heaps of tumbled stones, are all that remain of the great complex of pyramids, of platforms, of walls and terraces, of sunken courtyards, which once occupied the site. Buried and, under the mould, disintegrated by the thrusting roots of the tropical vegetation, a sacred city of pure geometrical forms once stood here. Its sharp-edged planes of hewn stone, of white or painted stucco, shone smooth, like the surfaces of a crystal, in the perpendicular sunlight. But toiling up and down through the scrub, among the fallen stones, I found it all but impossible to reconstruct in my imagination the Mayas' huge embodiment of a mathematician's dream. I had read the writings of the archaeologists and knew what sort of monument had been raised at Copan. But these almost shapeless barrows supplied my fancy with no visible foundations on which to rebuild the Mayas' prodigious works. Only the plastic decorations with which their mountains of solid geometry had been incidentally trimmed were still there, in unequivocal existence, before my eyes. The whole had gone ; but a few of the ornamental parts remained. In a maize field at the foot of the wooded mounds—the mounds were the acropolis and principal pyramid, the maize field had been a great forum—stood a group of magnificent stelae, floridly carved in such deep relief that the stone was sometimes pierced from side to side. Using neolithic tools, the Maya sculptors had displayed an almost contemptuous mastery of their material ; they had treated their twenty-foot monoliths as a Chinese craftsman might treat a piece of ivory. One is left bewildered by the spectacle of so much technical accomplishment displayed by people having such inadequate technical resources.

The stelae are not Copan's only monuments. Scrambling among the ruins, we found an astonishing wealth of carved stones. Here was a great cubic skull-symbol, its eye sockets glaring, its teeth deep in the grass and weeds ; here, at the base of a broken wall, a dado of small death's-heads in low relief ; here the famous altar with its frieze of fantastically adorned astronomer-priests in scientific conference ; here, carved in the round, a giant's head, grotesquely open-mouthed ; here a pair of statues, broken, but still violently alive. The finest specimens of sculpture in the round are no longer at Copan. I saw nothing to compare in grace, in plastic subtlety, in emotional expressiveness, with the torso of the maize god at the British Museum, or with the lovely head of the same god now at Boston. These two pieces and certain others in American museums, are stylistically so close to one another that one is tempted to think of them as the works of a single sculptor of outstanding ability. Of the other carvings in the round still at Copan, none exhibited the kind of approach to reality exemplified in these extraordinary statues. The beauty of most Mayan sculpture is felt by us to be profoundly, incommensurably alien. But with this particular group of carvings from Copan one feels suddenly at home, on familiar emotional ground. The mind of the man, or men, who made them seems to have been gifted with the same kind of sensibilities as ours. Now that these works have been taken away, the European visitor to Copan enjoys no such comforting conviction. He looks at the astonishing works around him, but looks at them from across a gulf; they exist in a universe of sentiment and discourse that is not his universe. Those colossal skulls, for example—they have nothing to do with the macabre of our later middle ages, or the florid horrors of baroque sepulchral art.

> The flesh is bruckle, the fiend is slee,
> *Timor mortis conturbat me.*

So wailed our ancestors. But I doubt if the Mayas were saying anything of the kind. In these great cubic monoliths, adorned (with what an unerring sense of the significantly decorative effect !) with eye sockets, nose hole, teeth, one finds no trace of our European lament for transience, our personal terror of extinction and decay. One finds—what? Confronted by the extraordinary objects themselves one can only ask the question, not hope to answer it. It is impossible to know by personal experience what the people who made such things felt and thought. Each life has its own private logic, and the logics of all the lives of people living at a given time, under a given cultural dispensation, have, at some point, a certain resemblance among themselves. The Mayas' life-logic was not the same as ours. The admiration with which

COPAN   Fragment of Sculpture.

we look at their works of art is tinged with a speculative incomprehension. What were they really up to?
Quien sabe?

We came back from the ruins to find the entire
population of Copan clustered round our aeroplane,
like a crowd of Breughel's peasants round a crucifixion.
Some were standing ; some, with the air of people who
had come out for a long day's pleasure, were sitting
in the shade of our wings and picnicking. They were
a villainous set of men and women ; not Indian, but
low *ladino*, squalid and dirty as only a poverty-stricken
half-caste, with a touch of white blood and a sense
of superiority to all the traditional decencies of the
inferior race, can be dirty and squalid. Before the
door of the cabin stood half a dozen ruffians, looking
like the Second Murderers of Elizabethan drama, and
armed with genuinely antique muskets of the American
Civil War pattern. The local police. We were
criminals.

It was, of course, our old friend nationalism at work
once more, creating labour and discomfort with a
punctual fidelity—creating also, it must be admitted,
a great deal of gratuitous amusement for the inhabitants of Copan. Our licence to land at Copan had
been issued by the central authorities in Tegucigalpa.
But the central authorities had omitted to tell the
local authorities of what they had done ; so that when
we dropped out of the blue, our arrival must have
had, for the *alcalde* of Copan and the General in charge

of the department, to whom he had immediately telegraphed, all the exciting characteristics of an unprovoked outrage, a wanton piece of Guatemalan sabre-rattling. ' *Aux armes, citoyens ! formez vos bataillons !* ' The Copanese had responded manfully to the call. Those Second Murderers, with their muskets, offensively refusing to allow us to sit in the cabin of our own aeroplane, were animated, I am sure, by the purest patriotism.

The hours passed, it grew hotter and hotter. Our pilot had telegraphed to Guatemala ; but goodness only knew how long it would take for the telegram to produce any effect in Copan. I began to wonder uncomfortably whether we should have to spend the night behind the bars of the local prison, in intimate companionship with the local bugs, ticks, lice and fleas. But happily, half-way through the afternoon, deliverance came. On the receipt of our telegram the aeroplane company had appealed to the Guatemalan Foreign Office, and the Guatemalan Foreign Office, justly indignant, had telegraphed to Tegucigalpa, and Tegucigalpa had telegraphed to the General at the head of the department, and the General had telegraphed to the *alcalde* of Copan. There was nothing for it but to let us go. With obvious reluctance the Copanese prepared to obey the orders from above. But, as though he could not bear to be deprived so soon of the exquisite pleasure of being offensive to his betters, the young man in charge of the Second

Murderers insisted on having yet one more look at our passports, and kept them a quarter of an hour, while he copied down all the names he could find, from our own to those of the Foreign Secretaries by whom the passports had been issued. Then, when there was really nothing more he could do to annoy us, he called away his men. We climbed into the cabin ; the pilot started up his engines and, after having paid—the final outrage—fifteen dollars for the use of the landing field, and a dollar a head for the privilege of photographing the ruins, shut the door behind us and prepared to take off.

A field not more than three hundred yards long, strewn with rocks and infested with cows ; at the end of it a river, with mountains rising steeply from the further bank. . . . Ignorance is bliss ; but even I could see that this was not the ideal taking-off place for an aeroplane. Our pilot, however, knew his job superbly well, and the plane was powerfully engined. We left the stony field in an astonishingly short space of time, wheeled round to avoid the rising ground beyond the river, and, corkscrewing up, were soon in the open sky a thousand feet above the mountains. Little more than an hour later we were in Guatemala.

' They told me,' said the pilot, as we walked towards the waiting car, ' that this was the second ship that ever landed at Copan.' He paused to light a cigarette. ' Well, so far as I'm concerned,' he went on, ' it's the last.'

Copan

COPAN is one vast monument to the Mayas' extra-ordinary preoccupation with time. Each stela marks the close of one of the shorter of the chronological periods, in terms of which they reckoned their position in endless duration—the close of a Katun of 7200 days or, more often, of a half- or quarter-Katun. The temples, the pyramids, the stairways were erected and then enlarged to celebrate the lapse of other significant spans of time. Of the hieroglyphs carved on mono-lith and staircase wall, those that can still be read are but the elaborate record of dates ; and of the rest many, if decipherable, would probably refer to astro-nomical occurrences, such as eclipses and the con-junctions of planets. Time was evidently at the very heart of the Maya religion. To grasp time intellectu-ally seems to have been the first duty of the initiated few. The uneducated masses could only passively accept the results of the priestly labours. It was their simple and exciting duty to rejoice in ceremonial unison when propitious seasons came round, to lament during the unlucky days, to express their terror at the critical close of some mysteriously significant period, to perform propitiatory rites against the coming of the predicted eclipse. Their relations with time were

COPAN   Mayan hieroglyphs.

fundamentally emotional ; those of the priests, intellectual.

At a certain level of consciousness, time inevitably becomes a preoccupation. Men are aware of the flux and of themselves within it. They may see themselves at rest in the current, at rest but doomed unceasingly to draw the potential into the actual, to go on drawing it until at last they draw the potentiality of death and, with its actualization, can draw no more. Or else, in their imagination, they are being swept along on the knife-edge of the present, between an unknowable future and a less and less known past, headlong towards a certain catastrophe. The first was the mediaeval conception of time, the second is Galileo's, Newton's and (except in the mathematicians' study) ours. Both conceptions are equally depressing. Indeed, any possible conception of time must be depressing. For any possible conception of time entails the recognition and intimate realization of the flux of perpetual perishing ; and to be made aware of the flux—the flux in relation to one's own being ; worse, as a treacherous and destructive element of that being—is intolerable. Regular, one, undifferentiated, time goes sliding on beneath and through all life, beneath and through its various pains and pleasures, its boredoms and enlightenments and seemingly timeless ecstasies—always the same mysterious dark lapse into nothing. The realization of it is, I repeat, intolerable. Not to be borne.

And, in fact, men refuse to bear it. Their method of escape is simple and consists in taking away from time the qualities they find unbearable and in giving it other qualities of a less distressing kind.

The endless continuity of time is appalling ; arbitrarily, therefore, men parcel up the flux into sections. It is always and everywhere horribly the same ; they impose imaginary differentiations and plant little landmarks of their own devising. The current flows implacably on, forthright and irreversible ; in their imagination, they distort it into a circular or at least a spiral movement with periodical returns to an identity. Time is unbearable. To make it bearable, men transform it into something that is not time, something that has the qualities of space. For we feel at home in space—at any rate, in the comfortable little space that belongs to this planet and in which we have our daily being. But in time, in the undifferentiated flux of perpetual perishing, we can never feel at home. Time, therefore, must be transformed, so far as our capacities for make-believe will allow of it, into space.

How shall time be spatialized ? Nature gives the first hint. The heavenly bodies march about the sky, and their marching is time made visible. The seasons recur, night and day recur, hunger and desire and sleep recur. It seems natural, therefore, to conceive of time as a series of circles—little round day, large round month, huge round year. On this natural system of spatialization men have grafted all kinds of arbitrary systems of their own. The rim of the year is studded with periodical festivals which serve to break up and differentiate the flux—to emphasize, by their regular recurrence, the essentially circular nature of the movement of spatialized time.

But this is not all. Between the round day and the round month they have slipped an intermediate round, the week, varying in size, at different times and in different places, from a circle three days in circumference to one of eight or ten. Sometimes circles are inserted between month and year. The Mayas, for example, had a sacred ' year ' of two hundred and sixty days, which went round and round in independence of the solar year. Similarly the Christians and the Moslems preserve within the solar framework a sacred lunar year, in terms of which Easter and Ramadan are dated.

The solar year is the largest of the natural circles. But man, being a long-lived animal, with an imagination capable of conceiving enormous durations, requires larger units. In a long period of time a year sinks into insignificance, becomes a mere dot, and finally vanishes out of consciousness, so that time is once more realized as a continuous and undifferentiated flux. Larger units have to be invented, in order that it may be possible to think of vast durations as composed of space-like fragments, of successive circles spiralling round a recognizable identity. By way of illustration I will cite only a few Central American examples. Thus, the Mayas and the Aztecs had a sacred fifty-two-year period, the conclusion of which was regarded as a potential world-ending and had to be celebrated with the most elaborate ritual. When reckoning dates, the Mayas ordinarily made use of a cycle of 144,000 days. It is probable that they also employed larger units—a Great-Cycle of 2,880,000 days, perhaps a Great-Great-Cycle of 57,600,000 days, and even, as Professor Morley thinks, a Great-Great-Great-Great-Cycle of more than 1800 million days. This last is an astonishingly large unit, and its use would indicate that the Mayas had an imaginative grasp of duration unparalleled until modern times. Indefinitely long durations can be reduced to something space-like only by the use of very large units. Many peoples—and among them very intelligent peoples like the Greeks—seem never to have been obsessed by the thought of indefinite duration, and therefore never to have felt the need for large time units, or indeed for any elaborately space-like calendarial construction whatsoever. Greek chronology before the time of Eratosthenes in the third century B.C. is absurdly inadequate, and the primitive ingenuousness of the Greek conception of time is well illustrated by the story that Herodotus tells of Hecataeus, the historian. Discoursing of his ancestry to the priests of Thebes in Egypt, Hecataeus ' traced his descent to a god in the person of his

COPAN

sixteenth ancestor ' ; whereupon the priests ' did to
him exactly as they afterwards did to me, though I
made no boast of my family. They took me into the
inner sanctuary . . . and showed me a multitude
of colossal statues in wood . . . the custom being for
every high priest during his life-time to set up his
statue in the temple. . . . Their colossal figures were
each, they said, a Pirômis, born of a Pirômis, and the
number of them was three hundred and forty-five.'
People who could imagine that the essential quality
of existence could be radically changed within sixteen
generations can never have been seriously bothered
with the horrible idea of indefinite duration. The
Greeks were, of course, acutely aware of short-term
duration and bewailed the transience of youth,
pleasure, life itself, with a rare eloquence. Like
every one else, they felt the need to turn this short-
term duration into the comforting likeness of space.
To this end they employed the usual recurrent units,
both natural and arbitrary, within the year, and
encrusted the circle of the year itself with the usual
festivals. Of larger units they also possessed a few—
but almost all of very modest proportions : four-year
Olympiads, nine-year renewals of Spartan kingship,
the eight-year period within which the lunar was
adjusted to the solar calendar—and so on. Meton's
' Great Year ' of nineteen solar years and Hipparchus's
304-year period were never generally accepted as
units of time. As for the enormous time units em-

ployed by the Mayas, no Greek even dreamt of using such things. For the good reason, I imagine, that none, as it happened, had ever urgently felt the need of spatializing indefinite duration. What causes a people, or at any rate the thinking part of a people, to become as acutely time-conscious as the priestly mathematicians of the Maya Old Empire? Not geography, not economics, not a high average of general intelligence. Rather a series of personal accidents. A man is born to whom, for whatever reason, time is an obsession. It also happens that he possesses the kind of abilities which enable him to solve his problem—the problem of the intellectual mastery and transformation of time—in comprehensible quantitative terms. Furthermore, as luck will have it, he is in a position to influence his fellows, to find colleagues, to make disciples. A tradition is formed, a technique and an intellectual discipline perfected ; it becomes ' natural ' for succeeding thinkers to turn their attention to time and the processes of spatializing it in terms of mathematics. But where the suitable philosophical tradition has never been established, and where no technique for thinking effectively about time exists, it is equally ' natural ' that even quite accomplished philosophers and mathematicians should ignore the subject.

Time can be spatialized in other terms than those of mathematics. There are artistic techniques for differentiating the undifferentiated, for parcelling up

the continuous flux, for bending an irreversible current
into the semblance of a circle. There is also a religious
technique for abolishing time in favour of an eternal
present. Nor must we forget those biological and
social devices for dulling men's awareness of the flux
—habit and its social equivalent, routine.

Habit and routine are artificial circular movements
superimposed on the natural circles of our physiological functioning. Thus, there are natural circles
of eating, sleeping, excretion and so forth ; and,
intersecting them, the circles of our 'second nature'
—circles of work, circles of habitual thought, circles
of conditioned feelings, circles of automatically repeated gestures.

Habit and routine are in part or wholly subliminal ;
the arts, on the contrary, are activities of full consciousness. Music, poetry, and the dance provide
methods for spatializing time on the highest plane
of awareness. The basic material is in each case
time, which is taken raw, so to speak, as mere duration,
and transformed, by means of rhythm and repetition,
into a pattern composed of qualitatively different
parts and involving circular returns to an identity.
For as long as it takes the music to be played, the poem
to be read, the dance to be trodden out, the trans-
mutation of time into space is as complete as it is
possible, in the nature of things, for such a trans-
mutation to be. And the effect is in some degree
an enduring one. A mind impregnated with music

will always tend to impose a pattern on the temporal
flux.

Religion makes use of every possible device for
rendering duration humanly acceptable. It takes
the calendar and, by means of its feasts and ceremonials, gives it an emotional as well as an intellectual
significance. It exploits the time-transmuting arts
of music, poetry and the dance. And finally it in-
culcates a philosophy, disparaging time in favour of
eternity and, along with the philosophy, a practical
technique for directly experiencing eternity. Of time
and eternity, Henry Vaughan wrote that :

> I saw Eternity the other night,
> Like a great Ring of pure and endless light,
>   All calm as it was bright ;
> And round beneath it, Time in hours, days, years
>   Driven by the spheres,
> Like a vast shadow moved, in which the world
>   And all her train were hurled.

For all its beauty, the imagery is inappropriate.
Eternity is an everlasting present. It is duration
spatialized, not as a ring, but as a glowing point.
Moreover, the time that Vaughan perceived ' moving
round like a vast shadow' was not real time (for real
time is an irreversible current for ever streaming in
one direction) ; it was the acceptably spatialized,
circular duration of the calendar-makers. Vaughan
makes the mistake of speaking too well of time and
not well enough of eternity.

COPAN

That time is somehow an illusion and eternity the only reality is a doctrine common to most of the great philosophical systems of Indian and European antiquity. But even if true—and personally I should like it to be true—the doctrine is not very efficacious against the obsessive consciousness of duration. For an illusion which is shared by all living beings, at any rate on our planet, is for all practical purposes indistinguishable from a reality. This being so, all the major religions have supplemented their theoretical disparagements of time with technical education in the art of escaping from time. Christianity, Islam, Buddhism, Hinduism, Taoism—all have their systems of mental and physical gymnastics for the production of ecstasy, which is the present experience of eternity. In the mind of the chronologist, the musician, the common creature of habit and routine, time has been transformed, by a variety of different processes, into the likeness of a circle. The mystic goes one further and contracts the circle to a point. The whole of existence is reduced for him to *here, now*. Time has been spatialized to its extreme limit. But, alas, when he emerges from his ecstasy, he finds the current still flowing—realizes that it has been flowing even while he imagined that he had altogether abolished it. The flux may be an illusion, but it is an illusion always and unescapably there.

Copan

WHEN the Spaniards arrived, Copan had been abandoned, at any rate by its civilized inhabitants, for nearly a thousand years. Dated stone monuments were set up at intervals during a single 144,000-day cycle; then they were set up no more. The site, presumably, had been deserted. Copan, therefore, had something less than four centuries of civilized existence. A short life—yet one of the longest of all the Old Empire cities. Only Uaxactun and Tikal were occupied for a greater span of time. Of the other cities, some, so it seems, were abandoned after an absurdly short occupation. Quirigua, for example, has dated monuments for little more than a century. By the beginning of the tenth Cycle all the Old Empire cities, from Palenque and Menchè in the north to Copan in the south, had been deserted, and new sites occupied in the peninsula of Yucatan.

What induced the Mayas to abandon the enormous capital represented by their sacred cities? Nobody knows. Almost certainly they were not invaded, and there is no sign of their monuments having suffered from destructive earthquakes. Some archaeologists believe that their agricultural methods exhausted the soil and that the population could no longer feed

222

itself; others, that there was an almost sudden change of climate, involving heavier rainfall, a more luxuriant and, for the Mayas, uncontrollable forest growth and an increase of yellow fever and perhaps malaria. Recently, a geological survey of the Peten district has shown that large areas that are now impassable swamps during the rainy season were once expanses of shallow water, and that these lakes were silted up in historical times. It is supposed that the Mayas built their cities on the shores of the lakes and put the higher land around them under intensive cultivation. The clearing of the forest led to erosion, and in course of time all the soil was washed off the fields into the lakes. The result was doubly disastrous : the fields became barren and the lakes were turned into enormous mud-holes. What had been a garden became a desert, and what had been a highway was converted into an impassable barrier. If this hypothesis is correct—and the geological evidence in support of it seems to be pretty convincing—then we can perfectly understand why the inhabitants of such towns as Tikal and Uaxactun migrated northward on to the dry limestone plateau of Yucatan. But conditions in the Peten district were totally unlike those at Copan. Copan lies in a narrow valley, drained and watered by a considerable river. There were no lakes here to be converted into swamps. And yet, punctually, at the end of the Ninth Cycle, and within twenty years of the abandonment of Uaxactun, the

Copanese (or at any rate all those among them who had the intelligence and the energy to raise and date a monument) deserted their valley and marched nobody knows whither, but presumably northwards, towards Yucatan.

An eminent authority on Central America, Dr. Gann, has recorded the curious fact that the modern Mayas will, from time to time, suddenly abandon their settlements and move for no apparent reason to another site. The 'no apparent reason' for such migrations is probably a religious reason. Some combination of evil auguries makes it in the highest degree unlucky to go on living in a certain place. Rather than run the risk of prophetically foretold calamities—and where people believe firmly enough in such prophecies, the calamities duly happen—the inhabitants decide to cut their losses and move to some spot with a more salubrious supernatural climate.

We smile ; but which of us, if he become convinced that his house was haunted, would not incur considerable financial loss in order to get rid of it ?

Increased rainfall, exhaustion of soil, erosion of farm land and silting up of lakes—to a varying extent the Old Empire Mayas may have been the victims of all these gradual disasters ; and the very accumulation of so many separate strokes of bad luck would naturally be interpreted as signs of divine displeasure. Other evil omens would not be lacking (they never are ; for the world is full of black cats, of hens with

deformed kidneys, of crows flying from left to right) ;
and a moment would come when the priestly diviners
would be convinced by irrefragable evidence that the
gods had abandoned their ancient home to the powers
of evil. Whereupon the only rational thing to do
would be to pack up and go somewhere else. Which
the Mayas accordingly did—by instalments : the inhabitants first of one city, then (since ill-luck is felt
to be something contagious) in rapid and accelerating
succession, of the rest. Within sixty or seventy years
the jungle was growing thick over every sacred place
from Palenque to Copan.

En Route

Six or seven sweltering hours in the train brought us
to Retalhuleu, which lies in the hot coastal plain some
twenty miles from the Pacific. A small Ford bus was
in waiting ; we stepped in, started. It was like a side-
show at Coney Island or Luna Park. The Wibble-
Wobble, the Flip-Flap, the *Montagnes Russes*. At forty
miles an hour, we bounded over the pocked and rutted
track towards the sea. With any other driver one
would have been scared out of one's wits. But our
young chauffeur was so evidently what the Germans
would call ' daemonic,' so unmistakably a genius, that

P   225

the experience was not in the least alarming, was even, apart from the physical discomfort, very agreeable. Even the old Ford had a bit of the daemonic about it. ' Many creatures are of a purely daemonic kind,' says Goethe, the recognized authority on this delicate subject ; ' in many, parts of it are effective.' In the case of our Ford, the daemonic parts were certainly the springs.

Our driver slowed down at last. We were in a street of decrepit shanties ; there were children in the dust and wandering pigs. Then, suddenly, vast and blank under a glaring white sky, the Pacific. One after another, with a succession of dreary bumps, the rollers broke on a flat beach. A long black jetty crawled like a centipede out into the water. The cranes gesticulated. Far out, a steamer lay at anchor.

At the door of the port authority's offices, we climbed out of our bus and said good-bye to its daemon driver. The air was like hot fly-paper. A sentry in khaki, with bare feet and a two-foot bayonet at the end of his rifle, ushered us into a room, where a young *mestizo*, extenuated with heat and malaria and the unspeakable boredom of life at Champerico, very slowly did what was necessary to our papers. A telegram of recommendation from a kind friend at the Foreign Office had preceded us, and was the reason why we were spared a large number of minor official annoyances. In what, at Champerico, must have been considered the twinkling of an eye—about fifty minutes—we were free to embark.

We walked out to the end of the jetty. There, twenty feet below us, a boat was wallowing among the rollers. One at a time, in an apparatus like a ducking stool, we were swung out into space and lowered towards the waves. When the boat heaved up within jumping distance, one jumped. A quarter of an hour later we were safely on board the steamer that was to take us up the Mexican coast.

Early in the century Salina Cruz was converted, at immense expense, into a first-class harbour for the largest ships. A railway was built across the isthmus of Tehuantepec to the Atlantic, and for a few years business flourished. It was cheaper to unload and reload than to send a ship round Cape Horn. Then in 1914 the Panama Canal was opened, and from one day to the next the prosperity of Salina Cruz, the very reason for its existence, was gone. To-day you could not land there even if you wanted to ; for the harbour has been neglected, and is so much silted up that ocean-going ships cannot enter at all. On the maps the name is still written large ; dotted lines, representing the course of imaginary steamers, connect Salina Cruz with San Francisco and Valparaiso, with Tahiti, New Zealand, Shanghai. Theoretically, it is still a great port. But our steamer made direct for Puerto Angel, two hundred miles further north.

Puerto Angel, as we discovered when we landed

there, is for all practical purposes non-existent. Three sheds on the shore of a rocky bay, a few huts, and that is all. There is no jetty. The whale boat which takes you from the ship comes to within about fifty yards of the land, and the passengers and luggage are transferred to a flat-bottomed canoe, like a coffin. You squat, cautiously balancing your weight ; the coffin shoots forward on a wave and runs aground ; then you wait till the retiring Pacific has left the sand relatively dry, and make a dash for it. When coffee from the plantations in the hinterland has to be embarked, the process is reversed. The stevedores carry the sacks waist-deep into the water and load there on to lighters. The lighters are rowed laboriously out to the waiting ships, and the coffee is hoisted on board.

Our travelling companion, Roy Fenton, was the owner of a plantation in the mountains, twenty miles inland. His agent at the port and the resident manager of the plantation, a charming young Norwegian, were there to receive us as we jumped ashore. Duly impressed, the customs officials showed themselves politely uninquisitive—anyhow, it was really too hot to bother very much about anything—and in a short time we were at liberty. The agent invited us to his house. He was a Spaniard and had once been handsome ; but life in this hot hole on the frontiers of nowhere had been too much for him. It was a bilious and emaciated eagle that hobbled up the rocky track before us. His house was a bungalow of three or four rooms, furnished with almost nothing but beds. On a veranda, hung with cages full of green parrakeets and cardinal birds, a table was spread for breakfast. The agent's wife, mother and sister, all three pale and haggard with tropical disease, did the honours. Preceded by an overwhelming smell, a dish of fried sardines made its untimely appearance. Luckily, we had eaten an early breakfast on the ship, so could refuse without giving offence. We got off with a cup of black coffee and some polite conversation.

It was after nine o'clock; the sun was growing hotter every minute, and as it climbed up the sky the parrakeets screamed with ever greater insistence. Grimly and without appetite, the cadaverous man, the three jaundiced and sickly women, ate their way through the fried sardines. 'But for the grace of God . . .' I thought, as I looked at them; and was filled with inexpressible thankfulness that I was in Puerto Angel only as a tourist, and in half an hour should be gone, probably for ever.

'When I went to Oaxaca last year,' said one of the women, her face lighting up at the memory of that almost fabulous event, 'when I went to Oaxaca . . .' From the cages a paroxysm of screaming interrupted her; and it seemed to me that if I stayed here much longer, I should start screaming too.

Puerto Angel is the terminus of a carriage road nearly twenty miles long. Some day it is to be continued across the mountains, till it meets the road coming from Ejutla and the provincial capital, Oaxaca. But all that is for the future, and 'to-morrow,' as the Mexicans judiciously remark, 'to-morrow is another day.' Between the end of one road and the beginning of the other there is still a gap that it takes two good days on a mule to overleap.

A car was waiting to transport us as far as a car could go. Hypocritically expressing our hopes for a speedy reunion, we said good-bye to our unfortunate hosts and started off. The road wound up through a dense forest, all silvery and rose-brown, at this dry season, like English oak woods in late autumn. In something under an hour we were at Pochutla, the administrative and commercial capital of the district, and as dismal a village as I have ever seen. It lay there, ankle-deep in dust under the blazing sun, irrevocably lost. No, not even lost; for there had obviously never been anything to lose. Just hope-lessly not there—the half-dead, pre-natal ghost of a place. In the huge glaring plaza a few Indian women in blue shawls were squatting in the dust. One had half a dozen scrofulous tomatoes arranged in a neat pattern before her; another had three bananas for sale; a third, in a cloud of flies, some gory bits of meat. In the centre of the square was the usual band-stand. Every Central American village has its band-stand—would consider itself disgraced if it hadn't. Does the band ever play? Except in the largest towns,

I never heard one. Those bandstands, it is obvious, have a mainly symbolic value. They somehow stand for public spirit—are in some sort the equivalents, psychologically, of the absent hospital, the non-existent drainage system. The bandstand once built, a citizen feels, I suppose, that enough has been done *pro bono publico*, and that he may return with a good conscience to his own affairs. The poor may die miserably, like dogs in a ditch, the municipal water supply may be crawling with typhoid, the streets may be full of holes, and unlighted at night. But, if there *were* a band, and if it *did* happen to know some music, it would be able to play to the assembled population from a handsome Moorish kiosk in the centre of the plaza.

The church had been built in 1912, and its curly painted façade was remarkably pretty. We entered. The last earthquake had left it half ruinous, and, looking up, we saw that the whole of the roof was encrusted with bats. . . .

It was time to go on. Half an hour through dry copse and maize fields, a wilderness of khaki-coloured dust, brought us to the end of the road. At the house of the local bandit, now transformed by success into a justice of the peace and a pillar of church and state, we got into gaiters and buckled on our enormous Mexican spurs. These last, so far as I was concerned, were wholly useless; for my legs hung down so far below the mule's belly, that it was only by withdrawing my feet from the stirrups and doubling up my knees

231

that I could bring the rowels into effective play. I had to be content with a stick ; and a stick is something to which no Mexican mule ever pays the slightest attention. I was always, in consequence, ignominiously at the tail of our caravan.

The bridle-path led up into the mountains, through a zone, first of all, of *tierra blanca*, slopes of white earth glaring incandescent in the ferocious sunshine, and thinly fledged with a leafless, skeleton scrub. As we mounted, a few greenish-yellow tufts of foliage began to appear : from autumn we had ridden up into the beginnings of spring. And then, almost suddenly, we were in perpetual summer. The mountain side was dark green with coffee bushes, and above the bushes rose tall trees, the larger of them, survivors from the original forest ; the smaller and younger ones, planted specially to give, not only shade, but also (since they are leguminous trees) a dose of gratuitous nitrogen to the plantations at their feet.

We were already on Don Roy's territory ; but the coffee *fincas* in these mountains are like small kingdoms, with outlying provinces, each with its separate name and capital.

Thus Pilas, the first of the provincial establishments to which we came, was more than an hour's ride from the metropolis of the estate, Progreso ; and above and beyond Progreso were other provinces— some cultivated, and centering round a dwelling and its drying-floors, some still under the aboriginal forest.

232

And twenty miles away was another Fenton kingdom, under another governor.

We reached Progreso at last and found a comfortable house on a terrace at the head of a valley that sloped away towards the coast. We were about three thousand feet above the sea, and at another season would have enjoyed an astonishing view. But the air was hazy with the dust of the long drought and, still more, with the smoke of the bush fires that the natives deliberately light at this time of the year. Mexican agriculture is a primitive and destructive process. The land is exhausted ; then, for a period of years, left fallow, while new fields are won from the jungle by the simple process of setting fire to the trees. The peasant may need only two or three acres for his *milpa* ; but often it happens that his fire will destroy square miles of forest. Sometimes, I suspect, he will indulge in this superfluous destruction for the mere fun of the thing. From the first introduction of gunpowder and saltpetre the Indians of Central America have always shown a consuming passion for fireworks. Even a funeral is a sufficient excuse for squibs and rockets. On nights of public jollification, you may see, even in quite modest little towns, the most astonishing displays of pyrotechny. Indians are desperately poor, but they are always ready to spend their last centavo on something that goes off with a bang and a bright light. I have seen a great many fireworks in the course of my life, but none that could compare for grandeur and beauty with a good forest fire. Moreover, for all but the owner of the forest, the show is entirely gratuitous. No need to spend that last centavo. The temptation to burn for burning's sake must sometimes be irresistible. The final results are, of course, disastrous. With the disappearance of the trees, erosion sets in. The soil disappears altogether from the slopes ; the level ground is scored with ever-deepening gullies. The land becomes either sterile or unworkable. The fathers enjoy a free display of fireworks, but the children pay, exorbitantly.

Progreso

TOWARDS evening, when the day had cooled off and the colours of things had begun to re-emerge after their long annihilation in the excess of tropical light, we would walk or ride among the *cafetales*. Our favourite path followed a level contour line round the flank of the extinct volcano that dominated the estate, winding out on to projecting bastions and round again into the valleys indented in the mountain side. One walked through an undergrowth of dark and glittering coffee bushes, and out of the undergrowth sprang great trees, each tree a column standing isolated from all the other columns and visible, in this

234

uncrowded forest, from its base among the coffee to its high green ceiling of spreading branches and leaves. It was the jungle, but domesticated ; a vast essay in tropical landscape gardening, richly, romantically beautiful. I thought all the time of that passage in the Fourth Book of *Paradise Lost*, where Milton describes the arrival of Satan in Paradise :

> So on he fares, and to the border comes
> Of Eden, where delicious Paradise,
> Now nearer, crowns with her enclosure green,
> As with a rural mound, the champaign head
> Of a steep wilderness, whose hairy sides
> With thicket overgrown, grotesque and wild,
> Access denied : and overhead up-grew,
> Insuperable height of loftiest shade,
> Cedar, and pine, and fir, and branching palm ;
> A sylvan scene ; and, as the ranks ascend,
> Shade above shade, a woody theatre
> Of stateliest view.

Admirable ; but still, I found, not quite satisfying. The description, it seemed to me, needed to be tighter, as it were, more closely involved upon itself. In Pope's ' Epistle to the Earl of Burlington ' there is a passage on landscape gardening that begins :

> Consult the genius of the place in all ;
> That tells the waters or to rise or fall ;
> Or helps the ambitious hill the heavens to scale,
> Or scoops in circling theatres the vales ;
> Calls in the country, catches opening glades,
> Joins willing woods, and varies shades from shades ;
> Now breaks, or now directs, the intending lines ;
> Paints as you plant, and, as you work, designs.

Those two final couplets came nearer to what I was looking for ; but were too short, too perky to render a reality on this vast scale and of such sublimely magnificent quality. But that Pope was on the right track I feel no doubt. An adequate description of this paradisial landscape would have to be woven intricately together, phrase into phrase, like the foliage of the jungle it sought to render ; would have to be heavy with repetitions and at the same time quickened with antitheses, so as to express simultaneously the enormous sameness of the forest and its startling contrasts ; all nature's endless variations on a few simple themes. Pope is in too much of a hurry, and his couplets make him jaunty. If he could have taken more time to develop his method ; if he could have allowed himself as much metrical space as Milton took for his descriptions—then, I believe, he could have given us the perfect, the completely adequate rendering of that tame jungle, which was the earthly paradise and is now almost any coffee *finca* on the Pacific slope of Mexico or Guatemala.

Progreso

THAT this Garden of Eden is less paradisial than it appears goes, I am afraid, without saying. The life of the planters is poisoned by the fear of blights and bad weather ; by the dismal prospect of yet lower coffee prices ; by labour problems, which they themselves have complicated by their own traditionally vicious system of paying out advances on future wages ; by the legislation which revolutionary governments have designed to inflict the greatest possible discomfort on capitalists ; and by the cynically corrupt local administrators of this legislation. As for the life of the labourers—that is poisoned by low wages (about fifteen gold cents a day, since the depression) ; by endemic venereal disease ; and by the interminable village feuds and family vendettas which make it necessary for every man to go about armed to the teeth, ready at any moment to shoot or be shot. For the tourist, it looks like Eden ; but for the inhabitants, it feels only too painfully like Mexico.

Progreso

THE permanent staff of a coffee estate amounts to only a score or two of men ; but when the picking season comes round, hordes of Indians descend from the mountain villages to work in the *cafetales*. A big *finca* will employ as many as six or seven hundred men to bring in the crop.

Coffee of inferior quality grows in the plains, and

the berries are allowed to ripen till they fall. Good coffee grows in the mountains, and the berries must all be picked by hand. It is the same with the leaves of the tea shrub. There is no conceivable labour-saving device to take the place of human pickers.

If coffee and tea grew in Western Europe and had to be picked by people drawing European wages, the cost to the consumer of these commodities would be, I suppose, about eight or ten times what it is at present. Which means that the consumer simply would not consume. 'The cups that cheer but not inebriate' will continue to cheer only so long as tropical countries continue to be backward in relation to temperate countries. Our afternoon tea and our after-dinner coffee depend on the existence of a huge reserve of sweatable coloured labour. An unpleasant thought. And if the labour is no longer sweated, then tea and coffee at once become luxuries beyond the reach of all but millionaires. In an economically equitable world we shall have to depend for our stimulants on the chemist rather than the farmer.

On the Road

IT was still pitch dark when we set out. Dark with a double night; for our road lay under trees, and the

black vault of foliage shut out the stars. There was
nothing to be seen ; but the mules picked their way
securely up and down the headlong windings of the
track ; one just sat still and left everything to their
better judgment.

The air was deliciously fresh against the face and
sometimes, in the darkness, one would ride through
the perfumed aura of an invisible lemon tree, exhaling,
for another sense, the symbolic counterpart of the
coolness that refreshed the skin—exhaling, indeed,
something much more than the mere equivalent of
an agreeable touch. For a perfume in the night is
charged with inexpressible significances.

> Elle se répand dans ma vie,
> Comme un air imprégné de sel,
> Et dans mon âme inassouvie
> Verse le goût de l'éternel.
>
> Sachet toujours frais qui parfume
> L'atmosphère d'un cher réduit,
> Encensoir oublié qui fume
> En secret à travers la nuit,
>
> Comment, amour incorruptible,
> T'exprimer avec vérité ?
> Grain de musc, qui gis, invisible,
> Au fond de mon éternité ?

The analogy is to some extent reversible. An incorruptible love may be likened to a forgotten
censer smoking in secret through the night ; and,
conversely, a perfume in the dark may seem, in

some mysterious way, a symbol of incorruptible love, an affirmation of eternal values, a recollection of immortality.

Sunrise, when it came, was a vulgar affair, streaky, like one of those loud rainbow silks that are made in Italy for the tourists. In a quarter of an hour, the colours had faded ; the day brightened to a flawless blue.

We had climbed some two thousand feet from Progreso ; almost suddenly there was a new flora. Enormous datura plants embowered the path. The great white blossoms hung in their thousands all around and above us. Most flowers strain up towards the light ; but these bells of the *galante de noche* hung patient, utterly resigned to the force of gravity. A lovely flower, but sad and seemingly hopeless.

Our road dropped into the valley of the Coppalita. Down, down, down, till we were not much more than fifteen hundred feet above the sea. We forded the river and it was now, five hours after starting, that the real business of the day began. The main range of the sierra was now before us ; ridge above ridge of vast, bald, shadeless hills. For five more hours we climbed uninterruptedly up one of the steepest paths I have ever seen. It was one of those vast, vague, chaotic landscapes that look as though they might go on for ever—a great desert of nonentity, endlessly not there, and empty, quite lifeless. There were no

240

ON THE ROAD   Between Progreso and Miahuatlan.

birds, no animals, no sign of a human habitation ; and the only travellers we met were two Indians with a train of loaded donkeys carrying the mail from Oaxaca to the coast. We drew aside respectfully to allow the representatives of the Federal Administration to pass. Their long ears flapping at every stride, their slender feet twinkling in small precise movements among the stones, the little asses stepped delicately by, one by one, each under an enormous burden of red, white and green mail bags. ' *Burr-rro !* ' the drivers shouted with that prodigious rolling of the *r* that is only to be heard in Mexico. And ' *Burr-rro !* ' yelled our *mozo*. It is automatic ; one always shouts ' *Burro !* ' when one meets donkeys on a narrow road. Not because it does any good, but simply for fun. And, indeed, few simple pleasures are more satisfying than watching donkeys pass and shouting ' *Burr-rro !* ' at the top of one's voice. I never missed an opportunity of doing so : nor of shouting ' *Perr-rro !* ' at any dog that strayed in my neighbourhood. With ten or fifteen years of practice, one might learn to roll one's *r*'s as grandly as the Mexicans themselves.

Scorched by the sun, immoderately thirsty and very sore indeed, we reached our destination in the middle of the afternoon. San Pedro is a small Indian village at the very top of the sierra, a good ten thousand feet or more above the sea. The sun was still hot when we arrived ; but its heat was a kind of veneer over an essential core of mountain cold. The village was built on a knife-edge between two gulfs. The tiny plaza was like the deck of a ship, a flat space, thirty or forty yards from gunwale to gunwale, and on each side a drop; in the distance the mountains rolled away, crest after crest, like waves.

Towards sunset, the boys of the village came out to play a kind of football in the plaza—deck football; if you kicked too hard the ball flew over the edge and you had to scramble down a couple of hundred feet to find it. In the last, almost level light, the scene was curiously moving—had the intensity, somehow, the more-than-reality of a work of art. It was partly, I suppose, because there was no background. We were on a little platform at the top of everything, with only the sky all around us. Every figure stood out clear and rather flat in strangely significant isolation, against that pale bright vacancy. A donkey, tethered to a post and compact, self-contained, detached, like Sancho Panza's ass in one of the Daumier paintings of *Don Quixote*; men passing, their heads stuck through the slits of their exiguous blankets, hunched and hugging themselves against the increasing cold; and in the centre of the narrow space the boys playing, brilliant in their white trousers and gaily coloured shirts, shining as though transfigured by the supernatural light of evening.

All at once it was piercingly cold. We went back to our quarters—a large storeroom belonging to the village shopkeeper, furnished, for the benefit of such

travellers of quality as pass this way, with three wooden
bedsteads, wholly innocent of springs, but clean and, as
the event surprisingly proved, also innocent of vermin.
Wrapped in all the wool we could lay our hands on,
we waited for our supper. It came at last, comfortingly
hot and remarkably good. The proprietor lingered for
a talk. Had we come far? Very far, from Europe.
Yes, he knew about Europe—but not, as it turned out,
very much about it : for he had a notion it was all
one country, like Mexico. What chiefly interested
him was the cost of the journey. I gave him the
figures—somewhat diminished, I confess ; partly out
of prudence ; for, though the country Indians are
proverbially honest, it is never wise to establish a
reputation for what must seem to such people inordinate and fantastic wealth ; and partly from a
certain sense of shame. Our host was doubtless one
of the richest men in the village ; but his whole annual
income would probably not have bought a single
first-class ticket across the Atlantic. He listened carefully : then, after a pause, ' I can't understand,' he
said at last, ' why you should want to *gastar su capital*
on coming to San Pedro.'

He had, I must admit, some excuse for his incomprehension. The cold was arctic, we were about to
spend a very uncomfortable night, should have to
rise, shuddering, next morning at daybreak. To
squander one's capital for this—yes, it did seem
rather odd. But, then, what was the alternative?

The alternative was to put it into Kreuger and Toll, or Insull. Squandering for squandering, I prefer my method.

On the Road

THE carriage road from Oaxaca ended in another mountain village four or five hours' ride from San Pedro. A car from Miahuatlan had been ordered by telegram to meet us at the terminus. It was not there when we arrived, and as the sun was already hot, we were glad to accept the invitation of an Indian woman to wait in her house.

It was a one-roomed hut walled with reeds and roofed with poles and thatch. There were no windows; the light entered, and the smoke of the fire went out, through the door and the countless chinks and crannies of the walls. The floor was of trodden earth, dry at the moment, but ready to become mud at the first shower. A wooden bench was the most considerable piece of furniture. There was a hearth, with two or three cooking pots ; one of those palaeolithic pestles and mortars, with which the Indian women grind their maize ; two blankets on a peg—and that, in the way of necessities, was absolutely all. Luxuries were represented by a rifle with a bandolier full of cartridges, an enormous felt hat, heavily embroidered with gold and silver thread, and worth at least ten pounds ; and finally (if anything so useful could properly be accounted a luxury) a sewing-machine.

Comfort is a modern invention, and the pursuit of it a very recent activity. Our ancestors lived in an austere squalor tempered (in the case of the rich) by magnificence. A Neapolitan nobleman of the eighteenth century might feed on chick-peas and, in winter, shiver in an unheated house ; but the house was a *palazzo*, and he went out in a coach, wore a jewelled sword and was followed by twelve lackeys. The Indian's scale of values is the same as the Neapolitan noble's. He is without furniture, his house lets in the wind and rain, he has no crockery, no washing place, no water supply, no chimney, no change of clothes. Innumerable wants to be supplied. But he does not feel them as wants and makes no attempt to supply them. What he laboriously saves up for, centavo by centavo, is, first of all, a gun, so that he can, if the need arises, murder his neighbour ; second, a princely hat in which to swagger abroad and excite the general envy ; and finally (more, no doubt, to show off than from any humane desire to spare his wife unnecessary labour) a sewing-machine. The pleasures we prize most highly are physical pleasures ; Mexican Indians prefer psychological pleasure. They get more fun out of satisfied vanity than out of pneumatically cradled flesh. In the hierarchy of concupiscences, theirs, I suppose, rank higher than ours.

Fame, of a rather ridiculous kind, no doubt, but still unquestionably fame, is their goal—' that last infirmity of noble mind.' Whereas we prefer the animal pleasures of the senses.

On the Road

HALF-WAY down to Miahuatlan we passed a dead man lying at the side of the road. Up to the present we had seen only the monuments of murder. Little crosses, festooned with paper roses, or with a bunch of withered flowers at the foot—one came upon them at every second turn of the road. A fight or an ambush, a corpse and, finally, a cross. And yet the country is not unsafe for travellers. The butchery is domestic, between friends : an affair of vendettas, of local patriotisms, of jealousies and rivalries. All that strangers need fear is meeting with a drunkard. A man who has swallowed a few glasses of the terrible raw spirit, distilled from the juice of the agave, is temporarily insane ; and since he will certainly be carrying a machete and almost certainly a revolver or a rifle, his lunacy is apt to be dangerous. It is as well therefore to be prepared to meet such emergencies. Our invaluable friend, Don Roy, had a pistol in his pocket. But happily all the few Indians we met were as sober as judges—a great deal soberer, I am thankful to say, than some judges I have known. So far as danger was concerned, we might have been riding from Dorking to Guildford. From time to time, when village feuds have resulted in some particularly savage outburst of fighting, the central authorities send a detachment of troops with orders to confiscate all the firearms in the district. The orders are obeyed ; but within a month or two every one has another revolver, a fresh supply of cartridges. A man, in this part of the world, hardly considers himself a man unless he is armed ; to buy a gun he is prepared to make almost any financial sacrifice. And, unfortunately, there are always guns to buy. Mexico must have an enormous stock of old, but carefully preserved firearms, in perpetual clandestine circulation. It will be a long time before her citizens are disarmed.

Miahuatlan

A MORE than ordinarily destructive earthquake shook the whole state of Oaxaca some two or three years ago. Oaxaca itself has been patched up, more or less. But outside the capital there is no money : only the most urgently necessary repairs have been undertaken. Miahuatlan is a still inhabited and therefore squalider Pompeii.

247

The scene, as it reveals itself to the wandering spectator, is typical—a standard Southern Mexican back-cloth. At the centre of things lies the great desert of a glaring plaza, with tortoise-eyed Indian women sitting in the dust, each with her three *pimientos*, her nine bananas, her half-dozen of tomatoes, arranged in geometrical patterns on the ground before her. Above the market towers the vast church, hopelessly dilapidated and shored up against irremediable collapse by a precarious structure of poles and beams. Along streets of half-ruined houses the donkeys come and go, flapping their ears ; bare feet move noiselessly through the dust, and under enormous hats, under close-drawn shawls one catches the reptilian glitter of Indian eyes.

The spectacle, I confess, always made my blood run pretty cold. Not so cold as the spectacle of an industrial town in Lancashire, say, or the Ruhr (*that* has power to chill the heart of man to its absolute zero) ; but cold, heaven knows, enough. The industrial town is intensely and positively, whereas these Mexican places are only negatively, appalling. They are appalling not so much because of what is there as because of what isn't there. A Black Country town is a fearful sin of commission ; Miahuatlan and its kind are sins of omission. Omission of the mental and the spiritual, of all that is not day-to-day animal living. ' Lilies that fester smell far worse than weeds ' ; the Black Country is more horrible than Miahuatlan

because it embodies the corruption of a higher good
than has ever been aimed at, at any rate since the fall
of the indigenous empires, by the Indians. The lily,
whose festering fills the industrial areas of every
continent with so fearful a stench, is the disinterested
love of truth. For the disinterested love of truth leads
to pure science ; and the application of pure science
to commercial ends is industry ; and when (as generally happens) the ends are silly or downright harmful
and the modes of application iniquitous, then, night-
marishly proliferating, appear the Pittsburgs and
Birminghams, the Osakas and Calcuttas of this un-
happy world.

Here, at Miahuatlan, there is no festering, because
there was never any lily. There was and there still
is just the deep-rooted weed of primitive human life.
If you happen to be a primitive human being, it must
be quite a pleasant place to live in. But if you happen
to have come within sniffing distance of the transcendental lilies, how unspeakably depressing ! Intrinsically worse than Miahuatlan, the Black Country
will yet seem to you preferable. For the festering
implies the existence, somewhere, of a lily, and the
lily will seem to you so immensely precious that you
will be ready, for its sake, to put up even with the
intolerable stink of its corruption. Lawrence wrote
eloquently of Oaxaca and Lake Chapala, with passion,
sometimes over-emphatically, of the merits of that
rank weed-life of the natural man. But it is signi-

249

ficant that he spent only a few months in Mexico and that, wherever he lived among primitives, he found it necessary, in spite of the principles he had made his own, to refresh himself by occasional contacts, through books, through civilized men and women, with the lilies of the mind and spirit. The attempt to return to primitiveness is both impractical and, I believe, wrong. For a lily is a lily and we know, by direct intuition and by discursive reasoning, that it is better than a weed. That it should fester is deplorable ; but the moral to be drawn from the stench is not that lilies are bad, but that our methods of preserving them should be improved. Lawrence so much hated the misapplications of science, that he thought that science itself should be abolished. But the only thing that can prevent science from being misapplied is more science of a higher quality. If Miahuatlan were the only possible alternative to Middlesborough, then really one might as well commit suicide at once. But luckily it is not the only alternative.

Miahuatlan

VICTORIAN ENGLAND, outside the villages, the country houses and the genteeler quarters of the large towns, was a land of indescribable ugliness and misery. To escape from it, Karl Marx went out imaginatively into the revolutionary future, Ruskin and William Morris into the pre-industrial past.

Twentieth-century industrial America is not quite so obviously frightful as the nineteenth-century industrial England ; moreover, its frightfulness was for some time concealed by a gaudy façade of success, behind which it was considered unpatriotic to peep. Some peeping, of course, there was ; but the records of it, such as the Lynds' classical *Middletown*, made little popular appeal. Then, in 1929, with a loud and terrifying crash, the façade fell down. The ugliness stood revealed, and an ever-increasing sum of misery cried aloud to heaven. History has repeated itself. In their desire to escape from the horrors of industrial reality—to escape from, and at the same time to find a remedy for, them—some American thinkers have run forward into the revolutionary future ; others, back into the pre-industrial past. But in Mexico the pre-industrial past still exists, is contemporary with the industrial depression across the border. The Ruskins and Morrises of modern New York do not have to use their imaginations to reconstruct the characteristics of a vanished way of life. They need only walk to the nearest Pan-American Airways office and buy a ticket. In a few hours they will find themselves in the midst of a fifteenth-century peasant society. Since the depression, books on Mexico have been almost as numerous, I should guess, as books on

Russia. The Marxes flee Northwards, the Morrises towards the South.

Many of these books are marred by an injudicious extravagance of admiration for everything Mexican, or rather, for everything Indian in Mexico. This is only to be expected. The Mexico of the Indians is more, for these writers, than a mere geographical and sociological reality ; it is a place where wishes are fulfilled, and the intolerable evils of the civilized world corrected. Morris gave his contemporaries *News from Nowhere* ; his successors give us news from Mexico. For critics of modern American society the Mexican Indians fulfil the functions reserved in the writings of Voltaire and his contemporaries to the Chinese and the Persians : they are alien cudgels for the beating of domestic malefactors. But whereas Voltaire never dreamed of actually visiting Peking, but was content to use his Chinamen as the disembodied symbols of a wisdom conspicuously absent from his own France, the Americans really take the train or the aeroplane and, having made the southern trip, are rash enough to affirm that their Noble Savages are genuine Mexican Indians.

The most judicious of the recent American books on Mexico is that of the well-known economist, Mr. Stuart Chase. I had read it on its first appearance in 1932, and now, *en route*, with the realities of Central America before my eyes, read it again more critically and understandingly. It is worth while, I think, to discuss this book in some detail ; for it attacks a problem which is surely of the first importance : the problem of reconciling the primitive with the civilized. Primitive societies have their characteristic virtues and their characteristic defects. The virtues of civilized societies are higher than those of primitive societies ; but their defects are more enormous. (The corruption of the best is always the worst.) The question which confronts us is this : can we evolve a new society which shall combine the virtues of primitives with those of the civilized, but exhibit the vices of neither ? Mr. Chase poses this general question in a particular form : How much of what is good in North American civilization can Mexico import and still remain Mexico ? His conclusion is that Mexico can, without danger, take over the following : modern hygiene *en bloc* ; two or three million horse-power of electric energy for the grinding of corn, the refrigeration of food, and the general development of small-scale village industries ; and finally, some few thousand more miles of metalled roads with a sufficient number of new Fords to transport the burdens at present carried by patient armies of mules and asses, of men and women, of little boys and girls.

The intrinsic desirability of such importations is undeniable. But the question at once arises : Could the Mexicans introduce them and still retain the characteristics which Mr. Chase finds so engaging ? The answer is, pretty obviously, ' No.' Let us consider the effects, measured in purely human terms, of these importations. We will begin with the rules of hygiene. Incidentally, it seems very improbable that the Indians could be persuaded to accept these rules unless they had received a fairly elaborate preliminary education —an education which would already have made them rather, perhaps very, different from the Indians Mr. Chase likes so much to-day. But let that pass. We will assume that the Indians have all gone hygienic. What are the results? An immediate and heavy decline in the infant mortality rate and an increase in the average expectation of life; consequently, within a few years, a rapid growth of population. But what happens when a population increases? Villages turn into towns and towns into cities. An urban and later, when cities have grown too large to be experienced as social unities, a suburban mentality is automatically brought into existence. The characteristic peasant virtues and defects cease to exist, and are replaced by the virtues and defects of townsmen. At the same time a heavy strain is thrown on the existing supply of food, clothing, shelter, and so forth. In order to meet the increased demand it becomes necessary to use scientific methods of agriculture and to mechanize the processes of manufacture. The electrically operated village industries may provide a sufficiency of cheap goods for this mounting population. Or they may not. It remains to be seen. In certain departments it may be that mass production will prove to be necessary.

But even the rationalization of agriculture and the mechanization of village industries (without which, it is obvious, the new population must miserably starve) are profoundly disturbing processes, fatal to the old traditional ways of thinking and feeling. Men do not retain peasant psychologies when they have ceased to be peasants.

It may be argued that undue rise in the population can be prevented by judicious birth control. But again, you cannot teach primitive Indians to practise the neo-Malthusian techniques and expect them to remain primitive Indians.

'Character,' says Mr. J. H. Denison in that valuable, but as yet little known book, *Emotion as the Basis of Civilization*, 'character is formed by enforcing a system of taboos which causes men to feel a sense of horror for acts harmful to the community '—and, we may add, for acts only imagined to be harmful to the community. To change a society's taboo-system, even in part, is to change the character of its members, and along with their character the kind of emotions they feel and the kind of thoughts they think. It is unlikely, for example, that Indians brought up on Stopes would continue to celebrate *fiestas* in honour of the ancient fertility gods. But an Indian who has given up his *fiestas* would not be the simple-mindedly happy peasant beloved of Mr. Chase.

And finally, there are the roads, the fleets of new Ford cars. What a huge intolerable load the Fords will lift from aching human backs ! But the minds to which these backs belong—they will be changed. For, over and above their material freight, the Fords will carry an invisible cargo of new ideas, of alien, urban ways of thought and feeling. There are schools, now, in even the smallest villages. But their influence is still inconsiderable. For what, after all, is the good of knowing how to read in a place where no reading matter ever makes its appearance ? Sometimes, it is true, a few scraps of print circulate in the far-off villages. But the stuff was written in the towns, by men with another philosophy of life. The village Indian can read ; but his mind is so conditioned that he cannot understand what he reads. Along the metalled roads the Fords will bring, not only reading matter, but also notions that will make the printed words fully comprehensible. Education can be as platonic as love—ardent but discarnate and sterile. School in Mexico is Dante, and the Indian mind has remained up till now barrenly Beatrice. Roads and motor cars will give to Mexican education a new potency. The untouched, untouchable Beatrice will conceive, bring forth. Backed up by the Fords, the village schools will at last begin to do what they were meant to do—transform the national character. And then good-bye—yet once more—to Mr. Chase's Indians. The more sensitive among us abhor the noisy restless vulgarity of our urban civilization ; we envy the primitive his serene, self-sufficing contentment. But

the primitive is fascinated by the very things we dislike. For example, Indians were taken from the wilds
to be given a course of instruction at a training centre
in Mexico City. The idea was that, when they had
passed their examination, they should return as school-
masters to their villages. But the great majority
refused to return ; they preferred to become wage-
slaves in the festering slums of the metropolis. It has
been decided now to train village teachers in the
provincial towns. Less vulgarly ' modern ' than the
capital, they will, it is hoped, exercise a less powerful
attraction. The metalled roads and the Fords will
have the effect of making large-scale urban vulgarity
accessible to almost all. And wherever urban vulgarity is made accessible to primitives, they rush
headlong to embrace it. This dismal truth is confirmed by daily examples from every corner of the
world.

From all this one conclusion evidently emerges :
Mr. Chase's programme is unworkable. You cannot
import North American virtues and North American
amenities into Mexico without causing the Mexicans
to lose their Mexican virtues and to abandon what is
best in their own Mexican way of life.

Must we then despair of this most desirable con-
summation—the wedding of primitive with civilized
virtues ? I think not. Partially to industrialize and
civilize primitives may be impossible. But to introduce
a salutary element of primitivism into our civilized

and industrialized way of life—this, I believe, can be done. The undeveloped consciousness of the primitive leaves him at the mercy of influences coming from civilization. Lacking a critical faculty, he is unable to take only the good and reject the rest. With him it is all or nothing ; he must accept everything that comes his way. But, for us, the case is different. A critical faculty has been developed, at any rate in the more intelligent members of every civilized community. Where primitives accept the world, society, tradition, unquestioningly, as fishes accept the water in which they swim, the civilized are able to stand back from their mental and material surroundings, to pass judgment upon them. It is possible for them to realize what is wrong with their own way of thinking and feeling and to appreciate all that is desirable in the primitive form of life.

It is easy to draw up a list of these desirable elements in the patterns of primitive existence ; difficult to say how many of these elements could possibly be incorporated into the pattern of civilization. Many primitive virtues are obviously incompatible with urbanism and industrialism (both to a great extent unavoidable, where population is dense), with individual self-consciousness, with education in scientific method, and with a high level of material prosperity. For example, the extreme stability of primitive communities is unattainable in our large heterogeneous societies, composed of individuals who have ceased to believe in the supernatural sanctions of traditional taboos. Nor can we expect people at a certain level of education to be content with the extreme simplicities of primitive life ; nor that, possessed of enough self-consciousness to make originality seem desirable and of enough material resources to make the expression of personality an easy matter, they should always observe the negative good taste of peasants who unquestioningly accept an old tradition and who lack the means to make more than a very small splash. Vulgarity is largely a matter of opportunity ; when people are given a chance to be vulgar, they generally are vulgar. Civilized people have many opportunities, and take them—alas, on what an enormous scale !

So much for what civilized men cannot take from their primitive neighbours. What *can* they take ? They can take, or at least they can try to take, the primitive's human wholeness. A primitive is forced to be whole—a complete man, trained in all the skills of the community, able to fend for himself in all circumstances ; if he is not whole, he perishes. A civilized man, on the contrary, is under no external necessity to be whole. He can go comfortably and, as we judge success, successfully through life, incapable of doing anything except, shall we say, writing detective novels ; within the strong economic and legal framework of civilization he is perfectly safe. A highly organized society protects him from the worst effects of his own incompetence ; allows him to be ignorant of all the useful arts and yet to live. So far as immediate physical disaster is concerned, he can be unwhole with impunity. But there are also psychological disasters—the gradual disasters of atrophy and decay. Our admirably efficient organization has no power to save a man from these. Indeed its very perfection is the cause of these individual disasters. All civilization, and especially industrial civilization, tends to turn human beings into the mere embodiments of particular social functions. The community gains in efficiency ; but the individual is maimed.

Man's biological success was due to the fact that he never specialized. Unfitted by his physique to do any one thing to perfection, he was forced to develop the means for doing everything reasonably well. Civilization reverses the evolutionary process. Generalized by nature, we impose upon ourselves, artificially, the narrowest specializations. Primitives are men who have never succumbed to the suicidal ambition to resemble ants. Generalization—this is the great, the vitally important lesson they have to teach the specialists of the civilized world. The problem is to evolve a society that shall retain all or most of the material and intellectual advantages resulting from specialization, while allowing its members to lead to the full the life of generalized human beings. To solve this problem will be hard, but not, I am convinced, impossible.

EJUTLA

Ejutla

OUR road wound across vast hills, bare and utterly dry—the grandiose emblems of a perfect hopelessness. A magnificent landscape ; but one looks at it with a sinking of the heart ; there is something profoundly horrifying in this immense, indefinite not-thereness of the Mexican scene.

The bus, of course, was crowded to overflowing. All means of transport always are crowded in this country. Crowded with shawled peasant women, withdrawn and silent ; with Indian men in soiled white cotton ; with city Mexicans, disguised, in their shoddy reach-me-downs and straw hats as New York bank clerks. The usual crowd, with the usual accompaniment of bundles and baskets and vegetables and live stock. Up and then down into *barrancas*, across unbridged streams, and up again, and down, the bus crashed on over the unmetalled road, through the huge, glaring nonentity of the landscape. There seemed no reason why it should ever stop. But at last it did stop. We were in Ejutla ; and it was as though we had never left Miahuatlan. For here was the same plaza, with the same tortoise-eyed women, selling the same six miserable tomatoes, in the shade of the same huge tumble-down church ; here were the same streets of half-ruined houses, the same donkeys, the same thick dust, the same . . . But luckily there were a few small differences. A bullock cart was standing in the plaza, fantastically loaded with the gilt and painted wooden horses of a merry-go-round. And in the ruinous church, fixed high up on one of the piers supporting the dome, was a really lovely statue of a flying angel—an Indian primitive, touched incongruously with the spirit of the baroque ; strange, but a genuinely beautiful work of art. And finally, in the hotel, what a pianola ! You touched a button, and suddenly the noise of the out-of-tune mechanical piano turned into the even more unpleasant noise of about twenty out-of-tune mechanical banjos. It was a pianola, the proprietress proudly explained, with a mandoline attachment.

Oaxaca

In spite of three major earthquakes, in spite of seven sieges, including one by a French army under Bazaine, in spite, above all, of four centuries of Mexican existence, Oaxaca remains a stately city, full of impressive buildings. Santo Domingo has been repeatedly pillaged, but is still, none the less, one of the most extravagantly gorgeous churches in the world. The cathedral has been shaken and cracked, yet continues to stand, enormous, at the centre of the town. The monks have fled, the clergy is without power or money ; but strolling through the streets, you find yourself at the portals of what were once magnificent monasteries, now transformed into warehouses and workshops and Indian dwellings ; you come upon handsome churches, in which the baroque saints still gesticulate above the altars and the gilded plaster still writhes in a tripe-like luxuriance over vault and ceiling. Yes, Oaxaca is a fine place. Fine and, as gaiety is reckoned in the provinces of Mexico, positively gay. There are two or three cafés in the plaza ; and at night a band discourses from the kiosk at the centre. The Indians squat on the pavements to listen, their dark faces melting into the night—invisible. High-heeled, in every tender shade of artificial silk, the flappers stroll giggling under the electric light. There is a rolling of eyes, a rolling of posteriors. The young men stroll in the opposite direction. In the roadway, the most correct of the *correctos* circulate very slowly in their automobiles—round and round and round. Our Oaxacan friend, Don Manuel, invited us one evening to join this endless procession. After revolving for about two hours in his car we grew, I must confess, a trifle bored. Some simple pleasures are really a bit too simple.

Oaxaca

POTTERY, *sarape* weaving, leather-work, the ornamental plaiting of string, and the making of *machetes* and swords—these are the principal local handicrafts. The last seems to be mainly a white man's and mestizo's industry. The other crafts are purely Indian and are practised in the outlying villages as well as in the town itself. The leather-work is poor ; but the pots are pleasant and the gaily coloured string bags and haversacks very pretty, in a rather childish way. Of the *sarapes*, some are quietly unpretentious—dark blankets with a minimum of pattern in grey or white on a black ground. But there are also more ambitious designs. One finds, for example, a lamb or a Mexican eagle, carried out in white, black and grey, with touches of red and green. Sometimes letters will be woven into the picture—a *Viva Mexico*, for example. A few of these blankets are excellent ; the rest are dull and sometimes downright ugly. This is only to be expected ; for the more ambitious the design, the greater scope for individual talent and the more narrowly restricted the influence of tradition. But individual talent is rare ; correspondingly rare, it follows, must be the designs whose excellence depends upon it.

264

OAXACA

Much nonsense has recently been talked about Indian handicrafts. Fleeing from the slump and with the hideous vision of Zenith and Middletown still painfully fresh in their memories, the new William Morrises from the United States have come to Mexico and, confronted by its peasant arts, have broken out into an intemperate and hysterical enthusiasm. Middletown and Zenith are nightmarish ; but this is no reason for asserting that the pretty little peasantries of the Mexican Indians are intrinsically significant works of art. Peasant art is hardly ever intrinsically significant as art ; its value is social and psychological, not aesthetic. Mr. Chase says of a well-known arts-and-crafts shop in Mexico City that it is ' as exciting to him as any art museum.' If that is so, then either Mr. Chase is wholly without a feeling for aesthetic values, or else he is mistaking for aesthetic excitement the pleasure which he derives, as a sociologist, from the mere idea of craftsmanship. The wage-slaves of Middletown spend their days alternately working at machines and being passively amused by machines. The craftsmen of Mexico simultaneously work and play at making pots and blankets, lacquer bowls and the like. The wage-slave's life is restless and un-satisfying ; the craftsman's life (at any rate in many cases) is serene and satisfying. Moreover, the crafts-man is unaffected by slumps ; the wage - slave periodically starves. Pots, blankets, lacquer, are the symbols of the Mexican craftsman's safer and more wholesome life. In the presence of these symbols, Mr. Chase, the sociologist, feels excited, and, through a roseate fog of mental confusion, the excitement communicates itself to Mr. Chase, the aesthete. This is, I think, the most plausible, as it is certainly the most charitable, explanation of Mr. Chase's remark. For, if he really finds a collection of peasant bric-à-brac as exciting as an art museum—*any* art museum, mark you : the Prado, for example, the National Gallery—well, then, heaven help him ! For he is a man to whom nature has denied all sense of the qualitative difference between things.

The whole subject of folk-art is in a state of great confusion and urgently demands to be clarified. Like Mr. Chase, most enthusiasts for handicrafts tend to attribute too much aesthetic merit to the result of activities whose real value is psychological, social and economic. It is good that large numbers of people should be craftsmen, not because there is the smallest prospect of their producing a correspondingly large number of good works of art, but because craftsmanship is something which most men and women find psychologically satisfying. I myself, for example, spend much of my spare time painting pictures. The exercise of this manual skill gives me extraordinary pleasure ; but I do not for that reason imagine that I am producing masterpieces. So far as the ordinary untalented, or slightly talented, individual is concerned, craftsmanship is its own reward. And because

it is its own reward, it is also socially useful. Craftsmanship brings psychological fulfilment ; a society
of craftsmen is a society of satisfied individuals ; and
a society of satisfied individuals tends to be a stable
society. Craftsmanship has a further social utility,
inasmuch as an economy based upon handwork is
less alarmingly liable to fluctuation than one whose
foundation is mass production. Thus we see that,
even if all craft-work and peasant art were uniformly
hideous, craftsmanship would still be of the highest
value. In point of fact, craft-work is never uniformly
hideous. In their own way, the productions of a people
of handicraftsmen are often excellent ; but the nature
of this excellence is essentially inferior to that of the
excellence we find in the work of a great artist.

The life of an epoch is expressed by, and at the same
time is itself an expression of, the art of that epoch.
Where popular art is vulgar, there the life of the people
is also essentially vulgar in its emotional quality.
The popular arts in our industrialized communities
are of an unprecedented vulgarity. Why should this
be ? And what is the precise nature of this vulgarity ?
What, again, is the nature of the relative refinement
of the popular folk-arts of peasants and craftsmen ?

The nature of contemporary vulgarity has been well
illustrated and analysed by Mr. Leavis and Mr. Denys
Thompson in their book *Culture and Environment*. So far
as it goes, it is an excellent little book. Its great defect
is that it does not go far enough. For its authors are

content merely to describe the symptoms of the disease and to suggest an educational treatment to combat them. But it is not by palliating symptoms that you can effect a real cure. Rational treatment must be based on a knowledge of the deep-rooted causes of the disease. Mr. Leavis and Mr. Thompson are like clinicians who should carefully describe the fever and the pustules, without ever mentioning the virus which is the cause of these symptoms of smallpox. This is the principal defect of their book. Another, less serious, but still grave, is their extremely uncritical assumption that the arts of pre-industrial civilization were not merely relatively refined, but always absolutely excellent. At the end of the book we find a series of questions, intended for the use of teachers. One of these is worded as follows : ' Do you know of any ugly building, furniture, tools, etc., before 1820 ? Account, as far as you can, for your findings.' The context makes it clear that one is supposed to answer this question in the negative. One is supposed never to have seen any ugly building, furniture or tools of a date anterior to 1820. And, of course, if one is an uncritical archaeolater, one never does see any ugliness in the productions of earlier civilizations. But for any sensitive and unprejudiced person, a walk through any museum of decorative art, through any old town, brings instant proof that the pre-industrial age was rich in all manner of ugliness and ineptitude.

The truth is, of course, that most art has always

been either bad or indifferent. This is inevitable. Artistic talent is an extremely rare phenomenon ; therefore good art is extremely uncommon. The only substitute—and it is at best a partial substitute—for personal talent is a good artistic tradition. This enables people with little talent to produce good work because it relieves them of the necessity for using their own second-rate, or tenth-rate, imaginations. A good tradition may be defined as the ghosts of good dead artists dictating to bad living artists. So long as the bad artists listen to the dictations, and so long as they make no attempt to launch out on their own account, they will produce good derivative work. But an artistic tradition need not necessarily be good. For generations the ghosts of bad artists may dictate to other bad artists ; the results, when that happens, are deplorable. But even at its worst the bad art of pre-industrial times is seldom quite so depressing and never so painfully vulgar as modern bad art.

The badness and vulgarity of modern popular art are the result of a number of interlocking causes. The most important of these are the increase of population ; the improvement of old techniques for treating raw materials and the invention of new ones ; the rise of the standard of living ; and finally, the development within the arts themselves of new and more powerful modes of expression. Let us deal with these in order.

The enormous increase of population during the last century is due to several causes. The cultivation of virgin soil in the New World and the introduction of Chilean nitrates into the Old, suddenly quintupled the world's available food supply. Power production made it possible to provide clothing and shelter for indefinite millions of new people. At the same time public hygiene reduced infantile mortality and raised the average age of death. Most of the new millions thus called into being collected in the towns, which were thus swollen to unprecedented dimensions. Now, it seems to me very doubtful whether it is mechanically possible for a very large city to be anything but ugly and depressing. Give to London all the town planning, all the civic centres, all the garden suburbs that the ingenuity of man can devise ; it will still remain an assemblage of a million houses sprawling over five or six hundred square miles of ground. And even if every one of these million houses were a masterpiece of architecture (which is humanly impossible), the total effect of their agglomeration would still be profoundly depressing. Avila is a city of extraordinary beauty ; but magnify it five or six hundred times, so as to make it as large as London, and Avila will be hideous, a place of interminable monotonies, of hopeless dreariness and suffocating oppression. All our great cities could do with an immense amount of improvement. But we must not flatter ourselves with the belief that these improvements will transform them into things of beauty. Only a ninety-per-cent. destruction can accomplish that miracle.

Undue increase of city population has a psychological effect which I can best sum up by saying that all urbanization, pushed beyond a certain point, automatically becomes suburbanization. The inhabitants of a small city can take part in all its activities ; they are able to experience their native place as a single living unit. A large city cannot be experientially known ; its life is too manifold for any individual to be able to participate in it. Every great city is just a collection of suburbs. Its inhabitants have lost the advantages of living in the country without acquiring the compensating advantages of living in a town. For they do not *live* in their city ; they merely inhabit it. Their minds are neither rustic nor urban, but suburban ; and experience seems to show that a suburban mind is not a soil in which good traditions of art easily flourish.

The mechanization of industry has deprived millions of people of the opportunity to practise a handicraft, and by so doing has destroyed many excellent traditions of applied art. Mr. Leavis and Mr. Thompson have expatiated at some length on this obvious point. But mechanization has had another and no less disastrous effect on the popular arts. The general improvement of technical processes has helped to bring about the general deterioration of taste. We pray that we may not be led into temptation ; and with good reason. For it is opportunity that makes most of the murderers, the thieves, the adulterers. Opportunity, too, that makes most of the vulgarians. One fact emerges clearly from the history of art : that whenever men have had the means to be vulgar, they have generally succumbed to the temptation and made use of them.

Vulgarity is always the result of some excess ; and the means to vulgarity are therefore means to the realization in practice of an inward tendency toward the excessive. These means to vulgarity are of two kinds, economic and technical. You cannot achieve excess, and therefore vulgarity, unless, first, you have enough money to undertake personally, or to buy from others, works of art on a considerable scale, and, second, unless you or your employees are equipped with enough technical ability to make possible the artistic expression of your inward urge towards excess.

Before discussing the technical means to vulgarity, it will be as well to say a few words about the economic conditions for its realization in terms of art. ' It pays to advertise ' is a maxim as old as civilization. The rich and eminent members of every society have always spent a certain proportion of their incomes on display. They have paid copy-writers and poster-designers to ' put them across ' in nation-wide publicity drives. Sometimes these copy-writers were called Vergil or Spenser, these poster-designers, Holbein or Velasquez or Tiepolo. But often the ruler's or the rich man's desire for publicity has been gratified by artists of inferior quality. Hence, from the tomb of Tutankhamen to the Queen Victoria Memorial, those

innumerable monuments of vulgarity which constitute, in such large measure, what is beautifully called
the World's Artistic Heritage.

Folk-art is often dull or insignificant ; never vulgar,
and for an obvious reason. Peasants lack, first, the
money, and, second, the technical skill to achieve
those excesses which are the essence of vulgarity.
Vulgarity has always been the privilege of the prosperous and the highly educated. The general rise
in the standard of living has meant a general increase
in vulgarity. For the first time in the world's history
the small bourgeoisie and even a part of the pro-
letariat have been able to treat themselves to the
luxuries previously reserved to members of the ruling
class. Conspicuous among these luxuries is artistic
vulgarity.

So much for the economic means to vulgarity.
The technical means are of two kinds—those concerned
primarily with the treatment of matter and those
concerned primarily with the treatment of the invisible entities in a work of art : ideas and emotions.

Wherever artists find much technical difficulty in
imposing form on brute matter, art tends to be simple,
severe and chaste. It cannot be anything else.
Luxuriance, unchastity and consequent vulgarity
become possible only when men have acquired almost
complete mastery over matter. It is when they can
express themselves freely that artists begin to reveal
their true character. The man of delicate and noble

S

talent will express freely his delicacy and nobility ; the man whose talent is coarse and vulgar will be able at last to give free rein to his coarseness and vulgarity. This is why any improvement in the techniques of subduing matter to spirit is always attended by an increase in vulgarity. Only an artist of exceptional austerity can make a temperate use of the resources of a highly developed technology. Significantly enough, many sensitive artists of this age have adopted towards modern technique an attitude analogous to that of a hermit towards the pleasures of the world. Fearful of temptation, they retire into the desert—an artificial desert of their own making, a little oasis of technical aridity in the midst of the prevailing luxuriance. They are perhaps wise. Personally, however, I should have admired them more if they had faced the problem a little more courageously—gone out into the luxuriance and tried to master it. But that is by the way.

Advances in technology have led not only to vulgarity, but also, indirectly, to the lowering of qualitative standards in all the popular arts. Process reproduction and the rotary press have made possible the indefinite multiplication of writing and pictures. Universal education and relatively high wages have created an enormous public who know how to read and can afford to buy reading matter and pictorial seeing matter. A great industry has been called into existence in order to supply these commodities. Now, artistic talent is a very rare phenomenon ; whence it follows (as I have already remarked) that, at every epoch and in all countries, most art has been bad. But the proportion of trash in the total artistic output is greater now than at any other period. That it must be so is a matter of simple arithmetic. The population of Western Europe has a little more than doubled during the last century. But the amount of reading- and seeing-matter has increased, I should imagine, at least twenty and possibly fifty or even a hundred times. If there were n men of talent in a population of x millions, there will presumably be $2n$ men of talent among $2x$ millions. The situation may be summed up thus. For every page of print and pictures published a century ago, twenty or perhaps even a hundred pages are published to-day. But for every man of talent then living, there are now only two men of talent. It may be of course that, thanks to universal education, many potential talents which in the past would have been still-born are now enabled to realize themselves. Let us assume, then, that there are now three or even four men of talent to every one of earlier times. It still remains true to say that the consumption of reading- and seeing-matter has far outstripped the natural production of gifted writers and draughtsmen. It is the same with hearing-matter. Prosperity, the gramophone and the radio have created an audience of hearers who consume an amount of hearing-matter that has increased out of all proportion to the increase of population and the consequent natural increase of talented musicians. It follows from all this that in all the arts the output of trash is both absolutely and relatively greater than it was in the past; and that it must remain greater for just so long as the world continues to consume the present inordinate quantities of reading-matter, seeing-matter and hearing-matter.

So far I have spoken only of technical improvements in the handling of materials. There have also been purely aesthetic advances in the technique of expression. Of these the most startling are to be found in the domain of music. Beethoven made it possible to give direct and poignant expression to a great number of thoughts and feelings which, owing to the absence of a suitable idiom, were inexpressible by even the most highly gifted of his predecessors. Beethoven's aesthetic discoveries were exploited by other men in order to express thoughts and feelings of greatly inferior quality. The same thing happened in the case of all the great musical innovators of the nineteenth and early twentieth centuries. Thanks to Beethoven, to Berlioz, to Wagner (himself a sad vulgarian), to Rimsky Korsakoff, to Debussy, to Stravinsky, the modern jazz composer is in a position to express (with what an appalling technical efficiency!) every shade of all the baser emotions, from a baboon-like lust to a nauseating self-commiseration, from the mindless mass hysteria of howling mobs to a languishing masturbatory *Träumerei*. The first popular waltz, as I pointed out some years ago, was *Ach, du lieber Augustin*. Compare that innocently silly little tune with a successful waltz or blues of to-day. The distance travelled has been enormous. Towards what goal? One shudders to imagine it. And the joke, the atrocious and deplorable joke, is that this Gadarene progress has been made possible by the labours of some of the most noble and delicate spirits known to history.

What is the upshot of it all? So far as I can see, it is this : that the vulgarity which characterizes our industrial civilization is part of the inevitable result or concomitant of our prosperity, our universal instruction, our technological progress, our urbanization. Mr. Leavis and Mr. Thompson seem to think that the remedy for vulgarity and the general lowering of qualitative standards lies in better education ; and certainly something can be done by teaching such children as are teachable to distinguish between the good and the bad, the bogus and the genuine. But I doubt whether education can restore us to complete emotional and artistic health. The psychological, social and economic forces, now making towards vulgarization, are too strong to be resisted by a handful of school teachers (themselves, incidentally, more or less seriously infected by the disease they are supposed to cure). A change in the existing organization of society might do some good. For example, it might be possible, while preserving the advantages of machine

277

production, to reintroduce, to some extent, the practice of handicrafts. Freed from the burden of competition, the organizers of industry could afford to create and artificially preserve little Red Indian Reservations of craftsmanship in the midst of a world of machines. Again, the state could train its citizens for a leisure in which the practice of handicrafts should play an important part. That love of ' hobbies,' so common in every class of society, could be systematized, could be given a new, more dignified status, a higher social significance. The psychological effects of such a policy would probably be excellent. But it does not follow that, because a man is contented, he will produce good art. I see no reason to suppose that the arts and crafts of a prosperous, technically efficient and relatively well-educated society would possess even the negative virtues of peasant art. For these negative virtues, as I have already shown, are the result of poverty and ignorance. A society of civilized handicraftsmen could never blindly accept an old tradition. There would always be attempts at origin-ality—attempts foredoomed, in the great majority of cases, to failure ; for only highly talented artists can hope to be original with success. The partial restoration of handicraft culture would probably make for personal happiness and social stability, but would do little, so far as I can see, to cure vulgarity. Vulgarity is the price we must pay for prosperity, education and self-consciousness. Nor must we forget the influence of quantity upon quality. So long as population remains at its present density, ugliness is inevitable. For, reduplicated a million times, even the most beautiful object becomes hideous. Even more hideous will seem the endless repetitions of objects originally and intrinsically ugly. And intrinsically ugly they must be ; for, in a large, prosperous, and educated population, it is impossible that the level of popular art should be high. It is impossible because, as I have shown, the consumption of the arts has increased far more rapidly than the natural production of men of talent. Great quantity inevitably creates bad quality and multiplies it till it becomes a nightmare.

So far, then, as the popular arts are concerned, the prospect is none too good. Perhaps the wisest thing to do is to abandon them to their inevitable vulgarity and ineptitude and to concentrate all available resources on the training of a minority that shall be capable of appreciating the higher activities of the spirit. *Il faut cultiver notre oasis.*

Monte Alban

URBAN architecture has to be looked at, too often, with the eye, not of common physiological vision, but of faith. Hemmed in by other buildings, some of the most splendid monuments of past and present times are all but invisible.

The architects of pre-Columbian America were more fortunate than most of those of Europe. Their masterpieces were never condemned to invisibility, but stood magnificently isolated, displaying their three dimensions to all beholders. European cathedrals were built within the walls of cities ; the temples of the aboriginal Americans seem, in most cases, to have stood outside. At Tenochtitlan, it is true, the great cathedral of human sacrifice was within the city ; but like the Pisans, the Aztecs had the wit to leave a wide open space all round the monument. One could see the great *teocalli* as an architectural whole, just as (and the case is almost unique in Europe) one can see the Leaning Tower, Cathedral and Baptistry of Pisa.

Monte Alban was evidently the cathedral of a whole Zapotec diocese. A cathedral without a cathedral town. For the Indians lived in the valley, and their capital occupied the site of modern Oaxaca. Monte Alban was a city of the gods—visited by men and women, not permanently inhabited. The site is incomparably magnificent. Imagine a great isolated hill at the junction of three broad valleys ; an island rising nearly a thousand feet from the green sea of fertility beneath it. An astonishing situation. But the Zapotec architects were not embarrassed by the artistic responsibilities it imposed on them. They levelled the hill-top ; laid out two huge rectangular courts ; raised pyramidal altars or shrines at the centre, with other, much larger, pyramids at either end ; built great flights of steps alternating with smooth slopes of masonry to wall in the courts ; ran monumental staircases up the sides of the pyramids and friezes of sculpture round their base. Even to-day, when the courts are mere fields of rough grass, and the pyramids are buried under an obscuring layer of turf, even to-day this High Place of the Zapotecs remains extraordinarily impressive. Few architects have had such a sense of austerely dramatic grandeur as these temple builders of the great Toltec tradition. And few have been given so free a hand. For—and this seems to be characteristic not only of Monte Alban and Teotihuacan, but of all Central American sites, Maya as well as Toltec—religious considerations were never allowed to interfere with the realization of a grand architectural scheme. Too often, in other countries, magic and fetishism have been given precedence over art. A particular patch of ground is holy, possesses *mana* ; therefore it is desirable that as many shrines as possible shall be built upon it, so that the benefits of the supernatural radiation from the soil may be shared by the greatest possible number of images and their worshippers. The sacred precincts at Delos and at Delphi, for example, were, architecturally, just sacred slums — unplanned collections of buildings crowded, higgledy-piggledy, into the

narrow enclosures within which the *mana* was supposed
to be active. Many Christian churches have been
ruined architecturally by the anxiety of the faithful
to cram the greatest possible number of tombs, altars,
and what not into the consecrated space. Like the
Egyptians, the pre-Columbian Americans preferred
art to magic—or rather had the wit to see that the
most effective magic is the magic associated with the
finest art. The most convincing way of proving that
a given place is holy, is to make it so grand and so
beautiful that when they see it, people will catch their
breath with astonishment and awe. Fine architecture
is one of the visible embodiments of *mana*. It is a
manifestation of ' the beauty of holiness,' of the beauty
that *is* holiness. The Zapotecs knew all this so well
that here, at Monte Alban, they allowed nothing to
get in the way of the architects. Here should be no
hole-and-corner sacred place, no slummy confusion
of little shrines and temples ; but one huge architectural complex informed from end to end by a single
artistic idea and overwhelmingly impressive, as only
a unified work of art can be.

The pre-Columbian architects were fortunate, no
doubt, in the religion they served. Astronomical
observation was a sacred rite in ancient America, and
immense importance was attached to the four cardinal
points. This necessitated an unimpeded view of the
sky and a clearly defined lay-out. A pious Toltec
would have found it impossible to worship in the holy

ETLA

Bull-fight : goring of the tax collector.

slums of ancient Greece. He needed space for the practice of his religion, and geometrical order. At Delos or Delphi he would have had overcrowding and confusion. Another point : as generation followed generation in the classical and Christian world, more and more new shrines were built in the sacred enclosures or tacked on to the existing temples. In America, each succeeding generation merely enlarged the existing works, by surrounding them with a new layer of masonry. In this way they could do great things for the glory of their gods without altering the original architectural design of the holy place. But however great their religious luck, we must still give credit to the ancient Americans for a quite astonishing amount of aesthetic good management. Monte Alban is the work of men who knew their architectural business consummately well.

Etla

THE Lord's Day was to be celebrated at Etla by the baiting of bulls, and Don Manuel kindly offered to drive us out from Oaxaca to see the fun. The road was a section of that hypothetical Pan-American Highway which is, some day, to link New York with Lima, or, more modestly, with Panama, or, yet more modestly, with Guatemala City. At present, no wheeled traffic can pass from Mexico into Guatemala, and even Oaxaca is hardly accessible by car from Puebla and Mexico City. In good weather, it is true, the journey can be accomplished. But it is not a pleasure trip—may even, as I learnt by personal experience on the way to Etla, be a trip of pain. A more than usually deep hole in the Pan-American Highway hurled me, like a stone from a catapult, head first against the roof of the car. It was several weeks before the bruised lump on my skull finally subsided.

The valley of Oaxaca is one of the most fertile pieces of healthy country in the whole of Mexico. But I was struck, as we advanced across the flat valley floor, by the amount of land under scrub and cactus. Well-cultivated fields would alternate with patches of mere wilderness. The fault is not with nature, but with man. These lands were once the property of rich *hacendados*. Under the provisions of the Agrarian Laws the great estates were broken up and distributed among the Indians of the neighbouring villages. These, like all primitive agriculturists, are concerned only to supply their own needs. If they have a surplus to sell, so much the better ; it will give them a bit of pocket money for pistols and gold-embroidered hats. But if there is no surplus, it doesn't really matter ; they can get on quite well without it. The idea of raising crops, on a large scale and more or less scientifically, for export abroad, or even to unknown parts of their own country, is one which does not, in many cases simply cannot, occur to them. They use as much land as they can conveniently cultivate, as much as will provide them with the food they need ; the rest they leave to the organ cactus. In a bad year Mexico is forced to import maize and other cereals from the United States and from Africa.

Even the worst road comes finally to an end, and here at last was Etla. A temporary *Plaza de Toros* had been built on the outskirts of the town—a circular fence with a precarious grand stand on the shadier side. We climbed into our seats and waited.

Painfully up-to-date, Etla had had a beauty competition. The results of it were sitting in the place of honour, just above the seats of the Authorities. Six Queens of Beauty, six Miss Etlas, 1933. I gazed at them, incredulously. The six were all dressed alike in bright pink artificial silk, the colour of those cheap sweets that one's nurse and parents never allowed one, as a child, to eat. Their faces were very dark, but powdered a bright mauve. As for their shape . . . There is a certain mingling of Indian and European blood which results, for some obscure Mendelian reason, in the production of an entirely new human type. The six Miss Etlas were all of this type. Their beauty would have won all the prizes at any cattle show. Such thickness of beef ! And have you ever looked into the eyes of the winning ox ? Like an awful warning, the mother of one of these oxen was sitting beside her daughter. The beauties were monsters, but young ; and the youth even of a monster is to some extent charming. The stigmata of insentience, of stupidity, of buffalo-like obstinacy were not yet very deeply marked on these still adolescent faces. Age permits of no disguises. *Eripitur persona, manet res.* What remained in the mother's case was frankly terrifying. One look at her would have been enough to cure any prospective wooer of a taste for beef.

The proceedings began at last and were gratifyingly unsanguinary. Four *charros*, magnificently hatted, armed and caparisoned, pranced round on their fine horses and did tricks with lassoes. And when they had finished with the bull, it was the turn of the amateur *toreros* to play him with their *sarapes*, and, if possible, stick a few pins into his hide. There was to be no killing. Most of the bulls were rather mild, foolish animals, and when one evidently very ferocious creature came snorting into the ring, the enthusiasm of the *toreros* instantly abated. The crowd began to yell—'*toreros, toreros!*' There were hoots and catcalls and howls of derisive laughter, so disgusting in their low animality that it was sickening to listen to them. It was a clamour for blood, for the delicious spectacle of pain. Shamed at last into action, various *toreros* ventured into the ring, waved feebly at the bull, and, when he turned and looked at them, scampered away as fast as they could go. Finally a middle-aged

MITLA   Ruins and Church.

mestizo in city clothes—the local tax collector, as we afterwards discovered—dashed heroically into the ring. It was evident that some at least of his courage was Dutch ; the man was drunk. He took off his jacket, he flapped it at the bull. Five seconds later he was on the ground and bleeding. There was a great shout of excitement : at last the crowd had got what it wanted. A man on the ground, quite still, and blood on his face. This was good, this was very good indeed. But, alas, how insecure is human happiness ! Before the bull had had time to start goring the prostrate tax collector, our friend, Don Roy, had jumped into the ring and lured the creature away. And, in a minute or two, the corpse got up and, supported by its fellow *toreros*, staggered out of the arena ; the disappointment was general. Still, there had been blood. Real blood. One must learn to be thankful for small mercies.

> Count your blessings, count them one by one ;
> And it will surprise you what the Lord has done.

Mitla

THE country seemed to grow drier and drier as we advanced. Great bald hills of baked clay rose on either side of the valley, and in the stony dust of the plain a hellish growth of cactuses ferociously flourished. Sometimes, but very rarely, we would pass a man walking, or perched on the rump of his ass ; but the emptiness of this parched landscape was so complete, the silence so absolute, that it was as though the man were not there at all. Human life seemed, somehow, too hopelessly irrelevant to be possible.

A village of mud huts, each surrounded by its impenetrable fence of bright green organ cactus. We were at Mitla. In the waste land beyond the huts stood a church, as large as a small cathedral, and, beside it, the Mixtec ruins which it had been built to exorcise and sanctify.

Mitla is strangely unlike any of the other pre-Columbian remains in Mexico and Guatemala. Within and without, the walls of the temples—if temples indeed they are—are decorated with geometrical patterns of a kind to be met with, so far as I know, nowhere else in Central America. The oddest thing about these patterns is this : all are manifestly inspired by and based upon textile designs. Patterns in a coarsely woven cloth have precisely those stepped outlines characteristic of the wall decoration at Mitla. The techniques of wood carving and wood construction have often enough been reproduced in stone. But petrified weaving—this, surely, is something extremely uncommon.

MITLA   Detail.

In the Train

THE journey from Oaxaca to Puebla is so frightful that its frightfulness describes, so to speak, a full circle and comes out at the other end of the qualitative barometer as a joke. Yes, a joke ; for, after a certain number of hours of steadily growing discomfort, a moment comes when, suddenly, you begin to find it all profoundly comic—comic, the genuinely antique coach in which you are sitting ; comic, the crowd of passengers with their vast and innumerable luggage ; comic, the occasional overflow from the second class of swarming families of Indians ; comic, even the heat. This last must be felt to be believed. I have, in the course of my travels, visited some pretty hot places ; but nowhere have I experienced anything that could compare with the heat in the valley of the Quiotepec, about half-way between Oaxaca and Tehuacan. The coach was an oven ; but if you opened a window it was like opening the oven door directly on to the fire. A gust of withering heat, that was at the same time a sand blast, rasped the face like a burning file. Hastily you shut yourself in again ; the oven, by comparison, was deliciously refreshing. Beyond the glass, the landscape was as infernal as the temperature. The train was running in a cleft be-

T   289

tween huge hills, bone dry, and covered as far as the eye could reach with a thin metallic forest of cactuses, shadowless under the perpendicular sun.

> Come forth into the light of things,
> Let Nature be your teacher . . .

But there are places where it is decidedly better to pull down the blind and read Spinoza.

Puebla

PUEBLA, in the eighteenth century, developed a style of domestic architecture all its own. The model was that Andalusian classic, of which you may see such admirable specimens at San Fernando, near Cadiz, and at Ronda and Arcos ; but the Pueblans embroidered on this originally austere architectural scheme till it became something altogether new, something extravagant and wholly fantastic.

Pueblan houses are tall (the district is not subject to earthquakes) and are built, in the ordinary Spanish way, round an arcaded patio. Their originality lies in the façades they turn towards the street. These are made of brick, alternating with brilliant yellow-and-white or blue-and-white *azulejos*. In many cases the bricks are arranged in elaborate herring-bone patterns, with a bright tile at the centre of each

PUEBLA   Casa del Alfenique.

diamond or lozenge thus formed. The colours, in their pied gaiety, have something mediaeval about them ; but all of the forms are incongruously neo-Roman. The proportions (and how rare this is in Mexico !) are classically correct. Classical, too, are the heavily carved stone cornices, the stone escutcheons over the entrance doors, the stone frames round each window. It is as though Sir Christopher Wren had dressed up as Benozzo Gozzoli. The effect is extremely queer ; but also, which is more remarkable, extremely charming.

Puebla

WE were in Easter week, and the usual jollifications were in full swing. At night the plaza was bright and noisy with the fun of the fair. Relatively noisy ; for the Mexicans are strangely silent people. Even when they sing, they contrive somehow to sing inwards, as though they were making a musical sound only in order to swallow it. There would have been ten times as much yelling and whistling, a hundred times as much provocative giggling and amorous squealing, at an English fair. Merry-making in Central America has a certain aquarium quality, which I always found a little sinister.

In tents at the foot of the dark and silent precipices of the cathedral two troops of strolling players were performing. We took our seats in one of these ephemeral theatres, among an audience of fat, rather unwholesome-looking burgesses, with a *charro* or two, very dashing, in skin-tight trousers and vast gold-embroidered hat. The performance began—a sort of cabaret show, each turn more astonishingly inept than the last. The only remarkable feature of the entertainment was the really staggering animality of the female performers. True, they were less ox-like than the beauty queens of Etla, looked a little more human. But this, precisely, was their undoing. Spirituality is not demanded of an ox; but in a human being you expect to find some trace at least of a soul. And when that trace is not perceptible, you have a very disagreeable shock. The animality of a bestial man or woman seems more intense than that of a beast, and is always incomparably more dreadful. There is a certain mixture of blood and a certain Mexican environment which evidently produces a type of woman more horrifyingly animal, more abysmally whorish in appearance, than any I have seen in any other part of the world. Appearances are often deceptive, and it may be that these unfortunate females are grossly slandered by their own physique. I cannot say. All I know is that, by comparison with theirs, the faces one glimpses in the *quartiers réservés* of Marseille, or Kairouan, or Singapore seem exquisitely refined and spiritual.

Cholula

' POETRY,' said Mallarmé, ' is not written with ideas ;
it is written with words.' Hence, if you are a man of
letters, those tears ; and hence, when the words have
fallen of their own free will or been laboriously bullied
into the proper, the inevitable pattern, hence also those
triumphant elations. Cholula, for example—how find
the words to render the magnificence, the queerness,
the general improbability of Cholula ? Happy Prescott ! He, it is evident, had no difficulties with the
place. ' Nothing,' he writes, and writes it obviously
without a qualm, ' nothing could be more grand than
the view which met the eye from the area on the
truncated summit of the pyramid. Towards the north
stretched that bold barrier of porphyritic rock which
Nature had reared around the Valley of Mexico, etc.
. . . At the foot of the spectator lay the sacred city
of Cholula, with its bright towers and pinnacles sparkling in the sun, reposing amidst gardens and verdant
groves, which then thickly studded the cultivated
environs of the capital. Such was the magnificent
prospect which met the gaze of the conquerors, and
may still, with a slight change, meet that of the modern
traveller, as from the platform of the great pyramid
his eye wanders over the fairest portion of the beautiful

plateau of Puebla.' And very nice too! But, alas, the days when verdant groves studded the environs are over. We are expected to use words that will give the reader an illusion of being close to the physical and psychological reality they express. Prescott had never been in Mexico. But for one who wrote in terms of verdant groves and sparkling pinnacles, this was no handicap, was actually an advantage. For, even if he had visited Cholula, his words would have been carefully chosen so as to conceal this somewhat compromising fact. Not having visited Cholula, he had nothing to conceal, but could devote himself whole-heartedly and without an afterthought to the description of the magnificent prospect. With us, the case is altered. The sort of words we use are meant to prove to the reader that we have been there, quiveringly in the flesh, even when in fact we haven't. Badly used, such words are much worse than Prescott's rhetorical proofs of a personal, an emotional alibi. They are worse, because they protest too much, whereas Prescott's words, for all their absurd pomposity, protest very little. A 'word picture' (the very name makes one feel slightly sick) by a fluent contemporary journalist has a poignant vulgarity unknown in earlier days. It is the old story of opportunity making the thief. During the last century certain prose stylists made possible the arranging of words so as to produce in the reader an imaginative conviction of personal intimacy with the reality that they

were artistically rendering. By their technical discoveries they enlarged the kingdom of literary art,
conquered new provinces of the inexpressible. Now,
the better a man's tools, the more effectively will he
be able to stamp his personality upon the raw material
of his chosen art—the more easily will he be able to
'express himself.' If the self he has to express is of
poor aesthetic quality (as it generally is), the possession of better tools will merely result in the production
of more vulgar art. In the course of the last ninety
years, good writers have provided the 'word-painter'
with a great number of technical resources entirely
unknown to Prescott. He was content to stud the
environs with groves and leave his pinnacles to sparkle
in the sun ; was content because, in the last resort, he
could do nothing else. Which was perhaps fortunate.
For when one *can* do something else, something more,
this is the sort of thing one does : 'The temple tapered
above the soft bronze of the river, above the dimmed
green of the palms, the spire of its tallest pagoda
stained with the drench of sunset. Its beauty was the
brutal beauty of blood-dark steel.' (The quotation is
from a novel which I found in the smoking-room of a
hotel.)

'Its bright towers and pinnacles sparkling in the sun . . .'
'Its tallest pagoda stained with the drench of sunset . . .'

Between those two phrases lie ninety years of stylistic
experiment. Prescott, in 1843, simply could not have
written the second of them. Pater, Rimbaud, Conrad,

D'Annunzio—these and a score of others had to live and work before such stuff became writable.

'And lead us not into temptation, but deliver us from evil.' With this prayer on my lips, let me return to Cholula, to the platform of that mountainous pyramid of Quetzalcoatl from which Cortes looked down on the holy city, '*y certifico a Vuestra Alteza que yo conté quatrocientas y tantas Torres en la dicha Ciudad, y todas son de Mezquitas.*' Even to-day one can still see almost as many 'towers of mosques.' But the mosques are no longer mosques of Quetzalcoatl and Tonantzin and Huitzilopochtli. They are the mosques of St. Joseph and St. James, of St. Francis and St. Dominick, of the Holy Trinity and Our Lady of Guadalupe. The Spaniards, it is evident, must have built a church, or at least a chapel, on the site of every pagan temple in Cholula. It was a sanitary precaution, a process of magical disinfection.

I did not bother to count the churches visible from the top of the great pyramid. But one did not have to invoke the aid of arithmetic to perceive that the town at one's feet was fairly bubbling with round domes, that all the plain for miles around was strewn with the fossil remains of ecclesiastical life. The religious emotions rank, with sunlight, hunger and falling water, as one of the great natural sources of energy. Harness this Niagara, and at once millions of horse-power are at your disposal. There are enough bricks in the Cholula pyramid to cover an area twice

CHOLULA   S. Francisco Acatepec.

as large as the Place de la Concorde to a depth equal to twice the height of the Louvre. And when Quetzalcoatl had gone, the missionaries recanalized the old energies in the imported name of Jesus; the towers of the new *mezquitas* sprouted everywhere like mushrooms on an autumn morning. It was the decay of faith that made it necessary to invent the steam engine.

Humboldt, in his *Essai politique sur la Nouvelle Espagne*, makes a remark which every enthusiastic pyramid-climber should strictly meditate. ' If,' he says, ' we analyse the mechanism of the Peruvian theocracy, generally so much over-praised in Europe, we observe that, wherever nations are divided into castes, and wherever men do not enjoy the right to private property and work solely for the profit of the community, we shall find canals, roads, aqueducts, pyramids, huge constructions of every kind. But we shall also find that these people, though for thousands of years they may preserve the air of external prosperity, will make practically no advance in moral culture, which is the result of individual liberty.'

Pyramids on the one hand; personal liberty on the other. We have an ever increasing number of pyramids, or their modern equivalents; an ever diminishing amount of personal liberty. Is this merely a historical accident? Or are these two goods essentially incompatible? If they turn out to be essentially incompatible, then, one day, we shall have to ask ourselves very seriously which is better worth having —pyramids and a perfectly efficient, perfectly stable community ; or personal liberty with instability, but the possibility, at least, of a progress, measurable in terms of spiritual values.

Descending from Quetzalcoatl's mountain of petrified energy, we set out to explore the Christian monuments. The most remarkable of these are San Francisco Acatepec and Santa Maria Tonantzintla. San Francisco, which stands on a little hill, quite alone in the rolling, campagna-like country, some three miles out of Cholula, is just the typical Pueblan church, raised, so to speak, to the nth power. In the city of Puebla all the churches have blue or yellow glazed cupolas ; and some have panels of the same bright tiles on their façades. San Francisco Acatepec is tiled from top to bottom. Dome, belfry, pillars, cornices—every inch is covered with blue and yellow *azulejos*. One would expect the church to glow like a flock of parrots. But, oddly enough, the total effect is drab. ' Jazzed up ' to the extreme limit of variegated brilliancy, San Francisco is like one of those ships one used to see during the war ; it has been dazzle-painted into indistinctness, almost into invisibility. Within, the wealth of moulded plaster and carved wood is astonishing. There is hardly a blank space in the whole church. The effect is queer, but not extraordinary. For the designs are all relatively orthodox—Spanish baroque only slightly Indian-

CHOLULA   Stucco work in church of S. Maria, Tonantzintla.

ized. To see how far Indianization can be carried, one must go to Santa Maria Tonantzintla. From the outside the church looks like any other Mexican church—the usual dome, the usual pleasantly pictur-esque but ill-proportioned façade and, since it stands near Puebla, the usual Pueblan *azulejos*. But enter ; you find yourself in what is probably the oddest church in Christendom. The whole of the interior is fairly crawling with stucco-work, brilliantly gilt and painted in red, green, blue and pink, on a spotless white ground. And what stucco work ! Cherubs, with Aztec feathers stuck in their back hair, peer out at you from the walls. On the vaulting, overhead, a group of Indian angels are playing the 'cello (the tom-tom, I suppose was too closely related to the old religion to be tolerated in a nominally Christian church). It is, as every-where in Central America, a baroque theme inter-preted by neolithically minded craftsmen—but inter-preted far more freely (and also with greater artistic power) than in any of the other churches I saw in Mexico or Guatemala.

Four or five Indians, all men, were busy, when we entered, decorating the church for Easter with palm branches and pieces of gold and silver foil. There was certainly no resident priest in the place ; perhaps no mass would be said even on Easter Day. But I doubt if the Indians minded. Since the Revolution, the church is wholly theirs ; they can do what they like in it, practise whatever queer blend of catholicism and Quetzalcoatlism pleases them best. The priests, it is true, could make strong magic ; but since their departure experience has doubtless proved to the Indians that, magic for magic, their own is just as effective as any one else's. There is not any less rain since the *padres* were turned out, nor any more disease. And there is certainly less to pay. We asked permission to take some snapshots. The Indians had no objection —were indeed delighted that we should find their church so interesting. But would we send them the photographs when they were developed ? We certainly would. The two most important members of the group wrote down their names and addresses for us. One was called Lorenzo Pancoatl, the other Encarnación Azcoatl. Merely from the names of the vergers one could have deduced the nature of the church.

Mexico City

THE dry season was at its last gasp. The air was thick with dust, and heavy, every afternoon, with the approach of thunder-storms that never broke. Even at sea-level the climate would have been trying ; at seven thousand feet its effects on the character were disastrous. I have never felt so thoroughly bad-tempered as during the weeks we spent in Mexico City.

MEXICO CITY

Between the inward weather of the mind and the physical climate of the external world there is evidently some connection. But our knowledge of its nature is no further advanced to-day than it was when Burton, in the *Anatomy of Melancholy*, wrote his 'Digression of Air.' 'The Clime changes not so much customs, manners, wits, as constitutions of their bodies and temperature itself. In all particular provinces we see it confirmed by experience ; as the air is, so are the inhabitants, dull, heavy, witty, subtle, neat, cleanly, clownish, sick, and sound.' That blood lust of the Aztecs, that still surviving preoccupation with death, those sudden Mexican violences—perhaps, in part at least, these are the products of the local air. Judging by my own state of mind, while I was in Mexico City, I should think it almost probable.

Mexico City

MEXICO is a country of peasants and handicraftsmen ; Mexico City, an oasis—or, if you prefer it, a small desert — of urbanism and industrialism. In the country men live almost without money, dealing directly in the real wealth of useful commodities which they themselves own or produce ; the inhabitants of the city—and there are more than a million of them

—depend on wages. In the country and the provincial towns the great masses of the population are almost untouched by the slump ; the people look well-fed, reasonably healthy and only reasonably dirty. In the capital everybody, workman as well as capitalist, has been more or less seriously affected by the slump. I never saw so many thin, sickly and deformed people as in the poorer quarters of the metropolis ; never such filth and raggedness, such signs of hopeless poverty. As an argument against our present economic system, Mexico City is unanswerable.

Mexico City

EASTER SATURDAY is Judas's day. In a top-hat and with the pale face of a foreign exploiter, his image is paraded through the streets, then strung up to a lamppost or a telegraph pole and set on fire. The swollen capitalist's belly is stuffed with crackers, and Judas ends in a terrific explosion that blows him to smithereens. So perish all *gringos* !

It is obvious, as one watches the rite, that the performers take not the smallest interest in the historic Judas and his crime. Like the little boys who, in England, burn the effigy of Guy Fawkes in commemoration of an event of which they have hardly

302

heard and about which they care less than nothing, these good catholics of Mexico are simply out to have a bit of fun with fireworks. The fun is heightened by the make-believe of murder. Victims are no longer gutted and eaten in honour of Huitzilopochtli or Tezcatlipoca, no longer drowned for the Tlalocs, flayed for Xipé, burnt for the god of fire and decapitated for the goddess of fertility. The modern Mexicans have to be content with the mere emblems of human sacrifice. But even a symbolical sacrifice is better than no sacrifice at all. To let off a firecracker is always amusing. But the pleasure is heightened when the explosion can be made to destroy the life-sized image of a man.

Mexico City

DIEGO RIVERA's frescoes in the *patio* of the Ministry of Education are chiefly remarkable for their quantity ; there must be five or six acres of them. For quality one must go to the Preparatoria and look at Orozco's paintings. These have a queer merit, even when they are most horrible—and some of them are about as horrible as anything could well be. Their unsuitability as decorations in a school for adolescent boys and girls is almost absolute. But they are real pictures,

303

by a man who knows how to paint. The formal inventions are often extraordinarily felicitous ; the colour subtle ; the modelling, for all the ferocious brutality of the subject, very sensitive and alive. They are pictures that remain, rather disquietingly, in the memory.

School, I suppose, was over, when we went to see the frescoes. At any rate, the cloisters of the Preparatoria were full of rather elegantly dressed youths, talking in groups, or singing to the guitar ; there was a continuous coming and going of schoolgirls, black-eyed, powdered and astonishingly nubile—like pomegranates, in their jumpers and their brightly coloured artificial satins, on the point of bursting. It was all most refreshingly unlike Rugby or Roedean.

Mexico City

In spite of the proximity of the United States, in spite of Fords and Frigidaires and Palmolive, Mexican culture still remains predominantly French. My Spanish is good enough for restaurants and railway stations ; but when it is a matter of talking about something a little more difficult than food or the registration of luggage, I feel as though my mouth were full of chewing-gum, stickily gagged. Luckily, in Mexico, most educated people speak French.

French, here, still occupies the privileged position which, from the middle of the eighteenth century to the 'twenties of the nineteenth, it occupied in Europe ; it is the language of civilization itself. Crazed with nationalism, Europe has long since unlearned this incomparable Esperanto ; and now Mexico is busily engaged in following the European example. In another generation French will probably be all but useless to the stranger visiting Central America. To-day it is still the next best thing to perfect Spanish. Thanks to French, I was able to talk without linguistic constraint, I was able (how profitably !) to listen, to the many men of letters who in Mexico showed me such extraordinary kindness. A contact was established between us, a bridge of words. A century from now, if the infectious idiocy of nationalism continues to spread at its present rate, the descendants of these universally cultured Mexicans will probably be talking some Indian dialect and mine will know no word of anything but cockney. Meanwhile, let us all be grateful for the existence of French.

Mexico City

AMONG the advertisements for pills and motor cars and soap and plumbing there would appear, morning after morning in the daily Press, an astonishing piece of sales talk, issued by the Ministry of Education. I forget the exact wording ; but the substance of the advertisement was as follows : ' The intellectual foundations of the modern world are constituted by Machiavelli's *The Prince*, Rousseau's *Social Contract* and Karl Marx's *Capital*. If you wish to understand the age in which you live, read these books in any of the Public Libraries of the City or the Federal District.'

Each time I read this advertisement I thought of those earnest young Indians we had seen in the mountains of Oaxaca, sitting round the school-house door and gravely listening, while one of their number read aloud from the ragged novelette which had somehow found its way into the village. Many Indians seem to have a real passion for reading. Reading for reading's sake ; the printed word is intrinsically magical. In my fancy I transported these young savages into the city, made them see the advertisement for culture, made them hurry to the nearest Public Library. ' *El Principe*,' they would ask at the desk, ' *El Contrato Social y el Capital de Carlos Marx*.' And they would proceed to read the volumes, from cover to cover, without skipping a word. And what would be the result ? What would they come to think about that Modern World, of which these books were said to be the foundations ? How would the reading affect their moral judgments, their political opinions, their religious beliefs ? Under the strain imposed by these questions, my imagination broke down. If one happens to have received a rather elaborate academic education, it is almost impossible to represent to oneself the mental processes of people who have been taught, for all practical purposes, nothing except the useful arts of day-to-day living. For the educated mind, all phenomena are interrelated. Take, by way of illustration, the immediately experienced facts of the Depression. From these, innumerable threads go out in every direction. They are so many bridges between universe and universe ; bridges over which the mind can pass, now this way, into history —to the great slump of 1837 to 1842, for example, or to the economic collapse of the Roman Empire—now into political economy and thence, in the effort to explain the fact of trade cycles, into mass psychology, or alternatively into the periodicities of the weather ; from which it is led in one direction to sunspots and the universes of astronomy and physics, in the other to . . . But obviously, for the educated mind, there is no end to the number of possible bridges. For the uneducated mind, on the contrary, there is no beginning. Each experience is unique, isolated, related intellectually to nothing else in the world. Between one star of consciousness and another the only connecting links are the physiological identity of the person who is conscious and perhaps some rudimentary system of religious philosophy. The world of the uneducated is a world of darkness, with a dim little light here and another there, and between them, invisible, mysterious objects with which from time to time the benighted traveller comes into often painful contact, but of which he cannot distinguish the form nor recognize the function. This nocturnal world must, I suppose, have its charm—the charm of a Grand-Guignol thriller. ' They say that miracles are past,' says Shakespeare, in *All's Well that Ends Well*, ' and we have our philosophical persons to make modern and familiar, things supernatural and causeless. Hence it is that we make trifles of terrors, ensconcing ourselves into seeming knowledge, when we should submit ourselves to an unknown fear.' Nevertheless, I prefer Spinoza's freedom through knowledge and understanding to emotional bondage, however deliciously creepy with ' unknown fears.' And so, it is evident, do the officials of the Mexican Ministry of Education. Their desire to enlighten the ignorant about the nature of the modern world is entirely laudable. It is only with regard to the means of enlightenment that one feels a little dubious.

Taxco

THE car in which we drove to Taxco was old, but large and powerful. A bit too powerful ; for we had no horn and no foot-brake—no means of warning people to get out of our way, and no means of stopping when they failed to do so. The hand-brake, it is true, was not quite dead ; at twenty-five miles an hour it could stop the car in about a hundred and fifty yards. I have seldom enjoyed anything less than that drive to Taxco.

It was the worst of a number of similar experiences. Only in India have I met chauffeurs as completely anti-mechanical as those of Mexico. The actual driving is good ; but there is a terrifying lack of knowledge about what goes on under the bonnet, and an even more terrifying lack of interest. It is the business of a car to go ; and if it does not go well, so much the worse ; the chauffeur makes the best of the bad job of driving it as it is. The idea of remedying the defect hardly seems to occur to him. And even if it did occur, he wouldn't know what to do.

Taxco is a sort of Mexican Saint-Paul largely inhabited by artists and by those camp-followers of the arts whose main contribution to the cause of Intellectual Beauty consists in being partially or completely drunk for several hours each day. In the eighteenth century, Borda, the mining millionaire, built for Taxco one of the most sumptuous churches in Mexico—one of the most sumptuous and one of the most ugly. I have never seen a building in which every part, down to the smallest decorative detail, was so consistently ill-proportioned. Borda's church is an inverted work of genius.

For some odd reason Mexican ecclesiastical architecture is inferior, on the whole, to that of Guatemala. Over-high for its width, the façade of the typical Mexican church has an uncomfortably hunch-backed appearance. In Guatemala, church fronts are wider in proportion to their height. The effect is more restful ; there is no suggestion of deformity. Why there should be a difference between the architectural traditions of the two contiguous provinces I do not know, but guess that one must seek the explanation in an accident—the influence in Guatemala of some architect who had seen the baroque churches of Rome, the absence of a corresponding influence in Mexico. But speculation is idle. One can only record the rather odd fact and pass on.

On the Ship

THE Gulf of Mexico was flat and dark blue and finely wrinkled by a steady breeze. It was as though we were gliding over an endless expanse of blue morocco leather, over the sumptuous, royal binding of some enormous folio. A book, I thought, as I looked over the rail. And what is written within ? *Quien sabe ?*

> Thrice happy he, who, not mistook,
> Has read in Nature's mystic book !

But what about him who *is* mistook? And how is one to tell when a mistake has been made? The poet is silent. True, the writing in the book is progressively decipherable; it is a matter of industry and scientific intelligence. But what is the meaning of the deciphered words? One can only guess, and, having guessed, hope and believe and obstinately insist that the guess is right. In other words, one has an intuition (or else accepts somebody else's intuition), and one has faith in its correctness.

I returned to my chair and the rereading of Lawrence's *Plumed Serpent*. I was nearly at the end. The heroine was at last resigning herself to being ' left immersed, drowned in the grand sea of the living blood, in immediate contact with all these men and all these women.' It is a conclusion which Lawrence himself has used all his extraordinary powers to make incredible. No one has ever written more forcibly than Lawrence in *The Plumed Serpent* of the hopeless psychological squalor and stuffiness of human beings who have not yet reached the spiritual and mental stage of consciousness. ' The curious radical opposition of the Indian to the thing we call the spirit . . . He understands soul, which is of the blood. But spirit, which is superior, and is the quality of our civilization, this, in the mass, he darkly and barbarically repudiates.' Lawrence illustrates this theme in passage after passage of wonderfully realized incident, each one of which violently moves us to share the heroine's ' hatred for these people, their terrible lowness, *à terre, à terre*,' to feel ' her passion of revulsion from these lice-picking, down-dragging people,' with their simultaneous yearning and loathing for ' that upper world of daylight and fresh air ' to which Kate herself belonged. And yet, in the end, we are asked to renounce daylight and fresh air and immerse ourselves in ' the grand sea of the living blood '—that blood whose natural and spontaneous flowering is hatred of spirit, lice-picking and ' the black thrill of the death-lust.' We cannot accept the invitation. Lawrence's own incomparable descriptions of the horror of unadulterated blood have made it impossible. It was impossible even for himself; he could not accept his own invitation. The facts of his life are there to prove it. Kate stayed, immersed in the primitive blood of Mexico ; but Lawrence went away. And, even if we did not know the facts of his life, the book itself would be sufficient proof. The first two-thirds of it are artistically perfect—as strong, as beautiful, as delicately sensitive and alive as anything could be. Then something happens. Lawrence has to prove, for his heroine, for himself, for his readers, that the immersion in blood is good—has to prove it in the teeth of his own doubts, of his heroine's nauseated revulsions (and with a scrupulous honesty he continues to record them all), of the scepticism which he himself has planted in the mind of the reader. Inevitably he starts to protest too much. Those descriptions of the ceremonials, in the course of which Don Ramón and Don Cipriano appear to the people as the living incarnations of the Aztec gods—they begin magnificently ; but as Lawrence feels the inner necessity of overcompensating his own doubts, they lose force and life even while becoming more violent ; fade into dimness in proportion as the tone is raised ; grow less and less persuasive with every increase and every prolongation of loudness. The artistic failure is evidence of some inner uncertainty of conviction. He had read in the mystic book and decided that what he had found there was the supremacy and the rightness of the blood. But this decision was made and sustained, one suspects, in defiance of many intuitions directly to the contrary. Lawrence deliberately cultivated his faith in the blood ; he wanted to believe. But doubts, it is evident, often came crowding in upon him. The questioning voices had to be shouted down. But the louder he shouted, the less was he able to convince his hearers. Art is convincing only when it springs from conviction.

Intemperate optimists talk as though you could get something for nothing ; or at worst, as though the only payments owing on account of human progress were payments in advance. But the truth is, that Destiny always charges twice for the benefits it sells us—once before the goods are delivered, and again, when the preliminary efforts have been crowned with success, in an indefinite series of deferred payments, afterwards. In other words, men have to work for every mental or material advance they make and, when they have made it, can enjoy the fruits of their labours, only on condition that they give up the privileges which were theirs before the advance was made.

In some cases the price of progress is fixed and cannot by any means be diminished. In others, Destiny is prepared to grant a substantial rebate to the intelligent. The advance from primitivism to civilization, from mere blood to mind and spirit, is a progress whose price is fixed ; there are no discounts even for the most highly talented purchasers. I thought once that the payment could be evaded, or at least very greatly reduced ; that it was possible to make very nearly the best of both worlds. But this, I believe, was a delusion. The price that has to be paid for intellect and spirit is never reduced to any significant extent. To Lawrence it seemed too high, and he proposed that we should return the goods and ask for our money back. When man became an intellectual and spiritual being, he paid for his new privileges with a treasure of intuitions, of emotional spontaneity, of sensuality still innocent of all self-consciousness. Lawrence thought that we should abandon the new privileges in return for the old treasure. But he was reckoning without himself and, since each one of us creates and largely *is* his own fate, without Destiny. In practice, he found that it was psychologically impossible to return the new privileges or be content with the primitivism that had been paid away for them. It was even impossible for him to make a fictitious personage do so, at any rate convincingly.

Human Bondage, in the words of Spinoza, is the price of Human Freedom. The advantages of the first state (and Human Bondage has many and substantial advantages) are incompatible with those of the second. We must be content to pay, and indefinitely to go on paying, the irreducible price of the goods we have chosen.

INDEX

Advertisements, 1, 152, 172, 305.
Aeroplane, 197.
Agrarian Laws, 284.
Alain, 77, 80.
Altars, pagan, 157, 186.
Amusements, 6, 102.
Angell, Sir N., 119.
Antigua, 127 *seq.*
Architecture, Indian, 48; Maya, 50; Spanish colonial, 130, 279; Greek, 281; Pueblan, 290; Mexican, 310.
Art, traditions of, 51, 219; generally bad, 268.
Atitlan, 139.
Augustine, St., 176.
Azulejos, 290, 298.

Baile de los conquistadores, 167, 193.
Bananas, 16.
Bancroft, 168, 181.
Bandstands, 231.
Barbados, 8.
Barrancas, 136.
Barrès, M., 94.
Baudelaire, 239.
Beethoven, 276.

Bergson, 180.
Birth control, 255.
Black, sacred colour, 203.
Borda, 309.
British Honduras, 291.
Bull dance, 171.
Bull-fight, 283.

Cabrera, 66, 115.
Calypso Tent, 18.
Cantharides, 96.
Caracas, 22.
Carrera, 111, 115.
Champerico, 226.
Character, 255.
Chase, Stuart, 252, 265.
Chichicastenango, 149 *seq.*
Cholula, 293.
Ciudad Vieja, 119.
Civilization, 253.
Climate, effects of, 301.
Cochineal, 127.
Coffee, 127, 237.
Colon, 26.
Colonel, the, 191.
Colonies, psychological substitutes for, 104.
Conditioning, 48, 79, 80.
Copan, 198 *seq.*
Cortes, 296.

316

INDEX

Costumes, traditional, 147.

Craftsmanship, social value of, 278.

Cruelty, 177.

Death, in art, 60, 208.

Democracy, emotional culture suitable to, 92.

Denison, J. H., 155.

Disestablishment, results of, in Guatemala, 159.

Domestic animals, 144, 199.

Education, 256 ; in Mexico, 306.

Ejutla, 261.

Encyclopædia Britannica, 114.

Esquipulas, 203.

Eternity, 220.

Etla, 283.

Eton, 92.

Fashions, 9, 22.

Fertility, gods of, 45, 51.

Fireworks, 233.

Five Republics, wars between the, 73.

Franciscan movement, 109.

Frederick the Great, 181.

French, value of as international language, 305.

Gage, Thomas, 158.

Gann, Dr., 53, 224.

Gide, A., 94.

Goethe, 226.

Goitre, 175.

Guatemala City, 66.

Half-castes, 139.

Hatred, 81, 94, 96, 111.

Hats, significance of, 9, 245.

Herbert, George (quoted), 179.

Herodotus, 216.

Hieroglyphs, as works of art, 195.

Humboldt, 117, 127, 297.

Illegitimacy, 26.

Imagination, limitations of, 32.

Imperial College of Tropical Agriculture, 16.

Independence, Central American, 90.

Indigo, 127.

Industrialism, 301.

Infantilism, 7.

Inferiority complex, 37, 70.

Jamaica, 27.

Japan, 112.

Jesuits, 80.

Judas, 162, 302.

Kingship, value of, 91.

Lawrence, D. H., 249, 311.
Leavis and Thompson, 267, 271, 277.
Lubricants, 130.

MacPhail, Dr., 39.
Magic, 157, 190.
Mahogany, 30.
Malaria, 40.
Malinowski, 53.
Mallarmé, 293.
Marimba, 119, 172.
Maudslay, 125, 134.
Mayas, their art compared with Indian art, 43; sculpture, 207 ; time reckoning, 216 ; migrations, 222.
Mexico City, 301.
Miahuatlan, 247.
Milton, 235.
Minerva, temples of, 65.
Mitla, 287.
Mixtecs, 288.
Momostenango, 186.
Monarchy, 92.
Monte Alban, 279.
Music, popular, 277.

Nationalism, emotional basis of, 81 ; compared to homosexuality, 94 ; supposed ethical justifications for, 97 ; 98, 201, 209.
Nature worship, 137.

Nazis, 112, 176, 179.
' New Stupidity,' 101.

Oaxaca, 262.
Old Man of the Mountain, 80.
Orchestral colour, 19.
Orgies, 83 *seq.*
Orozco, J. C., 303.

Palaces, 23.
Passions, as causes of war, 77.
Pavlov, 30.
Peasant art, 197, 264 (*and see* Vulgarity).
Peru, 164.
Pilgrimages, 165.
Pitch lake, 14.
Pochutla, 230.
Pope, A., 235.
Population, future constitution of, 3 ; effects of increase in, 255, 275.
Prescott, 293.
Primitive Indian paintings, 166.
Primitive and civilized psychology, 312.
Progreso, 232.
Prohibition, 97.
Puebla, 290.
Puerto Angel, 227.
Pyramids, 297.